The Gender

of

Modernity

Rita Felski

Harvard University Press
Cambridge, Massachusetts
London, England
1995

Library of Congress Cataloging-in-Publication Data
Felski, Rita, 1956–
The gender of modernity / Rita Felski.
p.   cm.
Includes bibliographical references and index.
ISBN 0-674-34193-7 (alk. paper)
ISBN 0-674-34194-5 (pbk. : alk. paper)
1. Feminist theory.   2. Civilization, Modern—19th century.
3. Civilization, Modern—20th century.   4. Women and literature.
5. Women in literature.   6. Feminist criticism.   I. Title.
HQ1190.F417   1995
305.42'01—dc20
94-44329

Contents

Acknowledgments   *vii*

Introduction: Myths of the Modern   *1*

1   Modernity and Feminism   *11*

2   On Nostalgia: The Prehistoric Woman   *35*

3   Imagined Pleasures: The Erotics and Aesthetics
of Consumption   *61*

4   Masking Masculinity: The Feminization of Writing   *91*

5   Love, God, and the Orient: Reading the
Popular Sublime   *115*

6   Visions of the New: Feminist Discourses of Evolution
and Revolution   *145*

7   The Art of Perversion: Female Sadists and
Male Cyborgs   *174*

Afterword: Rewriting the Modern   *207*

Notes   *213*

Index   *241*

Acknowledgments

My thanks are due first of all to the various institutions whose generous research grants made it possible for me to write this book: the Society for the Humanities at Cornell University, the Commonwealth Center for Literary and Cultural Change at the University of Virginia, and the Australian Research Council.

A number of individuals have helped me with this project in various ways over the last five years: by talking to me about my work or about theirs, by sending me relevant information and materials, by alerting me to unfamiliar references, or by correcting my more glaring errors. I am grateful to Janet Beizer, Charles Bernheimer, Abigail Bray, Jonathan Culler, Melanie Hawthorne, Missy Dehn Kubitschek, Dominick LaCapra, Janet Lyon, Allan Megill, Anne-Marie Metcalfe, Wendy Parkins, Michael Roth, and Peter Stallybrass. Discussions with Lindsay Waters helped me to formulate more clearly the aims of this book at a crucial stage of its development.

Having recently uprooted myself from Australia in order to take up a teaching position in the United States, I wish to pay tribute to the School of Humanities at Murdoch University in Western Australia, where I spent the previous seven years. I am grateful to all the friends, colleagues, and students who have helped make Murdoch a uniquely stimulating intellectual environment and a wonderful place to teach. I would particularly like to thank Ien Ang, Rachel Fensham, Mitzi Goldman, Adrian Montana, Zoe Sofoulis, and Jon Stratton for sending me off with a great song! Finally, I owe a special debt to my colleague Horst Ruthrof, whose intellectual passion, uncompromising vision, and generosity of spirit have been an ongoing source of inspiration.

Part of the argument developed in this book was first sketched out in two articles, "The Gender of Modernity," in *Political Gender: Texts and Contexts* ed. Sally Ledger et al. (New York: Harvester Wheatsheaf, 1994), and "Modernism and Modernity: Engendering Literary History," in *Rereading Modernism: New Directions in Feminist Criticism,* ed. Lisa Rado (New York: Garland Press, 1994). An early version of Chapter 4 was first published in *PMLA,* 106, 5 (1991).

Introduction:
Myths of the Modern

What is the gender of modernity? How can anything as abstract as a historical period have a sex? In the context of the current interest in the "historicity of textuality and the textuality of history," the idea is not as strange as it may initially appear.[1] If our sense of the past is inevitably shaped by the explanatory logic of narrative, then the stories that we create in turn reveal the inescapable presence and power of gender symbolism. This saturation of cultural texts with metaphors of masculinity and femininity is nowhere more obvious than in the case of the modern, perhaps the most pervasive yet elusive of periodizing terms. Accounts of the modern age, whether academic or popular, typically achieve some kind of formal coherence by dramatizing and personifying historical processes; individual or collective human subjects are endowed with symbolic importance as exemplary bearers of temporal meaning. Whether these subjects are presumed to be male or female has important consequences for the kind of narrative that unfolds. Gender affects not just the factual content of historical knowledge—what is included and what gets left out—but also the philosophical assumptions underlying our interpretations of the nature and meaning of social processes. This question of the gendering of history, as well as the historicity of gender, will serve as a leitmotif for the following analysis.

Consider, for example, one influential recent account of the politics of development. In Marshall Berman's *All That Is Solid Melts into Air,* the author hails Goethe's Faust as the exemplary hero of the modern age. In the character of Faust, Berman argues, the contradictions of modernity are portrayed with penetrating clarity: on the one hand, an exhilarating sense of liberation resulting from the challenge to tradition and established forms of authority; on the other, a nascent bourgeois individualism which asserts itself in the desire for uncontrollable growth and domination over nature. Thus Faust comes to stand for the adventures and horrors, the ambiguities and ironies of modern life, as exemplified in the creative destruction and constant transformation unleashed by the logic of capitalist development. And what, one might ask, of Gretchen, the young village girl who is seduced and abandoned by Faust in the course of his striving for new experiences and unlimited self-development? Berman notes that Faust is at first "enthralled by her childlike innocence, her small-town simplicity, her Christian humility," but gradually finds that her "ardor dissolves into hysteria, and it is more than he can handle."[2] "Drawn impatiently towards new realms of experience and action," Berman explains, Faust "has come to feel her needs and fears as more and more of a drag."[3] Although Berman is aware of some of the complexities of Gretchen's position, his sympathy clearly remains with Faust and his inevitable rejection of the closed, narrow world that Gretchen represents. Woman is aligned with the dead weight of tradition and conservatism that the active, newly autonomous, and self-defining subject must seek to transcend. Thus she functions as a sacrificial victim exemplifying the losses which underpin the ambiguous, but ultimately exhilarating and seductive logic of the modern.

From a reading of Berman's book, it would be tempting to conclude that the gender of modernity is indeed male. All the exemplary heroes of his text—Faust, Marx, Baudelaire—are of course symbols not just of modernity, but also of masculinity, historical markers of the emergence of new forms of bourgeois and working-class male subjectivity. Both in Berman's account of Faust and in his later evocation of Baudelaire's flâneur, the stroller who goes botanizing on the asphalt of the streets of Paris, the modern individual is assumed to be an autonomous male free of familial and communal ties. Here Berman's book fits comfortably into a long-standing tradition of writing that reads modernity as an Oedipal revolt against the tyranny of authority, drawing on metaphors of contestation and struggle grounded in an ideal of competitive masculinity. Feminism has in recent years developed an extensive critique of such idealized representations of the autonomous male subject, arguing that this ideal of freedom carries within it the seeds of domination in its desire to subjugate the other and its fear of a dependency aligned with the feminine.[4] From such a perspective, Berman's fascination with the ideal of restless, endless self-expansion embodied in the figure of Faust appears more problematic than he may originally have intended.

Yet Berman's equation of masculinity with modernity and of femininity with tradition is only one of various possible stories about the nature and meaning of the modern era. By contrast, a recent book by Gail Finney argues the imaginative centrality of *female* psychology and sexuality to representations of modernity in the European fin de siècle. Through readings of some of the period's most memorable dramatic heroines—Hedda Gabler, Salomé, Lulu—Finney demonstrates the profound interconnections between femininity and modernity in the late-nineteenth-century social imaginary. The psychic and social conflicts embodied in these heroines differ markedly from those examined in Berman's exclusively masculine pantheon. Most noticeably, intimate relationships emerge as a central arena within which the contradictions of the modern are played out. Whereas Berman's text tends to replicate an established view of modernity in terms of a polarized opposition between individual and society, Finney points to the centrality of familial ties and identities—as mother, daughter, wife—in the construction of modern forms of subjectivity. The so-called private sphere, often portrayed as a domain where natural and timeless emotions hold sway, is shown to be radically implicated in patterns of modernization and processes of social change. The analysis of modern femininity brings with it a recognition of the profoundly historical nature of private feelings.

The figures of the feminist and the hysteric emerge in Finney's analysis as key symbols of the gender politics of modernity, apparently opposed yet closely related images that permeated the culture of the fin de siècle. Just as the feminist expressed a rebellious, emancipatory, and outer-directed response to the condition of female oppression, so, she argues, the hysteric exemplified a rejection of society that was passive, inner-directed, and ultimately self-destructive. Yet both figures are equally implicated in modern systems of thought and representation: the apparently private, irrational behavior of the hysteric was itself a socially determined phenomenon, an index of the nineteenth-century preoccupation with sexuality as the truth of the self that found expression in the emergent doctrines of psychiatry and psychoanalysis and their hysterization of the female body. Indeed, the distinction between the feminist and the hysteric was regularly blurred in much of the writing of the period, which constantly sought to reduce the political actions of suffragettes to the irrational outbursts of a group of deranged and dangerous women. Thus, Finney writes, "this double spectrum—of women's responses to their oppression (feminism and hysteria) and of men's reactions to these responses (feminism and hysterization)—produced a field of conflicting currents of thought which inevitably left their mark on dramatists of the day."[5] The figure of woman pervades the culture of the fin de siècle as a powerful symbol of both the dangers and the promises of the modern age.

It is enlightening in this context to contrast Berman's discussion of Faust—the modern Prometheus—with Finney's reading of Lulu—the

modern Pandora. First brought to life by the German dramatist Franz Wedekind, the seductive, demonic, yet childlike Lulu was to become well known
to a wide public as a result of the success of G. W. Pabst's silent film *Pandora's Box*. Finney suggests in her reading of Wedekind's work that Lulu
should be seen not just as a product of modern society but as a quintessential
incorporation of its values. Actress, sex object, prostitute, performer, spectacle; all these identities render her the paradigmatic symbol of a culture
increasingly structured around the erotics and aesthetics of the commodity.
On the one hand, Lulu exemplifies the fin-de-siècle association of femininity
with nature and the primal forces of the unconscious; yet on the other, she
is also surface without substance, a creature of style and artifice whose
identity is created through the various costumes and masks that she assumes.
Here Wedekind's heroine joins an established repertoire of images of the
prostitute and the actress, whose paradoxical combination of eros and artifice
has frequently been seen as the quintessential manifestation of a feminized
modernity.

   Clearly, the versions of history proposed by these two texts are significantly
affected by the gender of their exemplary subjects. In Berman's account,
modernity is identified with dynamic activity, development, and the desire
for unlimited growth; the autonomy of the newly liberated bourgeois subject
is exemplified in the accelerating momentum of industrial production, rationalization, and domination over nature. Finney's text, by contrast, posits a
modern individual who is both more passive and more indeterminate, a
decentered nexus of textual influences, social roles, and inchoate psychic
impulses. The purposefully striving masculinity of Faust is replaced by a
fetishized, libidinized, and commodified femininity produced through the
textually generated logics of modern forms of desire. In these contrasting
visions of men's and women's modernity, Berman's primary reference point
is Marx, whereas Finney's is Freud. One obvious explanation for this difference lies in the period of time separating the works of Goethe and Wedekind;
clearly, the "modernity" of their texts is in many respects very different. Yet,
as Berman's book makes clear, the Faustian myth retains significant currency
as a symbolic articulation of the contradictions of the modern age, its resonances still powerful in our own time.[6] Indeed, the two stories I have just
recounted can be seen as competing myths of modernity that recur across a
range of both popular and academic, fictional and theoretical texts. For every
account of the modern era which emphasizes the domination of masculine
qualities of rationalization, productivity, and repression, one can find another
text which points—whether approvingly or censoriously—to the feminiza-

tion of Western society, as evidenced in the passive, hedonistic, and decentered nature of modern subjectivity.

Of course, these differing perspectives are by no means incompatible, and some writers have sought to bring them together into a single, overarching theory of modern development. One of the best known of such attempts is the *Dialectic of Enlightenment*, Theodor Adorno and Max Horkheimer's analysis of the self-destructive logic of Western society. Drawing on the work of Marx, Weber, and Nietzsche, Adorno and Horkheimer anticipate aspects of contemporary poststructuralist theory in their exposure of the fundamental irrationality of modern reason. The Greek myth of Odysseus and the sirens is read by the authors as a central text of European civilization and as an exemplary parable of the aporias of modernity. Ordering his sailors to bind him to the mast so that he cannot respond to the seductive song of the sirens, Odysseus epitomizes the disciplined male bourgeois individual, foreshadowing the repression of the body and the feminine that will determine the development of Western culture. As Douglas Kellner argues in a useful summary, "Homer's text is read as an allegorical journey in which Odysseus overcomes primitive natural forces (immersion in pleasure, sexuality, animal aggressivity and violence, brutal tribalism and so forth) and asserts his domination over the mythic/natural world. In his use of cunning and deceit, his drive toward self-preservation and refusal to accept mythic fate, his entrepreneurial control over his men and his patriarchal power over his wife and other women, Odysseus is presented as a prefiguration of bourgeois man who reveals the connections between self-preservation, the domination of nature and the entanglement of myth and enlightenment."[7]

This entanglement is exemplified in a central motto of the *Dialectic of Enlightenment*, the claim that "myth is already enlightenment; and enlightenment reverts to mythology."[8] Through the blind exercise of mastery over nature, reason is transformed into its opposite, as exemplified in the irrationality and barbarism of a modern capitalist society driven by the dual imperatives of instrumental reason and commodity fetishism. In an influential chapter on the politics of the culture industry, Adorno and Horkheimer argue that its mythological dreamworlds, seductive commodities, and promises of endless fun are one of the key means through which individuals are reconciled to the prospect of a totally administered society ruled by a logic of profit and standardization. The repressed feminine of aesthetic and libidinal forces returns in the form of the engulfing, regressive lures of modern mass culture and consumer society, which trades inauthentic pleasures and pseudo-happiness for acquiescence to the status quo. Thus for

Adorno and Horkheimer "masculine" rationalization and "feminine" pleasure are simply two sides of a single coin, the seamless logic of domination that constitutes modern subjectivity through processes of subjugation.

While Adorno and Horkheimer's thesis has been powerful and influential, particularly in Marxist circles, it has also been subject to criticism on a number of grounds. First of all, it can be argued that the *Dialectic of Enlightenment* espouses a highly pessimistic philosophy of history which conceives of modernity as an inexorable spiral of ever greater repression. Such an apocalyptic vision of history as domination denies the ambiguous and multidimensional aspects of modern development and allows little room for the possibility of contradiction, resistance, or emancipatory change within what is presented as a closed system. In particular, while ostensibly granting a key importance to the cultural domain, it ultimately reduces it to an essentially subsidiary role as a reflection of pre-existing economic, technological, and administrative logics. As a result, it does not make any allowances for the productive, interactive, and intersubjective dimensions of symbolic forms, the diverse and often contradictory constellations of discourses, stories, and images through which individuals interpret and make sense of their lives. By ignoring the hermeneutic agency of social subjects and the polysemic richness of cultural texts, Adorno and Horkheimer reproduce the very identity logic they claim to challenge through their representation of modern individuals as a passive, homogeneous, and alienated mass.

Second, the positioning of gender in Adorno and Horkheimer's thesis remains uneasy and ultimately unsatisfactory from a feminist perspective. On the one hand, their analysis emphasizes the fundamentally patriarchal basis of Western modernity, as exemplified in the tyranny of a logic of identity that requires a denial of autonomous difference. Here, as in more recent critiques of logocentrism emanating from French poststructuralist thought, the fantasm of the feminine plays a pivotal role, embodying a principle of resistance and a utopian alternative to the constraints of dominating reason. The exclusion of women from Western modernity thus allows them to function as a symbol of escape from all-pervasive systems of power.[9] On the other hand, this very critique risks the continuing identification of women with presymbolic otherness in its emphasis on the fundamental masculinity of the social. In particular, the reliance on a Freudian paradigm of repression reveals its limitations in encouraging a recurring equation of the feminine with a repressed and undifferentiated nature. Thus, as Patricia Mills notes in her critical engagement with *Dialectic of Enlightenment,* the female voice of the siren is linked with the song of the sensuous world of nature, the lure of the pleasure principle.[10] Mills goes on to argue that such an association of the feminine with the nonrational and the asymbolic does not allow for any independent conception of female identity, agency, or desire. Woman is reduced to the libidinal, inexpressible, or aesthetic, the repressed Other of patriarchal reason. The possibility of exploring women's varied and complex relations to processes of social change is excluded by a sweeping vision of Enlightenment as emblematic of a totalizing logic of patriarchal domination.

Adorno and Horkheimer's text thus points to some of the difficulties which arise in the search for a single explanatory account of the underlying logic of Western history. While their analysis has the obvious merit of acknowledging the male-dominated nature of modern development, the resulting vision of male agency and female powerlessness precludes any consideration of women's distinctive roles within and active contributions to historical processes. Within the constraints of a single mythic narrative, it is inevitably man who assumes the role of collective subject of history, while woman can exist only as Other, as the object rather than the subject of historical narrative. One possible avenue of response to this logic of exclusion is to reverse the roles of man and woman by constructing a counter-myth of emblematic femininity; thus Mills goes on to offer a feminist reading of the story of Medea, whom she describes as the female Odysseus, as a powerful allegory of the problematic of female desire.[11] Yet, as she simultaneously acknowledges, any attempt to encapsulate women's distinctive relationships to modernity through a single alternative myth risks becoming a new form of "reifying universal" in its assumption that the history of women can be subsumed and symbolized by a single, all-encompassing image of femininity. Retaining a belief in the univocal meaning of both woman and modernity, such a strategy does not address the multiplicity and diversity of women's relations to historical processes.

For precisely this reason, my own analysis does not attempt to provide a grand philosophical summation of the gendered nature and logic of Western history. Rather than creating an overarching feminist myth of the modern, I have chosen a different approach, which aims to unravel the complexities of modernity's relationship to femininity through an analysis of its varied and competing representations. Interweaving cultural theory with cultural history, I address more general theoretical questions about the gender politics of the modern via a reading of a diverse range of late-nineteenth-century and early-twentieth-century European texts. Through such an interpretive strategy I hope to analyze my topic from a variety of different vantage points, and to pay careful attention to the various genres and forms through which our sense of the modern has been constituted.

In opting for such a method, I do not wish to suggest that forms of abstraction or totalization are in themselves reprehensible or unacceptable practices. A degree of generalization is inevitable in any argument that wishes to go beyond empiricism and the mere notation of particulars to the construction of meaningful structures, connections, and arguments. In this sense, as Horst Ruthrof argues, there is an ineradicable teleological dimension within any interpretive strategy; rather than disappearing from poststructuralist theory, teleology has simply shifted from the interpreted text to the tools of interpretation.[12] Thus though I question the belief that modernity can be reduced to a single meaning and historical logic, my own arguments are themselves beholden to the implied telos of feminist theory and politics. The difference is one of degree rather than kind, and my choice of a multiperspectival approach to the cultural politics of modernity is itself driven by pragmatic rather than exclusively theoretical considerations. Abstract philosophical theories of the modern are of little *use* to a feminist analysis, insofar as they tend either to subsume women within a single unilinear logic of history or else to position them outside of modern discourses and institutions in a zone of ahistorical, asymbolic otherness. They are thus unable to illuminate women's complex and changing relationships to the diverse political, philosophical, and cultural legacies of modernity, a question, it need hardly be pointed out, that retains a continuing and urgent relevance in our time.

Furthermore, if there is any legitimacy at all to the claim that feminism constitutes a form of dialogical politics, this attentiveness to otherness surely needs to extend itself to a careful engagement with the voices of the past. Rather than simply subsuming the history of gender relations within an overarching meta-theory of modernity articulated from the vantage point of the present, feminist critics need to take seriously past women's and men's own understandings of their positioning within historical and social processes. It is here that cultural analysis comes into its own, as a means of approaching the history of the modern through an investigation of the diverse ways in which modernity has itself been represented. By examining some of the most significant and pervasive of these representations, I seek to elaborate the mobile and shifting meanings of the modern as a category of cultural consciousness. In this context it is by no means obvious, as is assumed by the more reckless claims within postmodern theory, that our present historical condition has freed us from those dogmas and blind spots that we typically project onto our modern past. Indeed, the modernity that is often caricatured as synonymous with a totalizing logic of identity reveals on closer examination a multiplicity of voices and perspectives that cannot be easily synthesized into a single, unified ideology or world-view. One of my aims is thus to emphasize the complexities and ambiguities of the modern against the reductive treatment it has received from some postmodernist and some feminist theorists.

By focusing my discussion on a particular period (the fin de siècle) and a set of interconnected cultures (France, England, Germany), I hope to unravel some of these ambiguous dimensions of the modern as they shape a particular and limited set of contexts. Given my interest in such particularities, the question arises as to the continuing usefulness of the modern as an analytical category. There are two important reasons why I have chosen to retain and complicate, rather than simply abandon, the term. First of all, the idea of the modern, in spite of (or perhaps because of) its polysemic and indeterminate meanings, serves to draw our attention to long-term processes of social change, to the multidimensional yet often systematic interconnections between a variety of cultural, political, and economic structures. The investigation of such structures is, in my view, a central task for feminist theory, whose critique of universal history should not be confused with a mere celebration of plural identities or a fragmentation of the social into dispersed and isolated sites. Hence the continuing relevance of the category of the modern as a means of coming to grips with long-term processes of structural change and equally important, of assessing the differing, uneven, and often contradictory impact of such processes on particular social groups. The intersection of femininity and modernity plays itself out *differentially* across the specifics of sociohistorical context.

Second, the idea of the modern saturates the discourses, images, and narratives of the late nineteenth and early twentieth centuries. It is an era profoundly shaped by logics of periodization, by the attempt to situate individual lives and experiences in relation to broader historical patterns and overarching narratives of innovation and decline. "Modernity" thus refers not simply to a substantive range of sociohistorical phenomena—capitalism, bureaucracy, technological development, and so on—but above all to particular (though often contradictory) experiences of temporality and historical consciousness. While the modern experience of historicity has for obvious reasons received significant attention from Marxist critics, it has been less systematically explored by feminists, whose explorations of nineteenth-century culture have been primarily organized around the spatial distinction of private versus public. By linking feminist theory to the analysis of different representations of temporality and history, then, I hope to elucidate some of the ways in which femininity and modernity have been brought into conjunction by both women and men. Gender, as my opening paragraph suggested, reveals itself to be a central organizing metaphor in the construction of historical time. Indeed, many of the myths of modernity that pervade the last fin de siècle can be detected again in our own, suggesting that we may yet have to free ourselves from the seductive power of grand narratives.

The starting point of my analysis was thus a deceptively simple one: a desire to reread the modern through the lens of feminist theory. I began by asking myself the following questions: How would our understanding of modernity change if instead of taking male experience as paradigmatic, we were to look instead at texts written primarily by or about women? And what if feminine phenomena, often seen as having a secondary or marginal status, were given a central importance in the analysis of the culture of modernity? What *difference* would such a procedure make? The stories resulting from such an investigation would not, I surmised, be completely alien or unrecognizable ones, given the complex entanglement and mutual imbrication of men's and women's histories. But they might well throw some significant new light on that seemingly exhausted issue, the aesthetics and the politics of modernity.

Modernity and Feminism

> I prefer to study ... the everyday, the so-called banal, the sup-
> posedly un-or non-experimental, asking not "why does it fall
> short of modernism?" but "how do classical theories of mod-
> ernism fall short of women's modernity?"
>
> Meaghan Morris, "Things to Do with Shopping Centres"

Even the most cursory survey of the vast body of writing about the
modern reveals a cacophony of different and often dissenting voices. Modernity arises out of a culture of "stability, coherence, discipline and world-
mastery";[1] alternatively it points to a "discontinuous experience of time,
space and causality as transitory, fleeting and fortuitous."[2] For some writers
it is a "culture of rupture," marked by historical relativism and ambiguity;[3]
for others it involves a "rational, autonomous subject" and an "absolutist,
unitary conception of truth."[4] To be modern is to be on the side of progress,
reason, and democracy or, by contrast to align oneself with "disorder, despair
and anarchy."[5] Indeed, to be modern is often paradoxically to be antimodern, to define oneself in explicit opposition to the prevailing norms and
values of one's own time.[6]

Clearly, there is no magical means of resolving this semantic confusion,
which derives from the complicated and many-faceted aspects of modern
development. Yet it is possible to identify certain key factors which contribute to this bewildering diversity of definitions. For example, the different
understandings of the modern across national cultures and traditions lead to
potential difficulties of translation when texts circulate within a global intellectual economy. Thus for Jürgen Habermas "die Moderne" comprises an
irreversible historical process that includes not only the repressive forces of
bureaucratic and capitalist domination but also the emergence of a potentially emancipatory, because self-critical, ethics of communicative reason.

Here Hegel emerges as a key figure, in whose philosophy the theoretical self-consciousness of modernity receives its first systematic articulation.[7] Vincent Descombes, by contrast, takes Habermas to task for such an unproblematic equation of modernity with idealist philosophy, a move which is, he argues, so closely rooted in the specific history and sociology of German culture that it remains "impossible" for those trained in French thought. For Descombes, it is the realm of poetics rather than philosophy and above all the figure of Baudelaire that define the parameters of a French *modernité* characterized by ambiguity, discontinuity, and a blurring rather than separation of art and life.[8] In this terminological dispute we can see a clear instance of one of the defining and recurring ambiguities of the modern: its use by some writers as more or less synonymous with the Enlightenment tradition and by others as antithetical to it.

This brings me to the related question of the influence of particular disciplinary traditions on the construction and circulation of theoretical concepts. The work of Michel Foucault in particular has sharpened our awareness of the ways in which structures of knowledge help to form our sense of the very objects they claim to analyze. Thus modernity can mean something very different in the work of political theorists, literary critics, sociologists, and philosophers, to take just a few random instances. This ambiguity relates not just to conflicting estimations of the nature and value of the modern but also to disagreements as to its actual location in historical time. Whereas a political theorist may situate the origins of modernity in the seventeenth century and in the work of Hobbes, a literary critic is just as likely to claim that modernity has its birth in the mid or late nineteenth century. Rather than a precise historical periodization, modernity thus comprises a constantly shifting set of temporal coordinates. As Lawrence Cahoone points out, "the historical starting point is impossible to fix; any century from the sixteenth through the nineteenth could be, and has been, named as the first 'modern' century. The Copernican system, for example, arguably a cornerstone of modernity, dates from the sixteenth century, while democratic government, which can claim to be the essence of modern politics, did not become the dominant Western political form until very recently."[9]

Cahoone's statement allows us to see that modernity is not a homogeneous Zeitgeist which was born at a particular moment in history, but rather that it comprises a collection of interlocking institutional, cultural, and philosophical strands which emerge and develop at different times and which are often only defined as "modern" retrospectively. In attempting to distinguish between these different strands, it is helpful to begin by clarifying the "family of terms" associated with the modern.[10] *Modernization* is usually taken to

denote the complex constellation of socioeconomic phenomena which originated in the context of Western development but which have since manifested themselves around the globe in various forms: scientific and
technological innovation, the industrialization of production, rapid urbanization, an ever expanding capitalist market, the development of the nation-
state, and so on. *Modernism*, by contrast, defines a specific form of artistic
production, serving as an umbrella term for a mélange of artistic schools and
styles which first arose in late-nineteenth-century Europe and America. Characterized by such features as aesthetic self-consciousness, stylistic fragmentation, and a questioning of representation, modernist texts bore a highly
ambivalent and often critical relationship to processes of modernization. The
French term *modernité*, while also concerned with a distinctively modern
sense of dislocation and ambiguity, locates it in the more general experience
of the aestheticization of everyday life, as exemplified in the ephemeral and
transitory qualities of an urban culture shaped by the imperatives of fashion,
consumerism, and constant innovation.[11] Finally, *modernity* is often used as
an overarching periodizing term to denote a historical era which may encompass any or all of the above features. This epochal meaning of the term
typically includes a general philosophical distinction between traditional societies, which are structured around the omnipresence of divine authority, and
a modern secularized universe predicated upon an individuated and self-
conscious subjectivity.[12]

The factual ambiguity implicit in the idea of the modern is, however,
combined with a distinctive rhetorical power. Modernity differs from other
kinds of periodization in possessing a normative as well as a descriptive
dimension—one can be "for" or "against" modernity in a way that one
cannot be for or against the Renaissance, for example. The symbolic force of
the term lies in its enunciation of a process of differentiation, an act of
separation from the past. Thus the famous Querelle des Anciens et des
Modernes in late-seventeenth-century Europe turned on the challenge to the
authority of classical texts as ultimate cultural reference points and bearers of
timeless truths. Matei Calinescu notes that while both sides in the dispute
retained a certain unquestioning adherence to neoclassical ideals, it was here
that the idea of the modern first acquired an explicit polemical edge as a
rejection of the dead weight of history and tradition. Increasingly, "modern"
was to become synonymous with the repudiation of the past and a commitment to change and the values of the future.[13]

It is easy to see that the politics of such an ideal are inherently double-
edged. On the one hand, the appeal to the modern could serve as a means of
legitimating rebellion against hierarchical social structures and prevailing

modes of thought by challenging the authority of tradition, custom, and the status quo. Such historical events as the French Revolution are often identified as key moments in the articulation of distinctively modern notions of autonomy and equality, grounded in the belief that there exists no authority beyond that of a critical, and self-critical, human reason. On the other hand, the idea of the modern was deeply implicated from its beginnings with a project of domination over those seen to lack this capacity for reflective reasoning. In the discourses of colonialism, for example, the historical distinction between the modern present and the primitive past was mapped onto the spatial relations between Western and non-Western societies. Thus the technological advances of modern nation-states could be cited as a justification for imperialist invasion, as the traditions and customs of indigenous peoples were forced to give way to the inexorable path of historical progress.[14] Similarly, the modern brought with it an ideal of equality grounded in fraternity that effectively excluded women from many forms of political life. Thus Joan Landes comments that "from the standpoint of women and their interests, enlightenment looks suspiciously like counterenlightenment and revolution like counterrevolution."[15] Tracing the history of women's roles in the French Revolution, Landes shows how the discourse of modern rights and republican virtues effectively served to silence women through a recurring identification of the human with the masculine.

Appeals to the modern and the new could, however, also be appropriated and articulated anew by dissident or disenfranchised groups to formulate their own resistance to the status quo. Thus in the early twentieth century the figure of the New Woman was to become a resonant symbol of emancipation, whose modernity signaled not an endorsement of an existing present but rather a bold imagining of an alternative future. In rather different ways, modernist and avant-garde movements sought to disrupt taken-for-granted assumptions and dogmatic complacencies, refashioning the idea of the modern to signify ambiguity, uncertainty, and crisis rather than an uncritical ascription to a teleology of Western progress and an ideal of reason. The "old new" of dominant bourgeois values was thus regularly challenged by diverse groups who defined themselves as "authentically new" and who drew on and revitalized the promise of innovation as liberating transformation implicit in the idea of the modern to forge an array of critical and oppositional identities.

Appeals to modernity have, in other words, been used to further a multifarious range of political and cultural interests. Rather than identifying a stable referent or set of attributes, "modern" acts as a mobile and shifting category of classification that serves to structure, legitimize, and valorize varied and often competing perspectives. My analysis thus begins with the assumption that modernity embraces a multidimensional array of historical phenomena that cannot be prematurely synthesized into a unified Zeitgeist. Hence I am skeptical of those writings which equate the entire modern period with a particular and narrowly defined tradition of intellectual thought stretching from Kant to Marx (as if several centuries of history could be reduced to the writings of a handful of philosophers!) in order to celebrate the emergence of postmodern ambiguity and difference against modern homogeneity and rationality. Such a purported critique of totalization is itself vastly totalizing, doing interpretive violence to the complex and heterogeneous strands of modern culture, which cannot be reduced to exemplifications of a monolithic world-view in this way. Within the specific context of late-nineteenth-century Europe, for example, appeals to science, rationality, and material progress coexisted with Romantic invocations of emotion, intuition, and authenticity as well as alongside self-conscious explorations of the performative and artificial status of identity and the inescapable metaphoricity of language. Rather than inscribing a homogeneous cultural consensus, the discourses of modernity reveal multiple and conflicting responses to processes of social change.

My intent here is not to claim that modern and postmodern are interchangeable signifiers; clearly, our own fin de siècle differs in crucial and fundamental ways from its predecessor, even as it also reveals some intriguing parallels. (Thus many of the topoi and catchphrases often seen as quintessentially postmodern—simulation, pastiche, consumption, nostalgia, cyborgs, cross-dressing—are suggestively foreshadowed in a number of nineteenth-century texts.) Nevertheless, feminist theory surely needs to question rather than uncritically endorse an opposition between a repressive modernity and a subversive postmodernity which has become de rigeur in certain areas of contemporary theory. As Gianni Vattimo has emphasized, such a view of the postmodern typically repeats the gesture of overcoming and futurity that is fundamental to the modern, naively re-enacting the very logic of history as progress that it claims to renounce.[16]

My own analysis is motivated by the desire to question existing theories of literary and cultural history in order to reveal their blindness to issues of gender. In this sense, I am in sympathy with feminist critics who argue that theories of both the modern and the postmodern have been organized around a masculine norm and pay insufficent attention to the specificity of women's lives and experiences. Yet I do not seek to demonstrate the illusory nature of the modern in order to position women and feminist concerns outside its logic. Such acts of attempted demystification are necessarily problematic because they fail to acknowledge their own inevitable enmeshment within the categories that they seek to transcend. Thus I hope to show that feminism, which has been highly critical of the concept of the modern, has also been deeply influenced by it, and that struggles for women's emancipation are complexly interwoven with processes of modernization. If women's interests cannot be unproblematically aligned with dominant conceptions of the modern, neither can they simply be placed outside of them.

"Heroines of Modernity"

The claim that most contemporary theories of the modern are male-centered will not, I imagine, come as a great surprise to most readers of this book. It is a constant feature that links together a range of otherwise very disparate texts. I have already cited Berman's richly textured, but in this sense frustratingly monological, account; within the area of literary and cultural studies alone one could easily list many other critical works which claim to offer a general theory of modernity but base themselves exclusively on writings by men and textual representations of masculinity. The issue is even more straightforward within the field of social and political theory, where the equation of modernity with particular public and institutional structures governed by men has led to an almost total elision of the lives, concerns, and perspectives of women.[17]

The identification of modernity with masculinity is not, of course, simply an invention of contemporary theorists. Many of the key symbols of the modern in the nineteenth century—the public sphere, the man of the crowd, the stranger, the dandy, the flâneur—were indeed explicitly gendered. There could for example, be no direct female equivalent of the flâneur, given that any woman who loitered in the streets of the nineteenth-century metropolis was likely to be taken for a prostitute.[18] Thus a recurring identification of the modern with the public was largely responsible for the belief that women were situated outside processes of history and social change. In the texts of early Romanticism one finds some of the most explicitly nostalgic representations of femininity as a redemptive refuge from the constraints of civilization. Seen to be less specialized and differentiated than man, located within the household and an intimate web of familial relations, more closely linked to nature through her reproductive capacity, woman embodied a sphere of atemporal authenticity seemingly untouched by the alienation and fragmentation of modern life.

This view of femininity has retained much of its rhetorical power, resurfacing in the work of numerous contemporary writers. Thus part of the common sense of much mainstream feminist thought has been a belief that such phenomena as industry, consumerism, the modern city, the mass media, and technology are in some sense fundamentally masculine, and that feminine values of intimacy and authenticity remain outside the dehumanizing and alienating logic of modernity. These assumptions received explicit articulation in works of cultural feminism which embraced a Romantic ideal of femininity as an enclave of natural self-presence in the face of the tyrannical onslaught of technocratic rationality. More recent feminist work has drawn upon psychoanalytic and poststructuralist theory to pitch a broadly similar critique at a more abstract level, arguing that the founding concepts and structures of modern thought are by nature phallocentric. In a recent book, for example, Juliet MacCannell claims that modernity is predicated on the elimination of woman and sexual difference. According to MacCannell, modern society no longer exemplifies the law of the father, but rather represents the regime of the brother, as the traditional and unquestioned authority of the patriarchal God or king gives way to a modern Enlightenment logic of equality, fraternity, and identity. Yet for women, this historical development brings with it more oppressive, because concealed, regimes of domination; the modern is predicated on the absence of the Other and the erasure of feminine agency and desire.[19]

Aspects of MacCannell's thesis are suggestive, and her reading of the modern through the lens of psychoanalytic theory usefully destabilizes the rational/irrational dichotomy by exposing the fantasmic and narcissistic dimensions of Enlightenment thought. Yet the difficulty with all such theories of the modern lies in the relentless generality of their claims. It is one thing to argue that particular institutional and cultural phenomena arising out of processes of modernization have been historically structured around a male norm, as does Joan Landes in her careful discussion of the symbolic politics of the eighteenth-century public sphere or Griselda Pollock in her account of the sexual topography of the nineteenth-century city.[20] It is quite another to claim that an extended historical period can be reduced to the manifestation of a single, unified, masculine principle. Such an absolute critique fails to account for the contradictory and conflictual impulses shaping the logic—or rather logics—of modern development. It does not allow for the possibility that certain aspects of modernity may have been or could potentially be beneficial for women. Instead, it engenders a dichotomy between an alienated modern past and an authentic (postmodern?) feminine future which can provide no account of the possible mechanisms of transition from one condition to the other.[21] Furthermore, such a view of the essentially masculine nature of modernity effectively writes women out of history by ignoring their active and varied negotiations with different aspects of their social environment. Accepting at face value an equation of the modern with certain abstract philosophical ideals and a male-dominated public life, it fails to consider the specific and distinctive features of women's modernity.

There also exists, however, a body of feminist work on the modern which has significantly influenced the arguments in this book. As well as drawing upon recent rewritings of the literary history of the fin de siècle by Elaine Showalter and Sandra Gilbert and Susan Gubar, I have found recent works by Elizabeth Wilson, Christine Buci-Glucksmann, Rachel Bowlby, Nancy Armstrong, Andreas Huyssen, and Patrice Petro to be enormously useful.[22] What these critics share is a self-conscious recognition of the complex intersections between woman and modernity, of the mutual imbrication as well as points of contradiction between these two categories. Rather than espousing either a progress narrative which assumes that modernization brought with it an unambiguous improvement in women's lives or else a counter-myth of nostalgia for an edenic, nonalienated, golden past, their writings offer a sustained engagement with the shifting complexities of the modern in relation to gender politics.

Thus on the one hand, as many feminist writers have noted, the nineteenth century saw the establishment of increasingly rigid boundaries between private and public selves, so that gender differences solidified into apparently natural and immutable traits. The distinction between a striving, competitive masculinity and a nurturant, domestic femininity, while a feasible ideal only for a minority of middle-class households, nevertheless became a guiding rubric within which various aspects of culture were subsumed. Mary Poovey notes that "the model of a binary opposition between the sexes, which was socially realized in separate but supposedly equal 'spheres,' underwrote an entire system of institutional practices and conventions at midcentury, ranging from a sexual division of labor to a sexual division of economic and political rights."[23] These material and institutional realities both shaped and were themselves shaped by dominant conceptions of women's relationship to history and progress, as spatial categories of private and public were mapped onto temporal distinctions between past and present. By being positioned outside the dehumanizing structures of the capitalist economy as well as the rigorous demands of public life, woman became a symbol of nonalienated, and hence nonmodern, identity. A proliferating body of scientific, literary, and philosophical texts sought to prove that women were less differentiated and less self-conscious than men and more rooted in an elemental unity. As a result, for a range of female as well as male thinkers, women could enter modernity only by taking on the attributes that had been traditionally classified as masculine.

On the other hand, however, a close consideration of nineteenth-century texts suggests that the divisions between public and private, masculine and feminine, modern and antimodern were not as fixed as they may have appeared. Or rather, they were unmade and remade in new ways. Christine Buci-Glucksmann refers to a "symbolic redistribution of relations between feminine and masculine," which she sees as a prevailing countertendency within nineteenth-century urban life.[24] Thus the ideology of separate spheres was undercut by the movement of working-class women into mass production and industrial labor, causing numbers of writers to express their fears that the workplace would become sexualized through the dangerous proximity of male and female bodies. The expansion of consumerism in the latter half of the century further blurred public/private distinctions, as middle-class women moved out into the public spaces of the department store and the world of mass-produced goods in turn invaded the interiority of the home. Finally, late-nineteenth-century feminists and social reformers provided one of the most visible and overtly political challenges to existing gender hierarchies. Asserting their rights to political and legal equality with men, they simultaneously appealed to a distinctively feminine moral authority as a justification for their occupation of the public sphere. Increasingly, images of femininity were to play a central role in prevailing anxieties, fears, and hopeful imaginings about the distinctive features of the "modern age."

In this context a number of critics have commented upon the significance of the prostitute in the nineteenth-century social imaginary and her emblematic status in the literature and art of the period.[25] Both seller and commodity, the prostitute was the ultimate symbol of the commodification of eros, a disturbing example of the ambiguous boundaries separating economics and sexuality, the rational and irrational, the instrumental and the aesthetic. Her body yielded to a number of conflicting interpretations; seen by some contemporary writers to exemplify the tyranny of commerce and the universal domination of the cash nexus, it was read by others as representing the dark abyss of a dangerous female sexuality linked to contamination, disease, and the breakdown of social hierarchies in the modern city. Subjected to increasing forms of government regulation, documentation, and surveillance, the prostitute was an insistently visible reminder of the potential anonymity of women in the modern city and the loosening of sexuality from familial and communal bonds. Like the prostitute, the actress could also be seen as a "figure of public pleasure," whose deployment of cosmetics and costume bore witness to the artificial and commodified forms of contemporary female sexuality.[26] This motif of the female performer easily lent itself to appropriation as a symptom of the pervasiveness of illusion and spectacle in the generation of modern forms of desire. Positioned on the margins of respectable society, yet graphically embodying its structuring logic of commodity aesthetics, the prostitute and the actress fascinated nineteenth-century cultural critics preoccupied with the decadent and artificial nature of modern life.

The changing status of women under conditions of urbanization and industrialization further expressed itself in a metaphorical linking of women with technology and mass production. No longer placed in simple opposition to the rationalizing logic of the modern, women were now also seen to be constructed through it. The image of the machine-woman is another recurring theme in the modern, explored in such texts as Philippe Auguste Villiers de L'Isle Adam's novel *Tomorrow's Eve*.[27] As Andreas Huyssen notes, this image comes to crystallize in condensed form a simultaneous fascination and revulsion with the powers of technology. Like the work of art, woman in the age of technological reproduction is deprived of her aura; the effects of industry and technology thus help to demystify the myth of femininity as a last remaining site of redemptive nature. In this sense modernity serves to denaturalize and hence to destabilize the notion of an essential, God-given, femaleness. Yet this figure of the woman as machine can also be read as the reaffirmation of a patriarchal desire for technological mastery over woman, expressed in the fantasy of a compliant female automaton and in the dream of creation without the mother through processes of artificial reproduction. There is a crucial ambiguity in the figure of the woman-as-machine—does she point to a subversion or rather a reinforcement of gender hierarchies?—which continues to mark her most recent reincarnation in Donna Haraway's cyborg manifesto.[28]

The prostitute, the actress, the mechanical woman—it is such *female* figures that crystallize the ambivalent responses to capitalism and technology which permeated nineteenth-century culture. The list can easily be extended. The figure of the lesbian, for example, came to serve as an evocative symbol of a feminized modernity in the work of a number of nineteenth-century male French writers who depicted her as an avatar of perversity and decadence, exemplifying the mobility and ambiguity of modern forms of desire. As Walter Benjamin notes in his discussion of Baudelaire, the lesbian's status as heroine of the modern derived from her perceived defiance of traditional gender roles through a subversion of "natural" heterosexuality and the imperatives of biological reproduction. Lilian Faderman and more recently Thais Morgan have explored some of the manifestations of this cult of lesbian exoticism as it shaped the texts of the nineteenth-century male avant-garde. As Morgan notes, the figure of the lesbian came to function as an emblem of chic transgression, allowing artists and writers to explore an enlarged range of pleasures and subjectivities without necessarily challenging the traditional assumptions and privileges of masculinity.[29]

As this example indicates, many prevailing representations of modern feminity are shaped by the preoccupations of masculine fantasy and cannot simply be read as accurate representations of women's experience. Yet this is not to argue for a counter-realm of authentic femininity that awaits discovery outside such representations and the textual and institutional logics of the modern. On the contrary, I hope to show that the nostalgia for such a nonalienated plenitude is itself a product of modern dualistic schemas which positioned woman as an ineffable Other beyond the bounds of a masculine social and symbolic order. Rather than pursuing the chimera of an autonomous feminity, I wish to explore some of the different ways in which women drew upon, contested, or reformulated dominant representations of gender and modernity in making sense of their own positioning within society and history. Women's experience cannot be seen as a pre-given ontology that precedes its expression, but is constituted through a number of often contradictory, albeit connected strands, which are not simply reflected but are constructed through the "technologies of gender" of particular cultures and periods.[30] Such an understanding of history as *enactment* situates femininity in its multiple, diverse, but determinate articulations, which are themselves crisscrossed by other cultural logics and hierarchies of power. Gender is continually in process, an identity that is performed and actualized over time within given social constraints.

To acknowledge the social determination of femininity is not, therefore, to advocate a logic of identity which assumes that women's experiences of modernity can simply be assimilated to those of men. To be sure, women's lives have been radically transformed by such quintessentially modern phenomena as industrialization, urbanization, the advent of the nuclear family, new forms of time-space regulation, and the development of the mass media. In this sense, there can be no separate sphere of women's history outside the prevailing structures and logics of modernity. At the same time, women have experienced these changes in gender-specific ways that have been further fractured, not only by the oft-cited hierarchies of class, race, and sexuality but by their various and overlapping identities and practices as consumers, mothers, workers, artists, lovers, activists, readers, and so on. It is these distinctively feminine encounters with the various facets of the modern that have been largely ignored by cultural and social meta-theories oblivious to

the gendering of historical processes. Thus an approach to literary and cultural history which focuses on texts by and/or about women may result in a
somewhat different set of perspectives on the nature and meaning of historical processes. Those dimensions of culture either ignored, trivialized, or seen
as regressive rather than authentically modern—feelings, romantic novels,
shopping, motherhood, fashion—gain dramatically in importance, whereas
themes previously considered central to the sociocultural analysis of modernity become less significant or recede into the background. As a result, our
sense of what counts as meaningful history is subtly yet profoundly altered as
the landscape of the modern acquires a different, less familiar set of contours.

Yet the feminist critic also runs the risk of reinforcing gender stereotypes
if she devotes all her attention to the uncovering of a distinctive "women's
culture." Many nineteenth-century women sought to question such a notion
by crossing traditional male/female boundaries, whether in overtly political
or in more muted and less visible ways. It is equally important to acknowledge the female presence within those spheres often seen as the exclusive
province of men, such as the realm of public politics or avant-garde art. By
appropriating such traditionally masculine discourses, women helped to
reveal the potential instability of traditional gender divides, even as their
versions of these discourses often reveal suggestive and interesting differences. Rather than reading such strategies as pathological signs of women's
subsumption into an all-embracing phallocentrism, I am interested in
exploring the hybrid and often contradictory identities which ensued. If
gender politics played a central role in shaping processes of modernization,
these same processes in turn helped to initiate an ongoing refashioning and
reimagining of gender.

Modernist Aesthetics and Women's Modernity

Among the various terms associated with the modern, modernism is the one
that is most familiar within the field of literary studies. Unlike modernity, it
can be situated in historical time with a relative degree of precision; most
critics locate the high point of modernist literature and art between about
1890 and 1940, while agreeing that modernist features can be found in texts
both preceding and following this period. The emergence of modernism in
continental Europe is often linked to the appearance of symbolism in France
and aestheticism in fin-de-siècle Vienna, whereas in England and America
modernist tendencies are usually supposed to have manifested themselves
somewhat later, from around the time of the First World War.

While modernist literature comprises a broad and heterogeneous range of styles rather than a unified school, it is nevertheless possible to list some of its most important identifying features. According to Eugene Lunn's useful summary, these include aesthetic self-consciousness; simultaneity, juxtaposition, and montage; paradox, ambiguity, and uncertainty; and the dehumanization of the subject.[31] These aesthetic features are conventionally explained with reference to the crisis of language, history, and the subject which shaped the birth of the twentieth century and left an indelible mark on the literature and art of the period. Thus Malcolm Bradbury and James McFarlane note that modernism "is the art consequent on the disestablishing of communal reality and conventional notions of causality, on the destruction of traditional notions of the wholeness of individual character, on the linguistic chaos that ensues when public notions of language have been discredited and when all realities have become subjective fictions."[32]

There is, however, much less agreement regarding the sociopolitical consequences of modernist innovation in the sphere of literature and art. Within such European countries as France, Germany, Italy, and Russia, the formal experimentation of late-nineteenth- and early-twentieth-century artistic movements was frequently linked to an explicit social agenda by both practitioners and critics: radical aesthetics was intimately intertwined with avant-garde politics. A crucial notion here was that of *ostranenie,* or defamiliarization, used by the Russian Formalist school to describe literature's capacity to disrupt automatized perceptions and draw attention to the materiality of language as a set of signifiers. For a variety of avant-gardes, this defamiliarizing potential allowed artistic innovation to acquire an integral connection to social change. Modernism was the art most suited to challenging political complacencies and ideological dogmas by disrupting the mimetic illusions of realist and naturalist traditions and articulating through its very form the radical contradictions and ambiguities which characterized modern life.

Within the Anglo-American context, modernism has been read rather differently, a fact at least partly due to the lack of a substantive avant-garde tradition in England and America and the more openly conservative and quietist politics of many of its key practitioners. As a result, modernism has often been defined in opposition to sociopolitical concerns, as critics have invoked the subtleties of modernist experimentation to defend an ideal of the autonomous, self-referential art object. Thus an elective affinity established itself between the often rarefied aesthetic concerns of writers such as T. S. Eliot and Ezra Pound and the formalist and antireferential emphasis of New Criticism as an institutional practice and technology of reading. Marianne

DeKoven writes that "the triumph of New-Critical Modernism has made it appear blunt, banal, even gauche to discuss modernist writing as a critique of twentieth-century culture—to approach it, in fact, as anything other than the altar of linguistic and intellectual complexity in search of transcendent formal unity."[33] DeKoven's perceived need to legitimate and defend her own socio-political interpretation of Joseph Conrad and Virginia Woolf underlines the entrenched nature of such assumptions and the marked differences in this respect between Anglo-American and European modernist traditions.

Both of these traditions, nevertheless, are united in their largely uncritical reproduction of a masculine—and often overtly masculinist—literary lineage that has come under scrutiny from feminist scholars. Some critics have drawn attention to a machismo aesthetic characterizing the work of male modernists that is predicated upon an exclusion of everything associated with the feminine. Here modernism's emphasis on a rigorously experimental, self-conscious, and ironic aesthetic is interpreted as embodying a hostile and defensive response to the seductive lures of emotion, desire, and the body. Other feminists have pursued a different line of argument, noting that many of the key features of modernist experimentation suggestively coincide with the feminist critique of phallogocentrism. Suzette Henke, for example, draws on the work of Julia Kristeva to read the work of James Joyce as a subversive challenge to the structures of phallocentric discourse, unleashing a plurality of signifiers that articulate the ambiguities of a libidinal desire aligned with the maternal body. The polysemic nature of modernist art is thus reappropriated for the feminist project through its radical unsettling of the fixity of gender hierarchy.[34]

Besides producing such revisionist readings of the male modernist canon, feminist critics are also bringing women to the fore as key practitioners and theorists of modernism. As well as rereading such well-known writers as Virginia Woolf and Gertrude Stein, they are beginning to recover a less well-known tradition of female modernists and hence to reshape and redefine the contours of literary history. Distancing itself from the more reductive, content-based analyses of early feminist criticism, this recent work is often at pains to acknowledge the subtleties and complexities of modernist writing through careful attention to its tropes, metaphors, wordplays, and textual rhythms.[35] Clearly, there are institutional grounds for such interventions and for attempting to bring more women into existing literary canons by drawing attention to the innovative and formally sophisticated nature of their art. Yet it is also evident that some of the women's texts discussed in such surveys are less informed by the credo of modernist experimentalism than by alternative literary traditions such as realism or melodrama. In this context, Celeste Schenk advocates a "polemic for the dismantling of a monolithic 'Modernism' defined by its iconoclastic irreverence for convention and form, a difference which has contributed to the marginalization of women poets during the period."[36] Rather than simply arguing for the inclusion of a few more women in the modernist canon, Schenk suggests that a sustained challenge to the fetish of avant-gardism and an expansion of the term "modernism" to cover all the texts written within a given period might help to counteract the marginal status of women and open up the critical gaze to the variety of styles of writing circulating within a given historical era.

The issue at stake here is that of the benefits and dangers residing in particular forms of categorization. While I am in overall sympathy with Schenk's concerns, her suggestion that modernism be expanded to include "anything written between 1910 and 1940" seems unsatisfactory for obvious reasons. If modernism is no longer defined by any distinctive stylistic or formal features, the dates that she advocates in turn become completely arbitrary; why locate the inception of modernism in 1910, rather than 1880, or 1850, or 1830, all periods which saw themselves as "modern" in important ways? To dissolve the specificity of "modernism" in this way is to render an already vague term effectively useless by robbing it of any meaningful referent. It is surely more useful to retain the term as a designation for those texts which display the formally self-conscious, experimental, antimimetic features described earlier, while simultaneously questioning the assumption that such texts are necessarily the most important or representative works of the modern period. Modernism is only one aspect of the culture of women's modernity.

In other words, the feminist critique of literary history is best achieved not by denying the existence of formal and aesthetic distinctions between texts, but rather by questioning and rethinking the meanings that are frequently assigned to these distinctions. These range from the liberal humanist celebration of the great male modernist as the heroic spokesman of his time to the belief, shared by various poststructuralist, neo-Marxist, and feminist critics, that experimental art exemplifies the most authentically radical challenge to the authority of dominant ideological systems. This isolation of the modernist text as a privileged site of cultural radicalism relies upon certain taken-for-granted assumptions about the uniquely privileged status of literary discourse that have become increasingly tenuous in critical theory. The first of these positions can be loosely described as a form of mimeticism; while purportedly rejecting the reflectionist frame of a realist aesthetic, it nevertheless assumes that modernism in some sense offers a truthful representation of the radically indeterminate and fragmentary nature of the social.

In this sense, the modernist text becomes the privileged bearer of epistemological authority, crystallizing in its very structure the underlying fissures that the realist text glosses over. Modernism is elevated over realism paradoxically because it is a truer realism; going beyond the superficial stability of surface literary conventions, it reveals that reality *is* fluidity, fragmentation, indeterminacy.[37]

A psychologist position, by contrast, places greater emphasis on the proximity of the modernist text to the fragmented and incoherent workings of the unconscious. Here the fascination of many modernist writers with the subterranean workings of the psyche coincides with the renewed impact of psychoanalysis on recent literary theory. Thus feminist critics have drawn heavily upon psycholinguistic theories of meaning to interpret the fissures and contradictions within modernist texts as eruptions of a libidinal desire that threaten to disrupt the fixed structures of a phallocentric system. Modernism's disruption of hierarchical syntax and of linear time and plot, its decentering of the knowing and rational subject, its fascination with the aural and rhythmic qualities of language, are seen to provide the basis for a subversively other feminine aesthetic linked to the impulses of the unconscious.[38]

Both of these positions assume in different ways that the modernist work bears a privileged relationship to a nonlinguistic reality which forms the basis of its transgressive potential. Through its articulation of repressed truths, the fractured text in some sense challenges, undermines, or otherwise calls into question the mystificatory discourses of a bourgeois/patriarchal order. The modernist text thus becomes the ultimate expression of the real contradictions of modernity. Yet I have already noted that the question of what modernity *is* is by no means as self-evident as such theories sometimes assume. Whereas Marxist theorists, for example, have tended to emphasize the crisis-driven logics of capitalist production, other writers have pointed out that cultural practices do not necessarily harmonize with economic development in any straightforward way. Alain Corbin, for example, notes the relative stability of religion, custom, and traditional networks of kinship and affiliation in nineteenth-century Paris, suggesting that claims for the radical transformation of social life under capitalism are often exaggerated.[39] If one accepts the legitimacy of such critiques of totalizing models of periodization, it becomes less easy to identify a single kind of text, whether the realist or high modernist work of art, as embodying the truth of the modern Zeitgeist in a uniquely representative way. In fact, any attempt to specify a single work as an authoritative index of an entire culture problematic (modernity, women) is revealed as a methodologically fraught enterprise in its positing of an isomorphic relationship between a literary text and the real. Rather, the

idea of the modern fractures into a range of often contradictory, if connected, strands which were not simply reflected but were in part constructed
through the different discourses of a particular period. Thus our own sense
of the modern as a period of radical instability and constant change is itself
at least partly indebted to the prominence of iconoclastic modernist artworks
in received histories of twentieth-century culture; a reading of other kinds of
texts may in turn engender a rather different view of the relationship between
stability and change within the modern period.

The epistemological problems inherent in appeals to the essence of modernity bear directly on the textual politics of modernism, suggesting that generalized claims for the subversive nature of experimental forms need to be
replaced by more contextually specific analyses of the relations between
particular discourses and different axes of power. Much of the avant-garde
art of the turn of the century, for example, expressed a profound antipathy
toward dominant ideologies and world-views on the part of marginalized
artistic and intellectual elites. In articulating this alienation at the level of
artistic form, such avant-gardes espoused a critical and contestatory aesthetic
that sought to explode the complacent certainties of bourgeois attitudes. Yet
a feminist reading often reveals striking lines of continuity between dominant discourse and aesthetic counterdiscourse in terms of a shared valorization of Oedipal models of competitive masculinity and an overt disdain for
the "womanly" sphere of emotion, sentiment, and feeling. As a result, the
introduction of gender politics radically complicates an existing opposition
between what Matei Calinescu has termed the "two modernities" of bourgeois rationalization and radical art, fracturing and reconfiguring existing
lines of power.[40] A text which may appear subversive and destabilizing from
one political perspective becomes a bearer of dominant ideologies when read
in the context of another. In this context the anxious pursuit of the authentically transgressive text within recent literary and cultural theory is revealed
as a singularly unproductive and uninteresting enterprise.

This argument in turn has significant implications for feminism's own
choice of methodology, indicating the problems inherent in trying to encapsulate the essence of women's modernity through the close reading of one or
two exemplary canonical texts. The works of Woolf or Stein, for example,
may reveal much more about the specific context of the aristocratic-
bohemian female subcultures of Bloomsbury and the Left Bank in the 1920s
than about some repressed and exemplary Ur-femininity. Such writings offer
us elegant and ironic explorations of the fragility of linguistic and sexual
norms, articulating an intellectual and artistic world-view that was shaped by
the impact of Freudianism and feminism, of linguistic philosophies and

artistic manifestoes. However, they tell us much less about those aspects of modernity that shaped the lives of other kinds of women: the modernity of department stores and factories, of popular romances and women's magazines, of mass political movements and bureaucratic constructions of femininity. Such concerns are not of course completely absent from modernism, but they are typically mediated and refracted through an aesthetic lens of irony, defamiliarization, and montage specific to an artistic and intellectual—though not necessarily political—elite of the period. The connection of such an aesthetic to the discourses, images, and representations of the modern shaping the lives of other classes and groups of women is by no means self-evident. As Martin Pumphrey notes, "Any adequate reading of the modern period . . . must take account of the fact that the debates over women's public freedom, over fashion and femininity, cosmetics and home cleaning were as essential to the fabrication of modernity as cubism, Dada or futurism, as symbolism, fragmented form or the stream-of-consciousness narrative."[41]

If epistemological claims for the truth of modernist writing may be in need of some modification, so too are political ones. Thus writers such as Gertrude Stein are often singled out for attention by feminist critics because of their defiance of linguistic and social conventions and their transgressive questioning of femininity. Such a reclamation of a female avant-garde tradition undoubtedly forms an important part of the feminist rewriting of literary history through its creation of a pantheon of major, inspiratory women artists. Yet it also often perpetuates an unfortunate dichotomy of literary and political value which identifies formal experimentation as the most authentically resistive practice, with a consequent stigma attached both to representational art forms and to the regressive, sentimental texts of mass culture. Such a future-oriented, progressivist rhetoric, I would suggest, may provide an insufficiently nuanced way of approaching the gender politics of cultural texts within the uneven histories of the modern. Thus a central aspect of feminist scholarship has been its concern with the everyday and the mundane, and its consequent recuperation of those areas of women's lives often dismissed as trivial or insignificant. In this context to equate modernity with modernism, to assume that experimental art is necessarily the privileged cultural vehicle of a gender politics, is surely to ignore the implications of the feminist critique not just for methods but for objects of analysis.

Here feminist scholarship enters into a productive relationship with semiotic theories, which have broken down rigid oppositions between art and society by demonstrating the sign-laden nature of the entire cultural domain. To argue that the world is textual in this sense is not to deny its political, institutional, and power-determined realities, but to recognize that these realities are concretized through a diversity of semiotically complex artifacts and activities. Such an expanded understanding of the cultural text can contribute significantly toward retheorizing the modern by breaking down traditional distinctions between a radical avant-gardism (often codified as masculine) and a mass culture that has often been depicted as sentimental, feminine, and regressive. In particular, recent feminist work in the area of popular culture and cultural studies has paved the way for a rethinking of women's modernity that can include a consideration of the politics of experimental art but that can go beyond the isolated hypostatization of the modernist text.[42] Such a culturally based reading of modernity may usefully supplement and rearticulate the existing but somewhat moribund discourses of modernization and modernism within sociology and literary criticism, respectively.

The Politics of Method

I have thus chosen to approach the issue of gender and modernity via an array of texts that span the factual/fictional as well as the high/popular divide. The particular forms of writing examined in the following chapters are drawn from a spectrum of genres, including sociological theory, realist and naturalist novels, popular melodrama, political tracts and speeches, and works of early modernism. All of these forms articulate in different ways an awareness of and response to the problematic of the modern that is crucially intertwined with their representation of the feminine. By linking together forms of writing which are often kept apart, I wish to scrutinize the metaphorical and narrative dimensions of sociological and political writing while simultaneously situating the self-conscious literariness of early modernist experimentation within particular sociopolitical contexts. If the establishment of New Historicism has helped to pave the way for such cross-generic readings, my argument is equally indebted to cultural studies for having irrevocably problematized the opposition between a "high" literature assumed to be inherently ambiguous and self-critical and a mass culture equated with the reproduction of a monolithic ideological standpoint. The meanings of all texts, it has become increasingly clear, are produced through complex webs of intertextual relationships, and even the most conciliatory and apparently monological of texts may show evidence of dissonance, ambiguity, and contradiction rather than simply reinscribing conformism.

To displace oppositions, however, is not to argue for identities. While it is important to identify images and clusters of ideas that migrate across texts,

it is equally necessary to give careful consideration to the distinctive conventions and logics governing particular discourses and kinds of texts as well
as to the specific contexts in which they operate. I thus wish, in Ludmilla
Jordanova's words, "to draw attention to the intricate transformations and
multiple meanings of fundamental ideas in our cultural traditions," to
explore the various ways in which concepts and images are taken up and
concretized within particular forms and genres of writing.[43] These "intricate
transformations" are immediately apparent when one begins to track the
figure of the feminine, whose meanings blur and change, sometimes dramatically, sometimes almost imperceptibly, as one moves across different
regimes of discourse and traditions of representation. Gender, as Jordanova
points out, contains many sedimented layers of meaning; it is a composite
whose boundaries are unstable and constantly shifting, even as it also reveals
significant elements of continuity across the differentials of period and
context.

With one or two exceptions, my corpus of texts is drawn from the period
1880–1914. The fin de siècle was a period in which conflicting attitudes to the
modern were staged with particular clarity, where invocations of decadence
and malaise were regularly interspersed with the rhetoric of progress and the
exhilarating sense of the birth of a new age. In this sense, of course, it is a
time which invites inevitable parallels with our own. It was also a period
which saw an increasing differentiation of discursive fields, as art became
increasingly self-conscious and aware of its own status as art at the same time
as such disciplines as sociology, psychology, and anthropology sought to
establish themselves as autonomous disciplines and scientific accounts of
reality. As a result, it was in the late nineteenth century that many competing
accounts of the modern received their first systematic articulation. Caught
between the still-powerful evolutionary and historicist models of the nineteenth century and the emergent crises of language and subjectivity which
would shape the experimental art of the twentieth, the turn of the century
provides a rich textual field for tracking the ambiguities of the modern.

The first half of the book is devoted to a detailed reading of some recurring
representations of the gender of modernity as they manifest themselves in the
texts of male writers of the fin de siècle. I begin by identifying what is still
perhaps the most common view of woman as existing outside the modern,
examining the ways in which this view is expressed and legitimated in early
sociological theory through its equation of modernity with a masculine
sphere of rationalization and production. In the following chapter, I analyze
what appears to be an antithetical view, the association of modernity with the
realm of irrationality, aesthetics, and libidinal excess, as exemplified in the

figure of the voracious female consumer. Why, I ask, are representations of modernity increasingly feminized and demonized, and what does this reveal about the relationship between the logics of capitalism and patriarchy in an emerging culture of consumption? Finally, I consider the migration of the trope of the feminine from the body of woman to avant-garde aesthetics, examining the emergence of a still-influential notion of literary modernity as linked to the feminization of (men's) writing. In these three ideational clusters, the metaphor of woman undergoes some striking transmutations as well as revealing significant continuities of emphasis.

The second half of the book, by contrast, centers upon women's own representation of the relationship between modernity and femininity, as manifested not simply in the content but in the styles and techniques of their writing. I ask: how did women position themselves in relation to the logics of temporality and the social, political, and aesthetic values associated with the modern? I begin with a discussion of the popular romance, a form often considered to be regressive and anachronistic but whose nostalgic yearning for an indeterminate "elsewhere" is, I suggest, a foundational trope within the modern itself. I follow this with an excavation of the philosophies of history evident in the speeches and tracts of first-wave feminists, focusing on their deployment of metaphors of evolution and revolution as markers of a particular experience of historical consciousness and sense of temporality. Finally, I contrast this politico-philosophical discourse of modernity with the literary modernity of the French decadent writer Rachilde (Marguerite Eymery), whose stylized explorations of the links between sexual perversion and the aestheticization of identity uncannily foreshadow some central concerns of contemporary cultural theory. By contrasting these very different genres—sentimental romance, political rhetoric, avant-garde aesthetics—I seek to highlight some of the very different imaginings of and responses to the modern among women writers of the fin de siècle.

My own analysis of these differing views makes certain claims to representativeness, as does any argument by definition. However, these claims do not rely on the presumed capacity of a single text to crystallize the underlying features of a social totality, to articulate the repressed feminine Other of the patriarchal logos or even to encapsulate *the* dominant ideology of the modern period. Rather, I aim to pinpoint and to analyze some of the most pervasive representations of women and modernity that recur within, and sometimes across, particular cultural boundaries and discursive fields, and whose traces extend well beyond the nineteenth century into our own. It is here that a comparative approach may prove useful, by highlighting different conceptualizations of the modern within particular cultural traditions, as well as allowing for a recognition of affinities that cross national boundaries. I have tried to select texts which illuminate such recurring themes with particular clarity, though the present selection is by no means a necessary or inevitable one. Similar arguments could easily be developed in relation to very different materials, though with obvious differences of emphasis.

While my approach has clearly been influenced by the new forms of cultural history as well as the more traditional discipline of the history of ideas, it retains an explicitly feminist interest in establishing connections between discourses and ideas on the one hand and systems of power on the other. I remain committed to the analytical value of positing broad systemic logics (hence my continuing and unembarrassed use of terms such as patriarchy and capitalism), while also believing that modernity contains a number of such logics which may often work in contradiction as well as collusion. Here I have found Nancy Fraser's notion of "axes of power" enormously useful; it has the merit of avoiding totalizing and functionalist models of society by highlighting the interactions and potential contradictions between different power hierarchies without, however, dissolving and dispersing the notion of power completely.[44] Such a model in turn yields a specific understanding of the politics of texts; rather than simply existing either in the center or at the margins, individual texts may possess different and often contradictory meanings in relation to particular power axes. My argument assumes, in other words, that the political meanings of particular discourses, images, and clusters of representation are not given for all time, but may vary significantly depending on the conditions of enunciation and the contexts in which they appear.

The following discussion also distances itself from an epistemological dualism which assumes that men's writing must invariably distort female experience whereas women's writing provides true access to it. Instead, it presumes that all knowledge of female (or male) experience—however intimate or seemingly private—is mediated by intersubjective frameworks and systems of meaning, but that these frameworks are heterogeneous rather than unified, and often are in conflict. The relationship of such discourses to the empirical fact of an author's gender is complex and variable rather than constant; one cannot predict the potential truth value or otherwise of a specific text simply from a knowledge of the author's sex. Thus the representation of femininity in works such as *Nana* and *Madame Bovary,* for example, interconnects in suggestive ways with recent feminist discussions of performance, desire, and consumerism; it is for this reason that I draw on these novels in my critical discussion of the sexual politics of modernity. Yet other aspects of these novels are misogynistic and otherwise problematic, invoking a critical rather than assenting response from this feminist reader. In other words, I am interested in pursuing the partial illuminations offered by particular texts rather than attributing to them a uniform essence of truth or falsehood grounded in authorial gender; these partial illuminations in turn derive from the points of correspondence and connection between the critical perspectives opened up by feminist theory and the ideologies operative within particular forms of nineteenth-century writing.

Such an oscillation between illumination and critique necessarily shapes my reading of texts by women as well as men; there is no unbroken substratum of communal identity which binds women together across history and culture. From the standpoint of the present, the texts of nineteenth-century women writers reveal their inevitable enmeshment within the ideologies and world-views of their time, so that their voices speak to us across a chasm of historical difference. This is true not only of self-identified conservatives such as the romance writer Marie Corelli, but also of those fin-de-siècle feminist writers and activists whose commitment to social change is deeply intertwined with what now seem anachronistic, and often overtly racist, Darwinian or Malthusian beliefs. The feminist desire to reclaim women's writing can surely only ground itself in a political commitment to recover the lost voices of women rather than in an epistemological claim for the necessary truth that is spoken by such voices. It is for this reason that my discussion retains a distinction between men's and women's texts—not because women's views of modernity are invariably more accurate than those of men, but because feminist criticism is in my view committed to giving at least equal weight to such views and to paying careful attention to the specific features of women's writing. This specificity, it should be emphasized, should not be seen as simply internal to a text; rather, it is fundamentally shaped by the particular meanings and effects which accrue to discourses publicly authored by women. The gender of authorship is a crucial factor influencing the circulation and reception of textual meaning.

I need only to conclude by noting my own investment in this project and the methodological implications of such an investment. I make no attempt to occupy a position of neutrality by limiting myself to a purely antiquarian recording of late-nineteenth-century discourses; rather, my analysis is an ideologically interested one which seeks to establish points of connection between the texts of the past and the feminist politics of the present. In this sense, it is a work of cultural theory as well as cultural history; if the value of "history" lies in drawing attention to the particularity of events, that of "theory" lies in the ability to make meaningful connections across these discrete particulars. From such a standpoint, the selective nature of interpretation is not just inevitable but desirable, given that social processes can only be constituted as meaningful objects of analysis in relation to a particular viewpoint and set of concerns. I thus subscribe to a belief in the inevitable hermeneutic dimension of any act of writing and the necessary construction of the past from the standpoint of the present. At the same time, however, I have tried as far as possible to avoid the obvious anachronisms which may result from an unreflecting projection of present-day truths onto the texts of the past in order to find them lacking. Instead, my discussion aims to retain an awareness of the discursive possibilities that were available at a given historical moment and to assess the political implications of particular representations of women and modernity in that light. This historical tightrope of empathy and critique is a difficult one to negotiate skillfully: it remains for the reader to decide how successfully this negotiation has been achieved.

2

On Nostalgia:
The Prehistoric Woman

The prevailing motif of nostalgia is the erasure of the gap between
nature and culture, and hence a return to the utopia of biology
and symbol united within the walled city of the maternal. The
nostalgic's utopia is prelapsarian, a genesis where lived and mediated experience are one, where authenticity and transcendence are
both present and everywhere.

Susan Stewart, *On Longing: Narratives of the Miniature,*
the Gigantic, the Souvenir, the Collection

The distance between the disciplines of literature and sociology remains
surprisingly large. While the sociology of literature enjoys a certain, albeit
modest, following, literary critics have for their part shown little interest in
reading the "great masters" of sociological thought. Yet recent intellectual
developments provide an opening for such interdisciplinary exchange by
rendering the distinction between these two genres a much less stable one.
Just as the most hermetic of literary works alludes, however elliptically, to the
very social conditions that it strives to transcend, so too texts that claim to
define the structure of social reality are themselves indebted to a range of
narratives, metaphors, and figurative schemata. Sociological theory is an act
of representation that draws upon a variety of descriptive vocabularies, classificatory systems, explanatory recipes, and enunciative rules.[1] My reading of
such representational logics will seek to unravel the significance of allegories
of gender, and specifically of a deeply nostalgic vision of femininity, in
shaping the parameters of modern sociological and critical thought.

This question of the connection between literature and sociology was of
great interest at the turn of the century, at a time when the latter was
struggling to establish its own legitimacy as an area of distinctive intellectual
inquiry. In his account of sociology's formation and development as an
unstable hybrid of literary and scientific traditions, Wolf Lepenies notes that

"from the middle of the nineteenth century onwards literature and sociology contested with one another the claim to offer the key orientation for modern civilization."[2] Like many of the realist novelists of the period, sociologists saw their task as defining and recording the essential features of their own historical era; within a relatively short time, the frameworks and vocabularies of sociological writing were to have a powerful impact on common-sense attitudes toward the nature and meaning of the modern age. Gradually permeating into everyday consciousness through such institutional channels as education and the media, the explanatory categories of social science continue to shape many of our taken-for-granted beliefs about modernity and gender. Thus the foundational assumptions and blind spots governing a particular form of knowledge reach well beyond its disciplinary origins to influence a much broader cultural and political arena. The discourse of sociology has affected the ways in which all of us envision the modern.

Sociology has been described as the quintessentally modern discipline, which could not have existed prior to the emergence of the liberal democratic state.[3] I am suggesting that this relationship between sociology and modernity should be seen as a mutually determining one; rather than simply analyzing a pre-existing social reality, sociology helps to constitute our sense of this reality in the very process of analysis. For example, the vision of modernity that shapes much sociological theory both relates to and differs from alternative images of the modern to be found in late-nineteenth-century literature, so that a comparison may usefully illuminate the specific ways in which periodizing terms are constructed and rendered meaningful in particular discourses. Just as the category of the modern reveals different qualities and components in its deployment across particular textual fields, so too the figure of woman accrues shifting meanings and metaphorical associations within the various vocabularies of the fin de siècle. As well as examining differences, however, I also hope to establish continuities across discursive registers by comparing some of the founding assumptions of sociology and psychoanalysis, tracing their parallel visions of a nondifferentiated, premodern femininity as they emerge out of a shared nexus of cultural reference points and frameworks.

Within this period of sociology's struggle to establish itself as a legitimate discipline, Georg Simmel was a major, yet in certain respects oddly atypical, figure. Though generally regarded as one of the founders of German sociology, he was unable to gain an established professorial position during most of his academic life and lacked many of the usual markers of institutional support. This intellectual and professional marginality has been attributed both to the pervasive influence of anti-Semitism within the German academy and to the eclectic and unorthodox nature of his writings.[4] Thus Simmel's interests stretched well beyond the typical concerns of sociology to embrace diverse topics in psychology, philosophy, culture, and art. He wrote about such seemingly random and disparate subjects as flirtation, ruins, handles, fashion, meals, prostitution, the sociology of smell, strangers, and Alpine journeys, teasing out the significance of the apparently inconsequential phenomena of everyday life as they shaped individual experience and social interaction. David Frisby describes Simmel as a sociological flâneur who indulged in impressionistic sketches of the fabric of modern urban life rather than the construction of grand theoretical systems.[5] Insisting that social reality could no longer be grasped as an ordered totality, he sought to explore the fluctuating and often fragmentary patterns and forms of modern experience. This proclivity made him an object of criticism in his lifetime, but it has rendered him highly attractive to a postmodern trend within present-day cultural theory often skeptical of totalizing frameworks and strongly interested in the aesthetic dimensions of modern society. Recent years have witnessed a dramatic resurgence of interest in Simmel's work; he is currently acclaimed as *the* sociologist of modernity, or alternatively as a postmodernist or deconstructive thinker *avant la lettre*. Simmel, it appears, is our contemporary.[6]

At the risk of doing a certain interpretive violence to the complexity of Simmel's thought, I am less interested in exploring his uniqueness as a social theorist than in highlighting the exemplary significance of his writings on gender. He is unusual among early sociologists in having written extensively on the subject of women and modernity, although these writings have been ignored by commentators until relatively recently. As Lieteke van Vucht Tijssen notes, Simmel is one of the few writers to have developed an account of gender relations as an integral part of a general theory of modernization.[7] In these writings, he renders explicit what remains implicit in much sociological and philosophical thought and thus clarifies many of the assumptions which have placed femininity and modernity in an antithetical relationship. Diagnosing yet simultaneously reproducing a pervasive cultural equation of the male with the modern, Simmel conceives of an authentic and autonomous femininity existing beyond the bounds of existing symbolic and institutional structures. Thus although he is often described as a theorist who refused the utopian lures of Romantic thought, woman is in fact positioned in Simmel's writing as the overt object of nostalgic desire.

This yearning for the feminine as emblematic of a nonalienated, nonfragmented identity is, I will argue, a crucially important motif in the history of cultural representations of the nature of modernity. Woman emerges in these discourses as an authentic point of origin, a mythic referent untouched by the strictures of social and symbolic mediation; she is a recurring symbol of the atemporal and asocial at the very heart of the modern itself. Thus an analysis of Simmel's work helps to illuminate a set of deeply ingrained assumptions about the necessary identity of modernity, alienation, and masculinity which underpin the work of an influential intellectual tradition stretching from Hegel to Jacques Lacan. Within this tradition, nostalgia and the feminine come together in the representation of a mythic plenitude, against which is etched an overarching narrative of masculine development as self-division and existential loss. Rather than epitomizing an anachronistic or marginal condition, in other words, nostalgia emerges as a recurring and guiding theme in the self-constitution of the modern; the redemptive maternal body constitutes the ahistorical other and the other of history against which modern identity is defined.

Desiring the Past

The sentence which originally aroused my interest in Simmel occurs in the introduction to his collected writings on women, sexuality, and love. Guy Oakes notes that Simmel assumes a fundamental equation between the male character and the objectified nature of modern culture; as a result, Oakes concludes that for Simmel "feminization would thereby qualify as demodernization."[8] In this succinct phrase, Oakes summarizes one of the most common views of women's relationship to the modern world. The assumption that an authentic female culture would reverse the instrumental and dehumanizing aspects of urban industrial society has been a recurring motif within both feminist and nonfeminist thought. Women's purported affinity with a nonalienated nature and organic community has been evoked both by conservatives nostalgic for an idealized premodern past and by Marxist and feminist thinkers for whom such a feminine principle embodies a utopian alternative to the domination of instrumental reason and the tyranny of Enlightenment thought.

This theme is already well established in the work of Rousseau, whose views on the appropriate psychic and social formation of male and female subjects exercised a powerful influence on subsequent conceptions of gender difference. The alignment of the feminine with an authentic realm of spontaneous feeling was reaffirmed in Romantic depictions of woman as a redemptive refuge from the constraints of a modern civilization identified with a growing materialism, the worship of scientific reason, and an alienating urban environment. Femininity thus came to stand for a prelapsarian condition, "a time before the fall into self-consciousness and into subject-object relations with nature."[9] An explicit temporal inflection underpinned this sentimental elevation of the feminine. Changing experiences of and attitudes toward time resulting from the industrialization of much of nineteenth-century Europe engendered a growing nostalgia for a continuity and tradition perceived to be under threat by the accelerated nature of social change. Woman, in other words, came to stand for a more natural past and to be identified with the lost cyclical rhythms of a preindustrial organic society.

This historical nostalgia can of course also be interpreted psychoanalytically, a move that is invited by the frequent invocations of "Mother Nature" within Romantic thought. From this perspective, the yearning for a lost golden age is explained in terms of a longing for the psychic plenitude of a pre-Oedipal condition. The maternal body is seen to embody a fullness of presence, a fantasmic image of originary harmony that is contrasted to the adult consciousness of alienation and lack. Although psychoanalysis tends to grant such fantasies a foundational status, they are themselves clearly shaped by broader historical shifts in the symbolic representation and material constitution of family relations. The psychic investment in an idealized maternal, precultural realm is itself a function of the privatization of the family within Western culture, with the mother assuming exclusive responsibility for the care of her children, and of emerging norms of the self which define women as natural and emotional creatures in the context of an increasing demarcation between the private and public worlds. "Women's time," rather than constituting an elemental, cyclical temporality outside linear and historical development, is itself related to processes of modernization which resulted in the emergence of the nuclear family and the construction of a redemptive realm of the maternal.[10]

This Romantic view of woman was to retain a significant purchase throughout the nineteenth century, reiterated not just in literature but in a wide array of scientific, anthropological, and historical texts which sought to demonstrate women's affinity with a premodern condition. In this context, repeated analogies between the development of civilization and that of the individual (the phylogenetic and the ontogenetic) played a central part in shaping patterns of gender representation in nineteenth-century culture. Woman was identified with a primitive or preindustrial era in the same way as she was linked through her maternal function to the unselfconscious being-in-the-world of the not yet socialized infant. The equation of woman with nature and tradition, already a commonplace of early modern thought, received a new impetus from the popularity of Darwinian models of evolutionary development, resulting in an explicit contrast between a striving, restless masculinity and an organic, nondifferentiated femininity. In the late nineteenth century, scientific theory repeatedly sought to demonstrate women's lower position on the evolutionary chain, with their development being invariably compared to that of children or savages. As Cynthia Eagle Russett and other feminist historians of science have shown, woman was thereby defined as an underdeveloped man, a lower biological form less differentiated from the common, primitive, embryonic type than her male counterpart.[11] Depending, then, on whether it was the narrative of progress or the myth of the fall that was uppermost in the writer's mind, femininity represented either a primitive condition of arrested development or an edenic condition of organic wholeness untouched by the ruptures and contradictions of the modern age.

A view of woman as existing outside of history was thus itself a product of a period imbued by historical modes of thought which interpreted the development of civilization in terms of philosophical meta-narratives of cultural progress or decline.[12] Such narratives suggest a magisterial confidence in the ultimate meaning and purpose of history. The rapid and often seemingly chaotic transformations of the social landscape of nineteenth-century Europe were ultimately to be explained in terms of a grand developmental plan which positioned the white bourgeois male at its apex. Yet the recurrence of idyllic images of an archaic past indicate an uncertainty and ambivalence regarding these same social processes. If the experience of modernity brought with it an overwhelming sense of innovation, ephemerality, and chaotic change, it simultaneously engendered multiple expressions of desire for stability and continuity. Nostalgia, understood as a mourning for an idealized past, thus emerges as a formative theme of the modern: the age of progress was also the age of yearning for an imaginary edenic condition that had been lost.

The history and etymology of nostalgia provides some illuminating insights in this regard. The term was first coined in the late seventeenth century as the name for a disease, a condition of extreme homesickness to which Swiss mercenaries were considered particularly prone. Its symptoms included despondency, melancholia, lability of emotion, profound bouts of weeping, anorexia, a generalized wasting away, and occasional attempts at suicide.[13] Michael Roth notes that the nineteenth century saw a proliferation of scientific writings on this puzzling medical condition, which subjected its temporal as well as its spatial significance to detailed scrutiny. The patients' overwhelming desire to return to their homes was simultaneously, doctors agreed, a longing to return to a specific and crucial locus of the past. Severing all connections to the present time, the patient withdrew into fond memories of family and birthplace and a process of mourning for that which had been lost. "The nostalgic person expressed an 'excessive' attachment to the past through a retreat from the world of the living. The retreat was such that patients did not even call attention to their malady, but quietly pursued their desire to return to the past until death."[14] This destructive desire to regress was attributed to the dislocations of the modern age, as increased mobility and demographic shifts caused significant sectors of the population to be uprooted from their native soil and hence to lose a natural sense of continuity with their birthplace and history.

Some doctors considered women less prone to the affliction of nostalgia because of their more sedentary and home-bound way of life. In other words, while women were the classic objects of nostalgic affection in their role as mothers, they were less likely to be subjects of it.[15] Rather than desiring the past, they *were* the past; identified with the domestic sphere, they suffered less frequently from a sense of homelessness and a longing for what had been lost. Nostalgia has now of course completely lost these medical associations, but the temporal division between an alienated present and a golden past is still regularly mapped onto a spatial opposition between public and private, masculine and feminine spheres. Women are deemed to suffer less from nostalgia because their lives are less marked by disruption and temporal discontinuity than those of men.[16] In turn, the maternal home offers a redemptive haven for those fleeing the chaos and instability of the modern world. Femininity continues to function as a signifier for the wholeness and self-contained completeness that modern man no longer possesses. Thus, to anticipate my discussion of Simmel slightly, woman "is always at home with herself," while man "has his 'home' beyond himself"; for Simmel, as for Freud, the female body signifies the originary birthplace, the familiar, yet enigmatic homeland from which the male subject has been irrevocably exiled.[17]

Femininity as Nondifferentiation

Between 1890 and 1911, Simmel published about fifteen essays on such topics as female culture, female psychology, the relationship between the sexes, and the German women's movement. In several of these essays, he goes to the very heart of the question of women's relationship to the modern. Simmel's account of the male-dominated structures of modern culture is informed by a critical vision of the identity logic pervading Enlightenment thought. Yet in reproducing the assumption that the logic of modernity is intrinsically and pervasively masculine, Simmel effectively closes off the possibility of women participating in modern society as women. Grounding his theory of gender relations in a dualistic ontology of fragmentation versus plenitude, mediation versus immediacy, alienation versus authenticity, he thereby uncannily foreshadows some of the aporias which continue to haunt contemporary feminist thought.

Simmel's understanding of modernity was adumbrated over many years in a wide variety of texts. This view, like that of many of his contemporaries, betrays a fundamental ambivalence that is repeatedly articulated in the structures of sociological writing. Simmel drew on an intellectual tradition which understands history as a gradual liberation of the individual from the constraints of traditional forms of life. Modernity is identified in this paradigm with a process of differentiation, a shift from homogeneity to heterogeneity, from absorption in the routines of a small world of tradition to participation in a wider world of multifaceted involvements and open possibilities.[18] The experience of the modern is thus one of differentiation and discontinuity. At the same time, however, this new freedom brings with it an increasing sense of disorientation and alienation stemming from the preponderance of objective over subjective culture. By this, Simmel means the rapid proliferation of cultural artifacts and institutions in modern society, such that no single human being can retain understanding of or control over them. Culture seems to become independent of human activity, to acquire a life and will of its own, so that individuals experience a sense of being dominated by and estranged from the products of their own creation. We live in a world of increasingly complex and diversified structures which cannot be rendered meaningful in terms of any overarching meta-value or purpose.

An obvious parallel suggests itself to the Marxist concept of alienation, except that for Simmel such historical processes of specialization and differentiation are an inevitable outcome of the complexity of modern society, which cannot be transcended through a hoped-for return to a communitarian ideal. Much of Simmel's work explores these simultaneously liberating and depersonalizing aspects of modern life, as exemplified both in the institutionalization of money as a general principle of exchange and in the new and distinctive modes of experience engendered by the modern city. Simmel's famous essay "The Metropolis and Mental Life," for example, addresses itself to the psychic and social dislocation that is endemic to modern urban culture, with its disorienting array of objects and experiences. Individuals are forced to adopt a blasé attitude to blunt their sensibilities to the excessive stimuli and infinite diversity of city life, even though the development of the money economy simultaneously encourages a form of rationality which reduces qualitative difference to quantitative difference and promotes a calculating intellect at the expense of emotional impulses. While in certain respects modernization promotes difference and diversity, then, it also paradoxically engenders an increasing sense of the homogeneity and interchangeability of things and persons.[19]

The crucial point, however, is that this ambiguous cultural dialectic is fundamentally gendered in nature. Simmel writes, "there is no sense in which culture exists in a domain that lies beyond men and women. It is rather the case that, with the exception of a very few areas, our objective culture is thoroughly male. It is men who have created art and industry, science and commerce, the state and religion."[20] The "tragedy of culture" is thus a tragedy of male culture, insofar as culture is composed of structures and artifacts that are objectifications of masculine ideas and values. It is man who constantly seeks to externalize himself in the act of performance, and who thereby exemplifies the principles of knowledge, becoming, and volition that typify the spirit of the modern. Man is defined as the transgressor of limits, impelled toward an expansive overreaching in restless pursuit of a significance that is never granted but always deferred. This Faustian striving is identified by Simmel as the ultimate motor of social development, even as it unleashes processes of change which in turn acquire their own independent momentum.

Modernity, then, is unambiguously gendered at the level of production; men's nature, according to Simmel, demands release through processes of self-objectification. As a result, women do not generally succeed in the creation of objective culture, which is antithetical to their distinctive and particular mode of life. At the same time, the modern brings with it an inexorable rationalization which leads to a weakening of sentimental attachments and personal ties and a resulting fragmentation of that which was originally unified. Modern life is increasingly compartmentalized and subject to the division of labor. Yet this process is not so much detrimental to male identity as it is a function of it. The autonomy and detachment of the male subject allows him to take part in various and specialized activities without feeling threatened by a sense of fragmentation, whereas the female psyche does not possess this same capacity for distantiation and yearns instead for immediacy and connection. Simmel thus establishes a series of rhetorical parallels between the ability of the male psyche to compartmentalize experience and the structural complexity of developed societies, which demand this capacity for dissociation of their members. The social characteristics of modernity both reflect and are reflected in the psychic features of masculinity; contemporary civilization is organized according to principles that are deeply antithetical to women's interests.

Simmel, moreover, goes beyond the diagnosis of male domination in existing social institutions to expose its broader philosophical implications for women. Here, aspects of his argument suggestively anticipate the insights of contemporary poststructuralist thought in its critique of a dualistic metaphysics within which "the male sex . . . acquires the status of the *generally human.*"[21] In an essay called "The Relative and the Absolute in the Problem of the Sexes," Simmel identifies the process whereby one member of a pair of dichotomous concepts acquires pre-eminence as an emblem of the objective and the absolute. Against such a view, Simmel insists that prevailing cultural norms of objectivity and universality are in fact derived from a specifically male mode of being. Expressions of maleness "claim normative significance on the ground that they exhibit the objective truth and rectitude that are equally valid for everyone, male or female";[22] yet such a claim is fundamentally illusory. Its very articulation results from a power structure which allows the master to conflate his own interests with the universal without needing to acknowledge his own particularity. The slave, by contrast, is constantly forced to confront the reality of her own difference. Simmel writes, "There is no doubt that the women loses a conscious sense of her being as a female much more rarely than holds true for the man and his being as a male. There are innumerable occasions on which the man appears to think in a purely objective fashion without his masculinity concurrently occupying any place in his perceptions. On the other hand, it seems as if the woman never loses the feeling—which may be more or less clear or obscure—that she is a woman."[23]

Thus the psychological superiority atttributed to men in a patriarchal society is translated into an expression of logical superiority, with masculine values appearing to attain a suprapersonal validity. As a result, Simmel concludes, the autonomy of the feminine cannot be articulated, because it is invariably defined in relation to a prior male principle. Either women are subsumed into supposedly general and objective norms actually derived from male experience, or they are represented as other, as the polar opposite of man. In both cases, they are judged by male norms masquerading as universal values. There thus appears to be no standpoint which would allow woman to be valued in and for herself. "Almost all discussions about women represent only what they are in their real, ideal, or value relationship to men. No one asks what they are for themselves . . . the conclusion is drawn that for herself she is *nothing.*"[24]

Thus far, much of Simmel's analysis may well seem both familiar and persuasive to feminist ears. One of his primary concerns was to address the limitations of the principle of universal commensurability, as exemplified in the belief that different forms of life can be encompassed in terms of an overarching logic of identity. As Susan Hekman notes, "Simmel's challenge to Enlightenment epistemology consisted of his argument that experience is defined and molded by a plurality of independent and irreducible forms."[25] This critique of the homogenizing imperative of modernity in turn caused Simmel to query the efforts of some sections of the German women's movement to achieve political parity with men. Such an ideal, in Simmel's view, would invariably fall prey to a conceptual framework derived from male experience. Rather, he insists, woman must be allowed to exist in and for herself, in her unique particularity, and women's distinctive psychological and social experiences cannot be encompassed by resorting to generalized notions of equality.

What, then, is the nature of this particularity? How can we imagine the specific nature of a feminine mode of life? Simmel's response to these questions interestingly anticipates present-day debates within feminist theory in its nostalgic figuration of an autonomous zone of femininity beyond the constraints of modern social and symbolic structures. Simmel's discussion rests upon a key distinction between two different notions of the feminine. A dualistic metaphysics defines woman as either the same as or the complementary opposite of man; this is femininity "in the traditional sense," as defined in terms of a prior orientation toward the primacy of the masculine principle. An authentic femininity, by contrast, must exist outside the social and symbolic hierarchies through which these very categories of sameness and difference are constituted. Woman cannot be contained within the binary structures of male thought; for her, the distinctions between subject and object, masculine and feminine, do not really exist. Against the discontinuities and hierarchies which characterize a male-defined culture, she embodies a condition of radical nondifferentiation. Femininity, in other words, exists beyond the boundaries of social structures and symbolic categories, including—paradoxically—the very distinction between masculine and feminine itself.

In many of these formulations, Simmel reveals his profound debt to a Hegelian conception of gender identity. For Hegel, as one writer notes, woman "is less alienated than man, but only because she is closer to nature. She is more *an sich*, less *für sich*, that is to say less blessed and cursed with self-consciousness than men, and so less divided but also less capable of rational reflection."[26] Whereas Hegel saw this feminine condition as a sign

of women's unfitness for social and public life, Simmel considered it a locus
of resistance to the male-driven division and separation that organizes yet
limits modern social experience. Thus in contrast to male becoming, woman
represents being; whereas he is dynamic, she is beyond historical time. The
center and periphery of female existence are integrated into a harmonious
synthesis, the ultimate example of a self-contained plenitude. The alienated
public culture of social institutions remains inimical to a feminine identity
that is unmediated, intuitive, directed toward process rather than production. Lacking the capacity for detachment which shapes the male ego,
women's whole self becomes invested in her experiences. Her relationship to
the world is intimate, unmediated, personalized in all aspects. As a consequence, concludes Simmel, "in the depths of their submersion into themselves, woman are at one with the basis of life itself."[27] Women's distinctive
way of being and knowing links them to the mystical and metaphysical, the
ultimate ground of being. Thus whereas the masculine is linked to dualism,
the feminine is "the absolute on which the unity of human nature rests in a
substantial and static self-contained completeness, in a sense prior to the
division into subject and object."[28]

   This condition of nondifferentiation is nowhere more apparent than in the
sphere of sexuality. For men sexuality is simply another specialized domain,
whereas for women it constitutes their entire being. Paradoxically, however,
this absolute and self-contained erotic plenitude renders the woman less
dependent upon a male other. Simmel writes, "The woman lives in the most
profound identity of being and being-a-woman, in the absoluteness of *imma-
nently* defined sexuality, the characteristic essence of which does not require
the relationship to the other sex."[29] This notion of the intrinsically erotic
nature of woman was of course a relative commonplace of the time. It is
echoed, for example, in Otto Weininger's notorious *Sex and Character*
(1903), an ambitious and influential meditation on the relationship between
sex and civilization. While conceding the bisexual constitution of all human
beings, Weininger nevertheless insists that women are less individuated than
men and more deeply submerged in the generic essence of their femaleness.
More generally, the feminine principle exemplifies inchoate matter, the
embodiment of the instinctual imperative toward biological reproduction.
This irrational, organic, and passive model of being is contrasted with the
individuated, monadic spirit of masculinity, from which derive all the moral,
legal, and institutional achievements of civilization.[30] Though sharing Simmel's view of femininity as nondifferentiation, Weininger arrives at the antithetical historical conclusion. He portrays modernization as synonymous not
with the sovereignty of the masculine principle but rather with an inexorable

and threatening process of feminization. A similar view of gender relations, in other words, gives rise to a radically divergent meta-narrative.

Against Weininger's view of the amoral and destructive nature of female sexuality, moreover, Simmel conceives of women as embodying a natural, even childlike piety, an unproblematic unity of morality and desire. Demonization here gives way to an idealized view of nonfissured, noncontradictory identity. This lack of conflict means that women do not suffer from the warring claims of sensuality and spirituality which do battle within the male psyche. In Freudian terms, they suffer from both an absence of libidinal drives and a weak superego. Thus femininity is situated outside the dialectic of desire and attempted gratification, as a state of being that is already complete within itself. This conceptualization of the female psyche casts a particular light on the gendering of historical processes. If the dynamic of modernity is typically equated with an unending generation of new needs and desires, then Simmel's attribution of a quasi-vegetative tranquillity to women places them outside this sociohistorical process, their psyche seemingly untouched by the conflicts and contradictions of the modern age. Indeed, if the irrevocable rupture of subject and object opens up the possibility of desire, then women's predualistic condition necessarily excludes the possibility of female desire or agency. Instead, in the memorable phrase of one of Simmel's explicators, "woman lies . . . like an immovable prehistoric boulder in the landscape of modernity."[31]

All these factors make it clear why for Simmel femininity and modernity are irrevocably opposed. Women almost inevitably fail in the creation of objective culture because they "do not translate their activity into an objective entity that continues to exist independent of that activity."[32] Production originates in a sense of lack, in the desire to struggle with and transcend limitations, and women, for Simmel as for later theorists such as Lacan, lack lack. Because they are already complete within themselves, women have no desire to objectify their spirit in a permanent fashion through the production of culture. Rather, their manifestations of self are fleeting and contingent, shaped by the demands of the moment and the everyday tasks of the household. This inclination toward reproduction rather than production confirms women's distance from a modern culture governed by a spirit of constant innovation, whether exemplified in the rapidity of technological development or in the creation of new forms and styles of art. The idea of the modern has become synonymous with the shock of the new, with an overwhelming sense of ephemerality and constant change resulting from capitalism's "creative destruction" of history and tradition. Described as a "maelstrom of perpetual disintegration and renewal," the modern is driven by a temporal logic that is viewed as one of "radical, total and violent rupture with the past."[33] Feminine culture, by contrast, is aligned with a very different logic of repetition and continuity: as presented by Simmel, it exists outside history and modernity, its daily rhythms undisturbed by the temporal dislocations occurring within the broader social domain. As a result, the anguish and ambiguity that often result from experiences of transitoriness and change are absent from the female psyche. Homogeneous and whole, woman is presented in Simmel's text as serenely free of alienation and contradiction, as the very opposite of a split subject.

To put it another way, woman does not need to create art because she *is* art. For Simmel, the aesthetic offers a promise of plenitude, exemplifying an absolute presence that transcends the fractured nature of modern experience and heals the split between subjective and objective culture. "The work of art," he writes, "in its impenetrable, circumscribed limits, separates itself from the heterogeneous confusion of things."[34] Woman is portrayed in a similar light; her distance from the social allows her to embody the redemptive promise of a transcendental unity. Femininity thus shares with the aesthetic a perfect integration of part and whole, as the utopian embodiment of a sensuous materiality which resists the tyranny of an abstract and one-sided reason. As a result, however, the feminine can retain its distinctive features only by remaining outside a male-defined objective culture. As Klaus Lichtblau notes in his reading of Simmel, "the idea of a genuinely female culture is utopian, a pure potentiality that must not be actualized for the sake of its own integrity."[35]

Simmel is not claiming here that individual women are incapable of producing works of art or of participating in public life. The question is rather whether such achievements contribute to the creation of a distinctively feminine culture or whether they merely reproduce existing male-defined forms of life. Simmel concedes that as women become more involved in the public world, such a distinctive culture may evolve. Yet his poetic vision of the feminine makes it difficult to see how this process could ever occur. If femininity is inimical to structures of mediation and differentiation, it cannot by definition be translated into modern social and symbolic forms. Thus, for Simmel, an objective female culture is ultimately a contradiction in terms. As women participate in modern life, they will simply be defeminized and subjected to the prevailing regime of masculine alienation. There thus seems to be no possibility in Simmel's work for the concept of a distinctively modern femininity.

In fact, the only cultural sphere which Simmel considers to exemplify the female mode of being is that of the household. "In its state of serene, self-contained completeness," he writes, "it assumes that real and symbolic relationship to the nature of the woman by which it could become her great cultural achievement."[36] The home, he suggests, is marked by the special interests and abilities and distinctive rhythms of female being; it is unified, concrete, and complete within itself. Although such an idealization of the home fits comfortably into an established nineteenth-century ethos of separate spheres, it appears oddly incongruous in the context of Simmel's other writings, many of which offer insightful accounts of the sociology of consumption and the invasion of the private sphere by the mass-produced commodities and artifacts of modern life.[37] This lame invocation of the idylls of domesticity can be contrasted with Simmel's brief but much more suggestive comments on fashion and femininity. As a paradoxical combination of conformity and uniqueness, standardization and individuality, fashion is seen by Simmel as a major medium of modern cultural expression, which he links to the distinctive features of the female psyche; yet he acknowledges that this psyche is itself formed within particular social constraints and is hence not an unproblematic site of authenticity. The preoccupation of women with fashionable dress relates to the limitations which they experience in other parts of their lives, constituting an ambiguous cultural phenomenon which may function both as a form of compensation and as an act of resistance.[38] In his speculations on women's interest in fashion as a (limited) expression of individuality and a symbolic articulation of a desire for innovation and change, Simmel moreover affirms a link between women and the modern sensibility which he appears elsewhere to deny. For the most part, his desire to define femininity in terms of a mystified ideal of absolute difference has the effect of reinforcing a view of women's necessary absence from society and history. While usefully exposing the limitations of an abstract logic of identity, Simmel's ascription of an ontological otherness to women simultaneously guarantees both their authenticity and their exclusion from a modernity that remains exclusively identified with masculine individuation and agency. Woman, it seems, is always elsewhere, her ineffable otherness beyond linguistic or political representation.

The Archaic Mother

At this point, I wish to contextualize Simmel's vision of femininity by relating it to a broader current of cultural pessimism within the European fin de siècle. While the association of women with nostalgia has an extended and multiply determined history, it was to gain particular prominence in the context of this powerful upsurge of antimodern sentiment. Such a current was evident in a number of European countries—in England the examples of William Morris and the Pre-Raphaelites come immediately to mind—but was particularly pronounced in Germany, where a long-standing tradition of Romantic organicism combined with a relatively late and rapid experience of industrialization to encourage a profound ambivalence vis-à-vis the supposed benefits and values of the modern. Artists, writers, and intellectuals sought to express their sense of estrangement from a positivistic world-view and an ever more urban and technologized society through an orientation to the past and an explicit cult of the mythic and the nonrational. In a wide variety of texts—historical, anthropological, psychological, literary—the narrative of the Fall was repeatedly deployed to highlight the insufficiency of an overcivilized, overrational present by contrasting it to an earlier, more primal, more authentic time.

In this fin-de-siècle fascination with the archaic and the elemental, woman played an important role as the repository of a lost truth that man had to regain. The mythology of the "eternal feminine" retained a particularly powerful resonance in German-speaking cultures, often overshadowing the competing claims of Enlightenment ideals of human equality. Its origins can be traced to the texts of early German Romanticism, which abjured the world of public politics and the tyranny of universal norms in favor of an aesthetic and sensual ideal of the multifaceted personality. Women's wholeness of experience provided in this context an ideal of liberation that could be counterposed to men's enslavement to a one-sided abstraction.[39] This idealization of the feminine recurs in the metaphorical linkage of woman, nature, and the archaic that pervaded numerous forms of fin-de-siècle cultural expression. From the paintings of Gustav Klimt to the writings of Lou Andreas-Salomé, the figure of woman emerged as an erotic-mythic creature, an enigmatic incarnation of elemental and libidinal forces that exceeded the bounds of reason and social order. In the modern yearning for a preindustrial world, she embodied everything that modernity was not, the living antithesis of the ironic self-estrangement of urban man.[40]

The work of the German classicist and myth scholar J. J. Bachofen was to have a powerful influence on such visions of an archaic femininity by challenging established perceptions of patriarchy as an inevitable and natural social form. In *Myth, Religion, and Mother Right* (1861), he developed the hypothesis that matriarchy formed a universal stage of all civilizations, a view which was to have a profound impact upon numerous late-nineteenth-century thinkers, including Engels, August Bebel, Nietzsche, and Freud. Bachofen's detailed narrative of the origins of Western civilization in the Mediterranean cultures of antiquity depicted the matriarchal basis of primitive societies and their gradual supersession by the Hellenic principle of patriarchal law. Elizabeth Fee provides a useful summary of Bachofen's overarching historical thesis.

> Bachofen saw the continuing struggle between male and female as the central theme in social evolution ... He believed human history to have consisted of three main stages: the haeterist-aphroditic, the matriarchal, and the patriarchal. During the haeterist-aphroditic stage, marriage was unknown. Sexual relationships were unregulated: women were at the mercy of male lust; promiscuity and sexual exploitation triumphed. Eventually, however, the women had rebelled and had staged a worldwide Amazonian revolt. Following their military success, they established the second stage of human history, the matriarchal stage. Women, as mothers, dominated social and cultural institutions; female sexuality triumphed; now they could force marriage and monogamy onto the reluctant males. In the final stage, men rebelled in their turn, triumphed, and replaced matriarchy with the patriarchal system. Women were dethroned and male supremacy everywhere recognized. In the matriarchal period, the female fertility principle had been glorified, while the transition to patriarchalism represented the emancipation of man from material nature.[41]

Such an imaginative depiction of a long-distant era governed by a feminine principle found a receptive audience among those seeking radical alternatives to the dominant values of their own time. Bachofen's writings equated matriarchy with a condition of homogeneity, materiality, and harmony with nature, a primitive social order embodying a lost happiness. He explicitly linked matriarchal prehistory to "childbearing motherhood"; both occupy a similar position on the developmental scale as embodiments of the rule of nature prior to the necessary alienation of culture. The emergence of civilization was understood in terms of a development from an archaic, chthonian feminine sphere of undifferentiated unity to a patriarchal culture governed by "higher spiritual laws."[42]

Parallels to Bachofen's etiology can be found in numerous other evolutionary narratives of the period, which were to reproduce the same associative chain linking premodernity, nondifferentiation, and the feminine. Freud's psychohistorical speculations on the origins of culture reveal a similar conception of woman as embodying a primal and static condition that is antithetical to the developmental logic of the civilizing process. In *Civilization and Its Discontents,* for example, women's allegiance to the interests of family and sexual life is seen as causing an antagonism to the demands of civilization, an antagonism which Freud traces back to the dawn of prehistory. Freud observes that their limited capacity for instinctual sublimation renders women incapable of participating in the development of higher cultural forms. "Thus the woman finds herself forced into the background by the claims of civilization and she adopts a hostile attitude towards it."[43] In the earlier *Totem and Taboo*, it is the rebellion of the sons against the father which provides the mythic foundation for the development of religion and morality; here again woman is positioned outside the Oedipal struggle between desire and authority which propels the trajectory of human progress.

Freud, of course, saw this process of sublimation as the necessary price to be paid for the development of civilization, with its attendant achievements of law, religion, art, and morality. The paternal principle epitomized the necessary if problematic renunciations and gains of culture and modernity, whereas the maternal merely served as an archaic symbolic reminder of a precultural and noncontradictory logic.[44] Some of Freud's colleagues, however, while sympathetic to the founding tenets of psychoanalytical thought, were less convinced of the inevitability and desirability of repression under the sign of patriarchal law. Thus Lou Andreas-Salomé, the well-known Russian feminist, writer, and psychoanalyst, interpreted the unconscious in a more positive light, as a source of creativity rooted in a primal experience of undifferentiation. In an essay entitled "The Consequences of the Fact That It Was Not Women Who Killed the Father," she uses Freud's etiological myth of the birth of civilization out of father-son conflict to argue that women are free of this burden of symbolic guilt and hence less subject to the rule of the superego. Instead, for Salomé, women are more closely aligned to a presymbolic state of primary narcissism. Against Freud's view of narcissism as a regressive phenomenon, however, Salomé reevaluates it as a token of woman's rootedness in an elemental unity, of her experience of a fusion of self and world, and hence as a sign of her superiority over man, who is torn apart by the contradictions of the social.[45]

In "The Human Being As a Woman" (1899), Salomé's representation of feminine difference is very close to that of Simmel. Woman exemplifies an elemental bisexuality, as an autonomous, undifferentiated being who contains both masculine and feminine within herself. She writes, "There is a self-sufficiency and repose in [the feminine,] in accordance with the deepest intentionality of being, which cannot be reconciled with the restlessness and disquiet of that which pushes itself forward with such passion to the outermost limits and splinters all its forces more and more intensively and pointedly in the service of specialized activities."[46] Salomé contrasts the goal-directed, specialized, individualized character of man with the self-contained circularity of woman. She too sees women as being more at home with themselves, less riven by the contradictions of modernity, symbolizing a unity and a rootedness in the body that men have lost. This unity is exemplified above all in the experience of motherhood, the ultimate symbol of a redemptive totality which allows woman to unite both masculine and feminine impulses within herself. Thus both writers draw upon an evolutionary schema which depicts the maternal as source or origin, a moment of authentic harmony and unity prior to the fall into culture. Simmel, for example, refers to the feminine as an absolute "whose first and unmediated expression is motherhood"; it is on this that "both the masculine and the feminine in the relational sense are preeminently based."[47] For him, as for Salomé, the more profoundly a woman is female in this fundamental maternal sense, the less she is feminine in relative, that is, male-defined, terms. She is integrated within herself, the embodiment of an ontological absolute. The key to an autonomous femininity lies in the domain of the maternal as a zone prior to cultural objectification and individuation.

In the writings of Simmel and Salomé, we can thus glimpse an identical rhetorical move. A conventional binary opposition of male-female complementarity is rejected so as to reinscribe this polarity at a higher level in the distinction between the principle of individuation and alienation (identified with masculinity) and that of nondifferentiation, bisexuality, and indeterminacy (identified with the maternal and the feminine). The difference of woman lies, paradoxically, in the fact that she is beyond difference; that which precedes the division of gender is itself gendered as feminine. This schema bears some obvious similarities to those more recent texts of French feminism which also reject a phallocentric notion of femininity derived from the subject-object dualism of Western metaphysics in favor of an alternative, quasi-utopian vision of the feminine as that which exists outside categories, distinctions, and patriarchal structures of individuation and socialization. The feminine and maternal body is seen to be that which resists classification, blurs boundaries, and collapses the distinction between subject and object, whether that body is idealized as the exemplum of a nonalienated plenitude or interpreted as an emblem of horror and abjection.

Such conceptual and metaphorical affinities are in one sense not surprising, given the reliance of both Simmelian sociology and the Lacanian framework underpinning much French feminism upon a very similar model of culture and the psyche. In her insightful critique of Lacanian theory, Anne McClintock notes that its combination of Freudian assumptions with a Hegelian structure robbed of its rationalist resolution serves to create a tragic existential narrative of self-division and alienation under the sign of paternal law. At the same time, McClintock writes, "women's difference is figured as a chronological difference; we inhabit an earlier space in the linear, temporal history of the (male) symbolic space . . . For Lacan, women do not inhabit history proper. We bear a pre-positional relation to history."[48] As McClintock suggests and as my own discussion has indicated, such an intellectual paradigm may reveal much more about the influence of specific nineteenth-century mythologies and narratives of gender than about the nature and form of a universal human destiny. Both sociology and psychoanalysis took shape at roughly the same time; the period 1895–1915, when some of the most important works of modern sociology were written, was also the time when Freud developed the model of psychobiological development which would form the basis for all his future writings.[49] In spite of their differences of focus and emphasis, these two disciplinary matrices thus reveal a strikingly similar emplotment of human destiny moored in a distinctively gendered rhetoric. Within this shared vision of individual and cultural evolution, the feminine remains forever subjugated—however uneasily—to the dictates of a patriarchal law that represents the civilizing process. Hence the evocative power of the primitive horde and the domain of the maternal as interchangeable symbols of a lost golden age in the fin-de-siècle reckoning with the costs of social progress.

The Nostalgia Paradigm in Modern Thought

The representative significance of Simmel's account of modernity should now, I hope, be apparent. The difference between masculinity and femininity underwrites not just a psychological but a philosophical and quasi-metaphysical distinction between the sexes which shapes an entire philosophy of history. Woman comes to represent nature in a dual sense: the inner nature of a bodily self-presence untouched by the constraints of the symbolic as well as the outer nature of an organic domain beyond the encroachment of industrial and technological forces. In the context of a modern ontology that posits the human condition as one of alienation from an originary identity, women are deemed to be less burdened by this self-conscious sense of existential homelessness than men and hence to be closer to a timeless point of origin.

In a recent book, Georg Stauth and Bryan Turner argue that the development of classical European sociology, in spite of important national variations, has been largely dominated by a nostalgic paradigm composed of four main themes. These they identify as follows: the idea of history as a process of decline from a lost golden age; an absence of wholeness and moral certainty; the loss of simplicity, spontaneity, and authenticity; and the belief that individual autonomy and genuine social relations have collapsed. These inter-related motifs are seen to provide the dominant metaphors and metaphysics of classical and contemporary sociology, linking together diverse writings which are conventionally regarded as very different. "In summary, the nostalgic metaphor suggests that we live in a world which lacks moral unity, in which individual autonomy is overwhelmed by administrative rules from a centralized state, and where direct expression of feeling is no longer possible, because need and desire have been rendered artificial and superficial by the spread of a consumer culture which exploits false needs."[50] This vision has in turn profoundly shaped the development of twentieth-century critical theory from Martin Heidegger to Theodor Adorno; as the narrative of history as progress has become exhausted and impoverished, argue Stauth and Turner, it has been largely replaced by the nostalgic paradigm.

While Stauth and Turner do not address questions of gender politics, woman is undoubtedly one of the central figures through which this paradigm has been concretized in sociological writing. In this context, Janet Wolff has critically addressed the assumptions of a still largely Weberian sociological tradition which locates modernity in the public world of work, bureaucracy, and the marketplace, with the result that women are positioned either tacitly or explicitly outside its frame.[51] Similarly, Marx's location of the revolutionary potential of modernity in the labor process and the transformation of modes of production has been called into question for encouraging a perception of women's reproductive and domestic work as situated beyond the dynamic of social change. A third graphic instance of sociology's nostalgic view of woman can be found in Ferdinand Tönnies's typology of community and society. Women, not surprisingly, are linked to the sphere of *Gemeinschaft*, or community, anchored within the home and a network of intimate and familial relationships and contrasted with the artificial and mechanical world of *Gesellschaft*. A woman's life echoes the pattern of premodern cultures in its adherence to religious belief, organic living, and forms of personal service to others. It is noteworthy that at a time of rapid industrialization and urbanization in Germany, when the metropolis was emerging as a site of social unrest in the context of both feminist and socialist politics, women are portrayed as essentially untouched by these diverse social transformations.[52]

The metaphorical and meta-theoretical dimensions of sociological thought have also been discussed by Robert Nisbet, who notes that its extensive reliance on images of growth—with their concomitant associations of directionality, cumulation, irreversibility, and purpose—tends to convey a sense of the historical inevitability of Western forms of development, while presenting alternative social forms as outdated and archaic.[53] This account of history as a single and unidirectional process of growth in turn gains much of its rhetorical power from the simultaneous deployment of various polar oppositions. The tradition/modernity distinction at the heart of sociological thought generates a whole range of further dualisms; uniformity versus differentiation, stasis versus change, competitiveness versus community, and so forth. Such oppositions efface all evidence of complexity, conflict, and change within premodern societies by projecting onto them a condition of simple and undifferentiated stasis. While such an ethnocentric perspective expels all traces of the primitive from its own locale in order to situate it in an external zone of racial and cultural otherness, the figure of woman serves as a recurring cipher of the premodern within modernity itself. Through a symbolic erasure of the complexities and conflicts within female experience, woman is seen to exemplify a blissful and nonalienated condition not unlike that of the noble savage.

In subjecting this nostalgic representation of femininity to critical questioning, I do not wish to imply that it is a purely arbitrary fiction that bears no relationship whatsoever to women's lives. Simmel's view of femininity as residing outside objective culture clearly contains a kernel of truth in identifying women's historical absence from many forms of institutionalized and public activities. Similarly, some feminists have noted that experiences such as mothering may offer forms of symbolic fulfillment and affective enrichment that remain invisible to theories of the modern derived from models of Weberian rationalization or Marxist alienation. There thus appears to be an intuitive fit between our everyday understanding of the differences between women and men and the sociological distinction between an intimate sphere of emotional relations and a public world governed by the impersonality of the market and the bureaucratic state. Yet it is equally important to insist that nurturing and motherhood constitute neither an autonomous enclave of intimacy untouched by changing discourses and ideologies of the self nor the essence or endpoint of female identity. Indeed, a number of writers from Nancy Armstrong to Jacques Donzelot to Friedrich Kittler have shown how ideas of feminine affectivity and motherliness have themselves been powerfully implicated and mobilized in the development of modern regimes of power.[54] In conceiving of the feminine as a self-contained plenitude outside social and symbolic mediation, the nostalgia paradigm cannot begin to address the complex and multifaceted nature of women's involvement in and negotiations with different aspects of modern culture.

Instead, a circular argument prevails within such a paradigm: it being assumed that modernity is a quintessentially masculine phenomenon, femininity must remain forever outside its reach. Underpinning this logic is an instrumental/expressive dichotomy central to much sociological thought whereby modernization is equated with an inexorable process of rationalization, whereas feelings, passions, and desires inhabit a realm of authentic interiority free of regulatory influence. The heritage of an Enlightenment world-view reveals itself in the assumption that society is composed of rational, autonomous individuals, an assumption which typically overemphasizes the impact of equalizing and instrumental logics and simultaneously underestimates the continuing importance of religious, ethnic, regional, and other "nonrational" identities within modern forms of life. At the same time, a countercurrent of Romanticism manifests itself in the longing for a sphere of redemption outside the iron cage of modernity, a sphere within which the figure of woman assumes a privileged place. The ostensibly dispassionate gaze of the social scientist thus frequently reveals itself to be impelled by a nostalgic desire not unlike that of the early Romantic artists, who were among the first to mourn the breakdown of organic connections and the domination of society by the cash nexus.[55]

Such a polarized distinction between the instrumental and the expressive is thus of symptomatic rather than analytical value in addressing the relationship between gender and modernity. The appeal to an ontologically prior emotional or bodily wholeness that is subsequently deformed by processes of modernization fails to acknowledge the ineluctably social nature of this Romantic myth of the authentic feeling self. Moreover, to focus only upon the rationalized character of the public world is to ignore the centrality of erotically and aesthetically charged representations in the formation of modern social experience. Rather than being limited to an autonomous private sphere, affectivity and sexuality permeated nineteenth-century social space and were intimately intertwined with processes of commodification and rationalization often regarded as quintessentially modern. Instead of being excluded by a masculine logic of development, women were in fact addressed in specific and multifarious ways by the culture of the fin de siècle, with such distinctively modern phenomena as fashion, consumerism, and the department store being explicitly geared to the desiring female subject. It is perhaps surprising that Simmel's often subtle and complex engagements with the contradictory dimensions of modernity gives way in the context of his account of femininity to a view of a static and unchanging female nature.

Nevertheless, such an idealized vision of Ur-femininity cannot simply be dismissed as an exclusively masculine fantasy of redemptive alterity. On the contrary, it underwrites a history of representations which have shaped the writings of women as much as those of men. Apart from Lou Andreas-

Salomé, many other female writers would also formulate their critique of a male-dominated society through a counter-vision of feminine plenitude; Karen Horney, for example, explicitly drew on Simmel's work in the 1940s in presenting her extensive criticisms of the patriarchal biases within the psychoanalytic profession.[56] More recently, aspects of Simmel's arguments have been adopted by contemporary feminists, particularly in Germany, to advocate a similar notion of women's unique particularity and ontological otherness. In fact, the mythologization of woman in Simmel's writing intersects at significant points with the self-definition of the German women's movement during much of its history. In contrast to English and American feminists, who stressed the importance of equal rights, German feminists have historically given much greater weight to notions of women's radical difference, a difference that has often been conceptualized through an idealization of the maternal feminine and the vocabulary of a nostalgic antimodernism. In her discussion of fin-de-siècle German feminism, Ute Frevert writes:

> For the bourgeois women's movement, the "pathology of the Modern" was . . . an intellectual and spiritual disorder whose symptoms could be summed up as mechanisation, objectification and the obliteration of the soul and the individual. Modern technology and industry seemed to be the incarnation of masculine principles, a rational system which dominated and exploited the vitality of nature, ignoring and subjugating all individuality and diversity to uniform, mechanical laws of production. Women were like foreign bodies in this object world of machines and bureaucracies: the "miserable impersonality" of economic life, cast as it was in a masculine mould, was no place for "natural" feminine interests and sensitivity.[57]

Thus many women as well as men agreed that the modern world was no place for a woman.

I therefore suggest that the politics of nostalgia may be complex and variable and by no means as clear-cut as is sometimes assumed. On this point, one can often find a rare instance of consensus between contemporary Marxists and poststructuralists: the latter tend to read any appeal to an originary unity as symptomatic of a reactionary metaphysics of presence, while many on the Left also tend to view nostalgia perjoratively as a sign of an inauthentic relationship to history and the past. Similarly, the repeated commentaries on nostalgia in diagnoses of postmodern culture almost invariably assume a condemnatory stance, as if the longing for an idealized past were automatically symptomatic of a regrettable political weakness and lack of moral fiber within the contemporary Zeitgeist. Yet it is not immediately clear why this should be so, or why an idealization of the past should be interpreted so much more harshly than a similar idealization of the present or the future. It is tempting to link such denunciations to the gendered subtext of the discourse of nostalgia that I have explored in this chapter. If nostalgia is conventionally associated with femininity, the home, and a longing for maternal plenitude, it is perhaps unsurprising that it has come under critical fire from those who pride themselves on the radical contemporaneity of their own ironized consciousness and their concomitant disdain for the taint of the sentimental.

Yet a simple dismissal of all manifestations of nostalgia as reactionary is scarcely sufficient. This is to turn one's back on the crucial insight that experiences of fragmentation and dislocation are not always perceived as liberating, but often engender a counter-response which seeks to establish a sense of continuity and stability by invoking the metaphorical power of an imagined past. Such strategies can be found in various and often very disparate texts that place themselves in an antagonistic or dissident relationship to aspects of the present. Within our own time, for example, a desire for an idealized past has helped to fuel the struggles of some feminist, ecological, and anti-imperialist movements as well as to inspire the more questionable forms of religious fundamentalism and calls for a return to traditional values. While on the one hand nostalgic desire glosses over the oppressive dimensions of the past for which it yearns, on the other hand it may mobilize a powerful condemnation of the present for its failure to correspond to the imagined harmony of a prelapsarian condition. The yearning for the past may engender active attempts to construct an alternative future, so that nostalgia comes to serve a critical rather than a simply conservative purpose.[58]

Seen in this light, nostalgia emerges as an ambiguous symptom of cultural malaise which can be associated with a whole range of political positions from the far Left to the far Right. There is a close relationship between modern fashionings of futurity and nostalgia; both bear witness to experiences of transition and flux which in turn engender a desire for an alternative center of stability and meaningfulness. "Nostalgia becomes possible at the same time as Utopia. The counterpart of the imagined future is the imagined past."[59] Rather than an ahistorical and unitary constant, a yearning for the past is itself a historically and culturally variable result of particular experiences of movement and transformation. In this sense, as Keith Tester points out, nostalgia simultaneously reaffirms the very condition that it seeks to transcend: "it is only possible for me to long for home if I know that I am without my home."[60] An idealized image of the feminine has historically functioned as a significant site of such nostalgic longing for home on the part of both men *and* women. It will perhaps continue to do so as long as women retain primary responsibility for the nurture and care of children and hence a privileged association with a fantasmatic and retrospectively imagined past.

3

Imagined Pleasures:
The Erotics and Aesthetics
of Consumption

The cultural logic of modernity is not merely that of rationality as
expressed in the activities of calculation and experiment; it is also
that of passion, and the creative dreaming born of longing.

Colin Campbell, *The Romantic Ethic and the Spirit
of Modern Consumerism*

To view modernity from the standpoint of consumption rather than
production is to effect a shift in perspective which causes taken-for-granted
phenomena to appear in a new light. The grand narrative of rationalization
becomes less persuasive as a comprehensive thesis of social change when it is
counterposed to the dream worlds and exotic-fantasmic images of urban
culture.[1] The belief that Western history has repressed erotic drives through
a prevalent ethos of discipline and self-restraint is called into question by the
central role of hedonistic desire and sexualized representations in the rise of
modern consumerism. Above all, a view of modernity as driven by the logic
of productive forces gives way to a recognition that consumer demand is not
simply a passive reflection of economic interests, but is shaped by a variety
of relatively independent cultural and ideological factors, of which gender is
one of the most significant.

In the late nineteenth century, the consumer was frequently represented as
a woman. In other words, the category of consumption situated femininity
at the heart of the modern in a way that the discourses of production and
rationalization examined previously did not. Thus consumption cut across
the private/public distinction that was frequently evoked to assign women to
a premodern sphere. Not only did the department store provide a new kind
of urban public space which catered primarily to women, but modern
industry and commerce encroached ever more insistently on the sanctity of

the private and domestic realm through the commodification of the household. Although the middle-class woman's responsibility for the purchase rather than the production of goods seemed to locate her outside of the dynamic of social change, in another sense her status as consumer gave her an intimate familiarity with the rapidly changing fashions and lifestyles that constituted an important part of the felt experience of being modern. The emergence of a culture of consumption helped to shape new forms of subjectivity for women, whose intimate needs, desires, and perceptions of self were mediated by public representations of commodities and the gratifications that they promised.

This feminization of modernity, however, is largely synonymous with its demonization. In the writings of many radical and conservative intellectuals from the mid-nineteenth century onward, the idea of the modern becomes aligned with a pessimistic vision of an unpredictable yet curiously passive femininity seduced by the glittering phantasmagoria of an emerging consumer culture. No longer equated with a progressive development toward a more rational society, modernity now comes to exemplify the growth of irrationalism, the return of repressed nature in the form of inchoate desire. As Rosalind Williams notes, "to a large extent the pejorative nature of the concept of consumption itself derives from its association with female submission to organic needs."[2] Women are portrayed as buying machines, driven by impulses beyond their control to squander money on the accumulation of ever more possessions. The familiar and still prevalent cliché of the insatiable female shopper epitomizes the close associations between economic and erotic excess in dominant images of femininity. Yet this irrationalism can simultaneously be seen as modern because it is a *managed* desire, manipulated by a logic of calculation and rationalization in the interests of the profit motive. Women's emotionality, passivity, and susceptibility to persuasion renders them ideal subjects of an ideology of consumption that pervades a society predicated on the commercialization of pleasure.

This current of thought continues to play an influential role in twentieth-century attitudes toward modernity and mass culture. Not only does woman remain the archetypal consumer, but an overt anxiety comes to the fore that men are in turn being feminized by the castrating effects of an ever more pervasive commodification. *Seduction* is a recurring term used in the writings of male intellectuals to describe the manipulation of the individual by marketing techniques, eloquently evoking the mixture of passivity, complicity, and pleasure seen to characterize the standpoint of the modern consumer. The subject is decentered, no longer in control of his or her desires, but prey to the beguiling forces of publicity and the image industry. Indictments of twentieth-century consumerism regularly invoke a nostalgia for a robust sense of individual self that has been invaded and feminized by an omnipresent culture of glossy media simulations. In an intellectual tradition extending from the Frankfurt School to the recent work of Jean Baudrillard, the discourses on commodity fetishism and the tyranny of the sign reveal a persistently gendered subtext.

Feminist theorists have until recently adopted and intensified this dystopian perspective, pointing to a systematic convergence of capitalist and patriarchal interests in the construction of modern femininity. Women have been portrayed as victims of the ideology of consumerism, trapped in a web of objectified images which alienate them from their true identity. Any pleasure derived from fashion, cosmetics, women's magazines, or other distinctively feminized aspects of consumer culture has been read as merely another symptom of women's manipulation by institutionalized mechanisms of patriarchal control. More recent arguments within feminism and cultural studies have rejected this manipulation thesis, insisting that greater weight be given to the potential for active negotiation and recontextualization of meaning in the process of consumption. The traditional Left and feminist discomfort with consumer culture has been criticized for an excessive puritanism and asceticism, often moored in a nostalgic vision of a premodern authentic subject and an untenable, utilitarian definition of "real needs."[3]

My intention at this point is not to present a straightforward defense of consumption; if anything, the celebration of the resistive agency of the female consumer is currently in danger of becoming a new orthodoxy, which often pays scant attention to the limited alternatives available to many women as well as the economic, racial, and geopolitical constraints determining the nature and extent of their access to commodities.[4] Nevertheless, feminist theory clearly needs to remain skeptical of a production/consumption dichotomy which persistently devalues the latter as a passive and irrational activity. This dichotomy is my primary focus in this chapter, where I aim to investigate the history of the metaphorization of consumption as it shapes our understanding of both economic and textual transactions. Representations of shopping and representations of reading, I will argue, reveal some striking similarities in their vision of the voracious female consumer.

Commodities and Female Desire

Perhaps the most common economic metaphor which has been used to describe women's position within capitalist society is that of the commodity. As Mary Ann Doane points out, "woman's objectification, her susceptibility to processes of fetishization, display, profit and loss, the production of surplus value, all situate her in a relation of resemblance to the commodity form."[5] Woman has been seen as an object exchanged between men in a capitalist economy, compelled to render herself as seductive as possible in order to attract the gaze of the male buyer. I have already noted the significance of the urban prostitute in this regard as the most graphic and literal embodiment of this phenomenon of female commodification. In nineteenth-century France in particular, the courtesan was to become *the* exemplary symbol of an eroticized modernity.

But if women could be seen as objects of consumption, some women were also becoming consuming subjects, as the advent of mass production and distinctively modern retailing strategies began to dramatically alter the everyday fabric of social relations between people and things. The introduction of the department store in the mid-nineteenth century was the most visible example of a burgeoning economy which would become increasingly oriented toward selling to women. Originally little more than a large draper's shop, the department store was to rapidly diversify its range of merchandise in order to cater to all the potential needs of the female consumer and her household, needs which it helped to create through its own enticing visual displays of commercial abundance. This transformation of the commodity into spectacle was further promoted by the late-nineteenth-century craze for great exhibitions, monuments of consumption that displayed exotic and disparate objects from around the world to the wondering visitor. Here again the figure of woman played an emblematic role; at the 1900 Paris exposition, for example, the monumental gateway was crowned by "the flying figure of a siren in a tight skirt, the symbolic ship of the City of Paris on her head, throwing back an evening coat of imitation ermine—La Parisienne."[6] Rosalind Williams notes that such symbols of feminized modernity coincided with an increased emphasis on pleasure and distraction rather than moral education as the legitimating function of the great exhibition. Finally, advertising at this time began to develop increasingly sophisticated marketing techniques, promoting repertoires of identities and lifestyles to which the consumer was encouraged to aspire. Given an extant gender division of labor which identified shopping as women's work, it was women above all who were interpellated in this way through mass-produced images of femininity, even as middle-class women's dependence upon the economic support of men required them to invest far more heavily in modes of fashionable adornment and self-display.

One of the most significant features of the expansion of consumption from a feminist standpoint is its preoccupation with women's pleasure. The discourse of consumerism is to a large extent the discourse of female desire. Whereas female sexuality remained a problematic notion throughout the century, its existence either denied or projected onto the deviant figure of the femme fatale, women's desire for commodities could be publicly acknowledged as a legitimate, if often trivialized, form of wanting. Late-nineteenth-century retailers and marketers eagerly sought to stimulate such desire through erotically saturated strategies of display and enticement, even as trade journals and newspaper articles spoke approvingly of women's inability to refuse commercial temptation and celebrated the inevitability of their seduction by the dazzling allures of new merchandise. Often depicted as an object in the domain of heterosexual relations, woman, it seemed, could only attain the status of an active subject in relation to other objects. The circuit of desire thus flowed from man to woman, from woman to the commodity.

But what if the female pleasure in shopping was not as harmless as it appeared? Perhaps, once awakened, this appetite would have disturbing and unforeseeable effects, reaching out to subvert the social fabric and to undermine patriarchal authority within the family. Thus fin-de-siècle responses to this new phenomenon of the consuming woman revealed conflictual and ambivalent attitudes. On the one hand, consumption was presented as a necessity, indeed as a familial and civic duty for the middle-class woman, even as retailers referred confidently among themselves to the docility of female shoppers, who would "follow like sheep in the path marked out for them by the softgoods merchant."[7] Such discourses framed women as the passive beneficiaries or victims, depending on one's viewpoint, of a new inexorable imperative of capitalist development. Yet on the other hand, the growth of consumerism was seen as engendering a revolution of morals, unleashing egotistic and envious drives among the lower orders and women, which could in turn affect the stability of existing social hierarchies. One American writer, for example, noted dangerous levels of self-indulgence in many women shoppers, citing "a certain lawlessness of disposition, an inherent dislike to live by rule, a breaking out of a wayward will at the point of least resistance."[8] The increasing influence of a new ethos of self-gratification could have problematic and unforeseen consequences for the natural relationship between the sexes.

The figure of the consuming woman was thus to become a semiotically dense site of cultural imaginings of the modern and its implications for the relations between women and men. The multifarious intensities of meaning accruing to this figure are clearly displayed in the texts which I discuss in this chapter, Emile Zola's *Au bonheur des dames* and *Nana* and Gustave Flaubert's *Madame Bovary*.[9] The preoccupation of French writers, social critics, and other intellectuals with the nature and significance of mass consumption arose almost inevitably out of the emblematic status of late-nineteenth-century Paris as a pre-eminent site of the modern "consumer revolution."[10] Their responses varied significantly according to ideological affiliation and cultural positioning; there was no univocal position on the nature and meaning of consumption per se. Nevertheless, a pervasive thread of anxiety about the social and moral implications of mass-produced luxury runs through many of these responses, which relates at numerous points to dominant conceptions of gender. The novels discussed in this chapter crystallize some of these contemporary uncertainties about the relationship between sex and capital, as evidenced in the circulation of contradictory assumptions about the female consumer. Depicted as the victim of modernity, she is also its privileged agent; epitomizing the subjection of women by the tyranny of capital, she simultaneously promotes the feminization of society through a burgeoning materialism and hedonistic excess.

These ambiguous meanings clustered around the female consumer suggest that the interrelations between patriarchal and capitalist structures may be more complicated than feminist theorists have often recognized. For if consumer culture simply reinforced women's objectified and powerless status, it becomes difficult to understand why the phenomenon was attacked so vehemently as a threat to men's traditional authority over women. If, as Gail Reekie has argued, "retailers, managers and marketing experts formed a fraternity, bound together by a bond *as men,* whose primary object was to reap profits from the compliance of the female customer," why did other men react so anxiously to mass consumption as a profoundly emasculating phenomenon?[11] Placing the question of femininity at the heart of the modern, the novels discussed in this chapter examine some of the complexities of consumer culture in the context of gender politics. In embedding middle-class women in circuits of desire and exchange, the growth of mass consumption threatened as much as it reinscribed established structures of masculine identity and authority.

Shopping and Sex

In Zola's novel *The Ladies' Paradise* (*Au bonheur des dames,* 1883), it is the department store named in the title and modeled on the well-known Parisian establishment Au Bon Marché, that remains in the reader's mind as the novel's most memorable character. Alternately described as an efficiently running machine and a fairy-tale palace of dreams, this emporium experiences a dynamic growth that drives the narrative momentum of the text.

Simultaneously destructive and seductive, this anthropomorphized "cathedral of modern commerce" ruins or drives to their deaths the small shopkeepers of the neighborhood even as it entices ever more female customers through its portals. In Zola's depiction of the department store as an ambiguous symbol of progress, the relationship between sex and capital is shown to lie at the very heart of modern social relations. The economic struggle for power is intertwined with and mediated by erotic relations between women and men and between women and commodities.

A number of contemporary writers have drawn attention to the importance of the department store in shaping the formation of cultural modernity.[12] The *grand magasin* brought about a number of significant innovations in merchandising: fixed prices, which made bargaining unnecessary; "free entry," which allowed customers to examine goods on display without any obligation to buy; and a dramatic expansion of the range and diversity of goods offered for sale under one roof. As a result, shopping came to be seen for the first time as a leisure activity; the department store offered an elaborate spectacle, providing enticing and elaborate displays of merchandise for the visual pleasure of shoppers and passers-by. It was to play a leading role in the aestheticization of the commodity and the marketing of lifestyles that simultaneously demarcated and blurred class distinctions, encouraging everyone to aspire to a middle-class way of life. The department store sold not just commodities but the very act of consumption, transforming the mundane activity of shopping into a sensuous and enjoyable experience for a bourgeois public.

It was this modernity of the department store which appealed to Zola, as an exemplary fictional site for exploring capitalism's impact on social and gender relations. His preparatory research for the novel included repeated, lengthy visits to various Parisian stores, interviews with retailers and managers, and the perusal of numerous journal and newspaper articles about shopping, marketing practices, and employees' working conditions. The preliminary note books for *Au bonheur des dames* were exhaustive; encompassing hundreds of pages, they contained excerpts from shopping catalogs, sketches of architectural features, and numerous other annotations on the mechanisms of retailing.[13] This voluminous documentation expresses itself in a novelistic form which enacts the very commodity fetishism it seeks to describe. *Au bonheur des dames* is a hymn to consumption, a novel dominated by the materiality of objects, given over to the exhaustive enunciation of the infinite multiplicity of modern consumer goods. Like the department store that it portrays, the novel displays commodities to readers/consumers, seducing or benumbing them through a monumental piling-up of wares.

Types of lace, colors and weights of silk, styles of carpets and rugs are enumerated in paragraphs of taxonomic description that simulate the precision and repetitiveness of a stock inventory. Even as it critically frames the irrational and impulsive excesses of the department store clientele, Zola's text reveals its own fascination with and seduction by the magical objects of consumer culture.

As the very title of Zola's novel suggests, the department store was a public space identified as distinctively feminine, offering the promise of indulgence, luxury, and fantasy to the middle-class woman. Not merely a place for making purchases, it allowed her to browse, to window-shop, to arrange a rendezvous with female friends, and to make use of the various facilities, such as libraries and tearooms, which it offered. Elizabeth Wilson suggests that "in a very real way the department store assisted the freeing of middle-class women from the shackles of the home. It became a place where women could meet their women friends in safety and comfort, unchaperoned, and to which they could repair for refreshment and rest."[14] In one sense, then, it provided a model of an egalitarian modern space that in principle, if not in practice, welcomed everyone through its open doors. At the same time, however, this public domain presented itself as an extension of the private sphere, providing the visitor with an experience of intimacy and pleasure intended to reflect, in magnified form, the comforts of the bourgeois home. Thus one writer observed, "it is necessary that she (the customer) consider the *grand magasin* as a second home, larger, more beautiful, more luxurious than the other."[15] As Zola's novel indicates, this feminization of the public domain brought with it an incorporation of distinctive architectural and decorative styles intended to put the female consumer at her ease. The feminine objects—laces, furs, dresses, lingerie—displayed within the department store, and soon disordered and rumpled by passing customers, helped to intensify this quality of boudoir-like intimacy. Thus the clientele of Au Bonheur des Dames, who use the store for both commercial transactions and romantic assignations, are indeed, as the owner, Octave Mouret, wryly acknowledges, very much at home.

The department store, then, was a paradigm of a new kind of urban public space linked not to an ideal of political community and rational debate but to the experience of sensuality and the commercialization of desire. Although the expansion of commerce was greeted by many as a mark of progress, benefiting the consumer and contributing to the economic health of the nation, it was also perceived to possess a darker side in its encouragement of pleasure-seeking and narcissistic self-gratification, a temptation to which women were particularly prone. The emergence of kleptomania, a disease that was codified as both feminine and modern, was a striking instance of the sexual disorder that was seen to lie at the very heart of consumer culture. Most disturbingly, it afflicted respectable women from bourgeois backgrounds whose behavior was otherwise impeccable, disrupting conventional assumptions about the moral probity of middle-class women. Contemporary doctors and psychologists sought to make sense of this puzzling new phenomenon by linking femininity, hysteria, and the dangerous freedoms of the department store. Prevailing conceptions of shoplifting as a form of monomania, which were often accepted and expressed by shoplifters themselves, encouraged a view of middle-class women as helpless rather than criminal, driven by irrational impulses beyond their control. At the same time, the startling incidence of theft was also attributed to the new and dangerous availability of consumer goods in a deregulated and morally disintegrating modern world.[16]

A similar unease about the ultimate social consequences of modernization is expressed in Zola's novel in an opposition between the celebration of production and the pathologization of consumption. Although the text depicts some of the human costs of unchecked growth, the passionate commitment to economic expansion of the store owner, Octave Mouret, is presented as an admirable and rational ideal, an embodiment of the awesome, unstoppable progress unleashed by capitalist development. Yet the equally powerful compulsion to consume which motivates Mouret's female customers is not endowed with the same heroic stature and world-historical dignity. Rather than symbolizing progress, *they* represent the regressive dimension of modernity as exemplified in its unleashing of an infantile irrationalism of unchecked desire. The distinction between the deviant shoplifter and the respectable customer is blurred in their common capitulation to the lure of the commodity.

The erotically driven nature of female consumption provides the leitmotif in Zola's novel. References to temptation and seduction abound; the department store customers described in the text are permanently breathless and excited, flushed with desire as if preparing to receive a lover. In a condition of sensual delirium, dazzled by the allures of the commodities spread out before them, they abandon themselves to the pleasure of shopping, a pleasure explicitly depicted as a sublimated expression of sexual passion. Here, for example, is Zola's description of one of the store's regular customers standing at the lace counter with her daughter. "She dived her hands into this increasing mountain of lace, Malines, Valenciennes and Chantilly, her fingers trembling with desire, her face gradually warming with a sensual joy; whilst Blanche, close to her, agitated by the same passion, was very pale, her flesh inflated and soft."[17] Consumption has here abandoned all pretense to being a rational transaction grounded in objective need, and is shown to be driven by the inchoate emotional and sensual impulses of the female customer. Usurping the role previously occupied by religion in women's lives, it encourages a euphoric loss of self through the surrender to an irrational cult of ideal feminine beauty.

While such scenes confirm a prevalent view of the instinctual and sexual nature of woman, this erotic euphoria is in turn channeled behind the scenes by the scientific marketing strategies of the retailer. Mouret's business success is attributed to his skill in arousing and orchestrating female desire. He introduces modern sales techniques—drastic reductions on selected items, the promise of immediate refunds to dissatisfied customers—which break down the resistance of even the most cautious consumers. He reorganizes the layout of the store in order to disorient his customers, so that, losing their way in the consumer labyrinth, they will be exposed to the temptations of ever more alluring goods. But it is above all the artistry of Mouret's displays which seduces his clientele. A Swiss chalet constructed entirely out of gloves, an elaborate display of opened umbrellas, an "Oriental" room of exotic carpets, waterfalls of dazzling white curtains, sheets and towels that reach as far as the eye can see—such lavish and quasi-surreal exhibits enrapture his customers. Everyday feminine objects are rendered strange and monumental through excessive quantity and bizarre juxtaposition. Modernist aesthetic techniques of defamiliarization and montage are pre-empted in these opulent displays, which anticipate the centrality of stylistic manipulation and aesthetic spectacle in twentieth-century consumer culture.

Visual pleasure thus emerges as a central stratagem in the incitement of female desire for consumer goods. If the flâneur was a masculine symbol of freedom of movement within the public spaces of the city, the department store, described by Benjamin as the flâneur's last haunt, gave women a space in which they could wander and observe in a similar manner. If the "flâneur embodies the gaze of modernity which is both covetous and erotic,"[18] then such a gaze was by no means limited to men, but emerged as a determining feature of women's voyeuristic relationship to the commodity. Yet the flâneur's aloof detachment was, perhaps, replaced by a more intimate relationship between surveyor and surveyed, a complex intermingling of active desire and surrender to the lures of images, objects, and lifestyles. Rachel Bowlby writes: "the boundaries of subject and object, active and passive, owner and owned, unique and general, break down in this endless reflexive interplay of consumer and consumed . . . Seducer and seduced, possessor and possessed of one another, women and commodities flaunt their images at one another in an amorous regard which both extends and reinforces the classic picture of the young girl gazing into the mirror in love with herself."[19]

At an economic level, Mouret's success in the management of this narcissistic female pleasure is unambiguous; he is a representative of the new type of capitalist entrepreneur whose daring innovations expose the limitations of traditional, hidebound forms of selling. Au Bonheur des Dames expands unchecked, swallowing up the buildings which surround it, until it finally employs over three thousand workers, a small microcosm of Parisian society ruled by its own hierarchies and struggles for power. This entrepreneurial mastery on the part of Mouret is in turn linked to his erotic mastery, to the seduction and domination of a crowd of compliant female subjects by a single man. Gazing down on the milling crowds of female shoppers from the vantage point of his office, Mouret is portrayed as master of all he surveys, confident of his ability to control the ebb and flow of female desire. His own superstitious fear of marriage derives from the fact that his primary erotic relationship is with his female clientele and his financial success is inseparable from his emotional investment in the control and manipulation of his customers. Rather than exemplifying a zone where abstract rationality and instrumental calculation hold sway, economic relations between producers and consumers are shown to be saturated with fantasies of sexual power and domination.

In one sense, the emergence of this distinctively new relationship between male capitalist and female consumer requires a relinquishing of traditional models of patriarchal authority. Thus Mouret is frequently described as an androgynous figure, "une homme-femme"; imaginatively anticipating and identifying with the desires of his customers, he takes on many of their qualities and becomes feminized in his turn. Success in modern commerce requires a new kind of subjectivity antithetical to old forms of rigid authoritarian masculinity, an identity mobile and sensitive enough to be able to respond quickly to the changing demands of an often fickle clientele. This feminization of male subjectivity will emerge as a key theme in late-nineteenth-century responses to capitalism's reconfiguration of gender roles. Yet Mouret's seductive flattery and his intuitive understanding of female taste is simply a strategy for exploiting women more efficiently. Empathy is combined with an underlying sadism, gallantry with a concealed contempt at the ease with which women allow themselves to be seduced. "Through the very gracefulness of his gallantry, Mouret thus allowed to appear the brutality of a Jew, selling woman by the pound. He raised a temple to her, had her covered with incense by a legion of shopmen, created the rite of a new religion, thinking of nothing but her, continually seeking to imagine more powerful seductions; and, behind her back, when he had emptied her purse and shattered her nerves, he was full of the secret scorn of a man to whom a woman had just been stupid enough to yield herself."[20] Commerce's assiduous and exhaustive attentiveness to the fulfillment of every female whim gives women's interests a previously unimagined prominence in the public domain, while simultaneously obscuring the exploitive economic relations which underpin the modern cult of femininity.

Zola's novel thus suggests that "capitalism triumphant," the purported theme of the novel, is ultimately to be equated with patriarchy triumphant; the march of economic progress brings with it an increasing male sovereignty over female desire. Yet the text also suggests a more complicated view of power relations between the sexes than is encapsulated by such a summary. Thus the theme of female vengeance disrupts a unilinear narrative of male mastery; in Zola's own words, the novel describes "Octave exploiting woman, then conquered by woman."[21] The obvious vehicle for this theme is the novel's romance plot; the masterful Mouret is finally brought to his knees by his love for one of his own employees, a demure young woman from the provinces. Denise Baudu is thus shown as avenging her sisters by emotionally subjugating the man who has exploited them. According to the logic of such archetypal romance narratives, the hero is feminized by his love for the heroine, who thereby gains a certain, albeit limited, ascendancy and power over the male.[22] It is striking, however, that Zola's heroine, while a staunch supporter of commercial progress, is shown to be completely free of the compulsion to consume which affects almost all the other female characters. Young women who moved to the city in search of work were considered to be highly susceptible to promiscuity and ultimately prostitution, because their appetites for luxury, once awakened by their proximity to an alluring profusion of material goods, could only be satisfied by selling their bodies for financial gain. Numerous journal articles depicted female shop employees as particularly endangered in this regard, given their constant exposure to middle-class lifestyles and their ambiguous class status, which helped to encourage envy and dissatisfaction.[23] In other words, a desire for commodities was closely associated with moral laxity and the transgression of sexual mores. In this context, it is unsurprising that Zola's novel presents the good woman as the premodern woman, free of urban artifice and false allures, who retains the unassuming modesty, frugality, and innocence of her provincial origins.

By contrast, the consuming woman refutes this model of femininity as chaste self-denial, and exemplifies the potentially threatening and destructive consequences of unassuaged female desire. This threat becomes explicit in the crowd scenes of Zola's novel, where the seething mass of female shoppers assumes a sinister, even demonic, quality. The manufacture of crowds is an essential part of Mouret's commercial stratagem, a means of turning the consumers themselves into spectacle and advertisement and thereby luring yet more customers through the doors of the department store. But Zola's descriptions also invoke the more sinister connotations of the urban crowd as explored by such contemporary sociologists and social psychologists as Gustave Le Bon and Gabriel Tarde. Bourgeois representations of the crowd in the nineteenth century, as present-day critics have often noted, typically resort to feminizing metaphors of fluidity and liquidity; the anonymity of the mass embodies a labile, chaotic, and undifferentiated force that threatens the boundaries of autonomous individuality.[24] A crowd of consuming women was thus the ultimate instance of uncontrolled irrationality, as evidenced by descriptions such as the following.

> The ladies, seized by the current, could not now go back. As streams attract themselves to the fugitive waters of a valley, so it seemed that the wave of customers, flowing into the vestibule, was absorbing the passers-by, drinking in the population from the four corners of Paris. They advanced but slowly, squeezed almost to death, kept upright by the shoulders and bellies around them, of which they felt the close heat; and their satisfied desire enjoyed the painful entrance which incited still further their curiosity. There was a pell-mell of ladies arrayed in silk, of poorly dressed middle-class women, and of bare-headed girls, all excited and carried away by the same passion. A few men buried beneath the overflow of bosoms were casting anxious glances around them.[25]

In this description of a busy sales day at Au Bonheur des Dames, an amorphous mass of feminine corporeality flows into the store, driven by an overriding and unstoppable desire to consume. The crowd exercises an irresistible attraction, enticing ever more women to attach themselves to it and allow themselves to be propelled forward by its inexorable momentum. Class distinctions are blurred by the women's shared instincts and passions, by the common bond of primordial, desiring femininity. Yet, if class difference is minimized in the promiscuity of the crowd, gender difference is accentuated; the nervous and isolated men squeezed among the compress of excited female bodies do not share, yet are unable to escape, the feverish delirium that envelops and threatens to suffocate them. Masculinity is hemmed in and restrained from all sides by female passion. Such representations of hordes of insatiable and excitable women evoke the possibility that the commercial incitation of desire may have unforeseen effects, subverting rather than encouraging a proper relationship between the sexes. Once inflamed by the temptations of consumerism, women's animalistic impulses may express themselves in violent attempts to dominate the male. Like a band of furies or a horde of invading locusts, the crowd of women shoppers pour through the store, ravaging the merchandise and forcing the exhausted male clerks to obey their every whim. "And, at this last moment, amidst this over-warmed air, the women reigned supreme. They had taken the whole place by storm, camping there as in a conquered country, like an invading horde installed amongst the overhauling of the goods. The salesmen, deafened, knocked up, were now nothing but their slaves, of whom they disposed with a sovereign's tyranny."[26] The department store was the primary instance of a gendered public space in which many men were to feel insignificant, helpless, or out of place.

The All-Consuming Woman

This suggestion that the conjunction of women and consumerism may undermine rather than simply consolidate certain forms of male authority is reinforced in Zola's portrayal of Mme. Marty, one of the regular customers at the store. Unable to resist the temptations proffered by Mouret, she spends compulsively and recklessly, squandering her husband's meager earnings on the acquisition of ever more feminine luxuries. A weak and ineffectual figure, Marty can only stand by and watch helplessly as his wife gradually brings about his financial ruin; every new piece of lace brings closer the threat of impending economic disaster. The culture of consumerism reaches into and disrupts the sanctity of the private sphere, encouraging women to indulge their own desires in defiance of their husbands and of traditional forms of moral and religious authority. In other words, the promotion of hedonism brings significant economic benefits for the individual male capitalist, but its effects on intimate relations between the sexes and the structure of the patriarchal family are destabilizing and potentially destructive.[27]

In *Nana* this motif of the woman whose lust for commodities leads to her lovers' ruin is magnified in an apocalyptic vision of consumerism run rampant. Here, Zola paints a lurid picture of insatiable female greed as an agent of destruction. The crumbling of an established social fabric based upon frugality, decorum, and the accumulation of wealth is attributed to the contamination and corruption emanating outward from a desiring femininity. Nana, together with her aristocratic alter ego, the Comtesse Sabine de Muffat, symbolizes an emerging tide of reckless sensuality that is sweeping away the values and traditions of an earlier epoch. An ethos of scarcity and self-denial recedes before the inexorable logic of materialism, abundance, and reckless excess that will embody the new spirit of consumer capitalism.

In his depiction of the rise of Nana from her origins in the Parisian slums to the status of celebrated courtesan and woman of fashion, Zola offers a complex exploration of the interrelations between femininity and modernity. Nana is above all a product of the city, her class mobility a function of changing social conditions that allow her to make use of the new erotic and aesthetic possibilities of urban culture for her own advancement. Rather than existing outside modernity, Nana is clearly revealed to be constructed through it; prostitute, actress, avid consumer, she is situated at the very heart of the cash nexus, her social and sexual identity shaped by fashion, image, and advertising, her perverse erotic desires linked to modern urban decadence. Nana first appears in the novel as an unknown actress making her debut, yet her name is already on everyone's lips, a titillating enigma generated through skillful publicity techniques. In the words of Peter Brooks, Nana is revealed as a "representation of a representation, a consciously created and self-creating sex object."[28] The same will hold true for her later career as courtesan and demimondaine, where her sexual magnetism cannot be separated from the public perception of her image and appearance. Constantly playing a role whether she is on or off the stage, Nana exists in a symbiotic relationship with her audience, her erotic aura a projection of the desire of the crowd.

As in *Au bonheur des dames*, public space is associated in *Nana* with a fear of contamination and disorder arising from a leveling of class distinctions. At the theater, the races, the balls, and the soirées depicted in the novel, the anonymity and promiscuity of the crowd subvert established social divisions; hierarchies are undermined in the public domain as disparate individuals rub shoulders in the common pursuit of pleasure. At one point, the text states that Nana's bedroom has also become a "veritable public place, so many boots were wiped on its threshold."[29] The metonymic identity of the bedroom and its inhabitant is explicit; Nana herself emerges as the ultimate threat to class difference, her body a private site of public intimacy, within which the seminal fluids of workers, bourgeois men, and aristocrats indiscriminately commingle. In Zola's novel, anxieties about the female body and the modern city merge indistinguishably, as twin zones of social instability which engender the risk of contamination, corruption, and the subversion of the law by the tyranny of desire. Indeed, in modernist culture the metropolis will increasingly come to be depicted as a woman, a demonic femme fatale whose seductive cruelty exemplifies the delights and horrors of urban life.[30]

Most critical discussions of *Nana* have focused on the theme of prostitution as the ultimate symbol of the moral corruption of France at the end of the Second Empire. However, equally crucial is Nana's status as consumer, her economic as well as her sexual profligacy. The aggressive dimensions of women's passion for commodities are exemplified in the boundless desire of Zola's heroine. Apart from its economic meaning, consumption retains an association with exhaustion, waste, and destruction, signaling a process oriented toward the negation of matter and death.[31] Such negative associations clearly color the representation of Nana's endless and insatiable spending.

> This was the period of her life when Nana lit up Paris with redoubled splendour. She rose higher than ever on the horizon of vice, dominating the city with her insolent display of luxury, and that contempt for money which made her openly squander fortunes. Her house had become a sort of glowing forge, where her continual desires burned fiercely and the slightest breath from her lips changed gold into fine ash which the wind swept away every hour. Nobody had ever seen such a passion for spending. The house seemed to have been built over an abyss in which men were swallowed up—their possessions, their bodies, their very names—without leaving even a trace of dust behind them.[32]

Such revealing descriptions of men being engulfed and annihilated by the ferocity of female desire point to a set of metaphorical linkages between money, sex, and death. Nana, whose constant spending in fact promotes the circulation of money, is nevertheless depicted as draining it out of the economy, as a bottomless pit into which capital endlessly disappears. It is hardly necessary to refer to the double meaning of the French term "consommation"—both economic consumption and erotic consummation—to detect in such references to engulfment and incorporation a manifest anxiety regarding the prospect of an unleashed female sexuality. Indeed, the economic and social implications of consumption as a monetary transaction here recede completely in the face of its psychic and sexual symbolism in Zola's quasi-mythic depiction of the struggle between the sexes. A fear of the "carnivorous vagina" can be glimpsed in the depiction of Nana's destructive orality;[33] she is a man-eater ("une mangeuse d'hommes"), consuming men one after another, cannibalistically devouring and destroying the very men who desire her. "In a few months, Nana gobbled them up, one after the other. The growing needs of her life of luxury sharpened her appetite, and she would clean a man out with one snap of her teeth."[34] Recurring references to mouths, hunger, and eating underscore the animalistic and instinctual nature of female appetite. In the novel, to consume is indeed literally to destroy—the voracious female passion for commodities not only undermines the authority of the male but brings about his annihilation, and shakes the very foundations of the culture he represents.

In one sense, sex and money appear to exemplify antithetical principles in Zola's novel; the libidinal chaos identified with woman undermines the proper operations of the capitalist economy, as enshrined in principles of economic rationality, leading Nana's lovers to incautious speculation, bankruptcy, and even suicide. But sex and money are also subject to a process of metaphorical equation; as Bram Dijkstra notes, women's sexual hunger and their desire for gold were to become closely associated in the nineteenth-century social imaginary.[35] Psychoanalysis has drawn attention to the symbolic valency of money as a token of phallic power and authority, an interpretation that is echoed in Zola's depiction of Nana's cupidity as arising out of an unconscious desire to emasculate and destroy the male. Consumption is presented as an act of tacit female aggression; women's economic exploitation of their husbands and lovers not only allows them to indulge in hedonistic self-pleasuring but becomes their primary form of retaliation against male authority and their own lack of power in the public domain.

Yet if money possesses a latent psychic and sexual meaning, the opposite is also true; economic metaphors were frequently used to describe sexual activity in nineteenth-century texts.[36] Within the context of such a libidinal economy, Nana's promiscuous coupling exemplifies profligacy and waste, engendering an unstoppable flow of money, of semen, of desire—the text refers at one point to the river of gold running between her legs. According to a model of sexual energy shaped by imperatives of accumulation and conservation, any activity not geared toward production must be considered profoundly wasteful. Nana's one sickly child is an eloquent symbol of the separation of desire from reproduction and social utility and of the sterility of modern forms of sexuality. She thus crystallizes in her person the symbolic affinity between emerging sexological definitions of polymorphous perversity and the new focus on the pleasures and dangers of unrestrained consumption.

What is ultimately most disturbing about this female desire is that it lacks an object. Nana herself remains serenely indifferent to almost all the men who pursue her; it seems as if they serve merely as a means of gaining access to the money and the commodities that she craves. Yet it is soon apparent that Nana's contempt for commodities echoes her disdain for the men who provide them; she spends simply for the sake of spending, squandering money indiscriminately on luxurious furnishings and cheap knickknacks, soiling and destroying goods as soon as she has bought them. Her household is a "river of wastefulness"; Nana allows herself to be cheated by her servants, buys food only in order to throw it away, clutters her house with useless objects which she buys on impulse, never to look at again. It is this indifference toward money and what it can buy that embodies her greatest offense against a traditional bourgeois ethos of respect for prosperity and the accumulation of wealth. The very materiality of the commodity is rendered unstable as it is swallowed up in a vortex of free-floating female desire that moves restlessly from one object to the next. Rather than worshiping at the shrine of the commodity, Nana takes delight in desecrating it. "It's funny how rich men fancy they can get anything with their money . . . Well, and what if I say no? . . . I don't give a damn for your presents . . . And as for money, you poor thing, I can get plenty of that when I want it! I don't give a damn for it! I spit on it!"[37] Her contempt for money is simultaneously an expression of disdain for the entire system of cultural values premised on the assumed authority and prestige of traditional symbols of masculinity.

Although this mobility of desire is at odds with bourgeois norms of thrift and self-restraint, it renders Nana an ideal subject of a society increasingly structured on the imperative to consume. As Colin Campbell points out, the spirit of modern consumerism is defined by an unfocused and insatiable longing which latches onto a succession of objects in a potentially endless sequence.[38] What is desired is not the object per se, but the imaginary gratifications with which it is invested by the fantasizing subject. The inevitable disjuncture between anticipated and experienced pleasure in turn generates a yearning for a new fantasy object and a rapid decathexis from the old. Within such a logic of desire, things in themselves are interchangeable and expendable; what is at issue is not the discrete particularity of the object, but the symbolic meanings and generalized aura of desirability with which the object-as-commodity is invested. Satisfaction is thus by definition impossible because there is no objective need that is being addressed; rather, the commodity comes to stand for an imaginary fulfillment that remains necessarily unattainable.

It is immediately apparent why such a consumerist ethic is a threat to the stability of traditional social and moral norms. Translated into the sphere of sexual relations, the yearning of the desiring woman manifests itself in an endless "consumption" of lovers, none of whom can satisfy her unfocused yearning for gratification and plenitude. For Nana, as for my next subject, Emma Bovary, economic and sexual profligacy derive from a logic of abstract equivalence, which renders each object of desire—whether lover or commodity—interchangeable with the next in the relentless pursuit of the unattainable. Nana's "perversity," as evidenced in her turn toward lesbian and sadomasochistic sexual practices, provides further confirmation of the triumph of an individualistic libertarian desire emancipated from any allegiance to moral and social imperatives. On the one hand, her insatiability is presented as a natural manifestation of an all-consuming primordial female desire; on the other, it simultaneously exemplifies the unnatural condition of the modern woman whose perverse cravings are stimulated by capitalist decadence.

To Read Is to Eat?

At one moment in the text, the narrator describes Nana's literary tastes in a manner clearly intended to provide an overt contrast to Zola's own aesthetic:

> During the day she had read a novel which was causing a sensation at the time. It was the story of a prostitute, and Nana inveighed against it, declaring that it was all untrue, and expressing an indignant revulsion against the sort of filthy literature which claimed to show life as it was—as if a writer could possibly describe everything, and as if novels weren't supposed to be written just to while away the time! On the subject of books and plays Nana had very decided opinions: she liked tender, high-minded works which would set her dreaming and uplift her soul.[39]

The irony here is palpable. Zola's own commitment to an unflinching exploration of the grim realities of modern urban life stands in explicit contrast to the platitudinous tastes of his heroine. Incapable of comprehending the aims and purposes of an uncompromising realism, Nana can appreciate only the kind of fiction that promises entertainment, escapism, and moral edification. As a literary heroine, she serves as an evocative symbol of modern immorality and decadence; yet as a reader of literature she takes refuge in the very romantic idealism that Zola professed to despise.

In this brief passage is encapsulated an entire ideology of women and reading. As Naomi Schor has noted, the devaluation of idealism in the late nineteenth century had the effect of pushing once celebrated female writers such as George Sand to the margins of the French literary canon.[40] Although the male intelligentsia disputed whether naturalist or modernist techniques were more suited to representing the complexities of the modern age, they were largely united in their disdain for an idealist aesthetic associated with an outmoded and cloying feminine sentimentality. The hegemonic status of realist representation during this period should not, of course, be exaggerated; as the trial of Flaubert in 1857 and of Vizetelly, Zola's English publisher, in 1888 made clear, many of the texts of French realism remained objects of public controversy and condemnation, their affinity with immoral topics deeply at odds with the official aesthetic ideology espoused by the courts, state censors, churches, and various other institutions.[41] My concern is thus not to negate, but merely to complicate, the received view of the radical artist struggling heroically against the *bêtise* of bourgeois morality by showing how this struggle is in turn informed by a fantasmic and conflictual relationship to the feminine. This motif, in turn, lies at the very heart of *Madame Bovary,* where, as Andreas Huyssen points out, Flaubert's position as a founding father of modernism rests "on the uncompromising repudiation of what Emma Bovary loved to read."[42]

The disapproval of the uncritical and overly emotional nature of women's reading habits is of course nothing new. Similar laments were already familiar in the eighteenth century, when the growing popularity of the novel as a genre devoted to romantic love caused much anxiety about its possible effects on susceptible female readers. Yet this debate took on increased vigor in the second half of the nineteenth century, with the emergence of what Fredric Jameson describes as the opposed but dialectically interrelated poles of high and mass culture.[43] Cheaper and more efficient techniques of mass production combined with the growth of literacy and an expanding reading public to give popular fiction an ever greater visibility. At the same time, artists and intellectuals sought to distance themselves from the vulgarity and sensationalism of this nascent mass culture by taking refuge in esoteric credos and practices. This division between elite and popular culture gradually acquired an explicit gender subtext; a "remasculinization of culture value" took place in the late nineteenth century, in which the ostensibly distanced and unemotional aesthetic stance embraced by both naturalists and early modernists was explicitly valorized over the feminine sentimentality associated with popular fiction.[44]

While Emma Bovary's frenetic purchasing of commodities as a symbolic expression of unsatisfied desire clearly relates to my previous discussion, I now wish to shift gears slightly and consider the relationship between consumption and reading. In an economic sense, the connection is obvious enough; like other mass-produced objects, literature becomes increasingly integrated into commodity culture, its production and distribution inextricably entangled with the profit motive. But it is striking how frequently an unconscious slippage takes place from the economic to the symbolic domain, so that consumption comes to denote not simply an economic transaction between seller and buyer, but an extended set of assumptions about the uncritical and passive reception of texts by mass audiences. The pejorative connotations of the term, in other words, are deployed within the aesthetic domain to underwrite given hierarchies of literary value and cultural prestige. An already extant dualism which elevates production over consumption is appropriated to distinguish between the intellectual labor demanded by high art and the mindless pleasure and escapism promoted by popular fiction.

What does it mean exactly to speak of "consuming" a book? I have already explored some of the oral and sadistic connotations of consumption, its association with fantasies of incorporation and destruction. Such metaphors occur repeatedly in the critical commentary on *Madame Bovary,* as in the following statement by Larry Riggs: "From the old maid's addictive 'swallowing' of adventure novels in the convent and her encouraging the girls to do the same, through Emma's 'devouring' of fashion magazines, to the corrosive action of the ingested arsenic, with the course of events punctuated by feasts, *Madame Bovary* is a case study of *bovaryste* consumption."[45] Here the literary is reduced to the alimentary; reading becomes a form of eating. Riggs is not alone in this regard; Leo Bersani, for example, refers to the romances on which Emma "gorges herself."[46] It is striking how frequently oral metaphors are used to describe the process of reading, though such metaphors are more likely to be attributed to some kinds of readers than others. As Janice Radway has pointed out, it is primarily critics of popular fiction who rely on metaphors drawn from biological processes of ingestion, incorporation, and absorption, reducing the cultural practices of nonintellectual and particularly female readers to a quasi-mechanical satisfaction of instinctual appetite.[47]

The phrases I have quoted are those of contemporary critics of *Madame Bovary,* not of Flaubert himself. I do not, however, dispute their accuracy—on the contrary, they convey well the tenor of Emma's literary response—rather I question their frequently unreflective endorsement of the ideologies embedded within Flaubert's own text. In the context of a critical tradition which has—with honorable exceptions—reacted to Emma Bovary by desiring, dismissing, or degendering her, such interpretations underline the continuing power of an ideology of the aesthetic which defines literariness in opposition to woman as commodity culture. The assumptions endemic to this aesthetic are well encapsulated in Larry Riggs's reference to Emma's "perversely utilitarian romanticism." The paradoxical nature of such a statement seems obvious: the idealist, spiritual impulse of romanticism seems to stand in blatant contradiction to an ethos of practical use-value. Yet it is precisely such a contradictory blend of idealism and instrumentality, of the yearning for transcendence and earthbound vulgarity, which underlies the representation of Emma Bovary as the prototype of the reading woman.

The romantic elements shaping Emma's literary preferences are obvious

enough. Like Nana, she assigns a utopian and idealist significance to literature as a means of escape into a better world. Seeking exotic scenarios as far
removed as possible from her own mundane existence as a provincial doctor's wife, she yearns for a romantic sublime, for exaggerated emotion and
passionate excess. Flaubert offers a dry account of the books she reads as an
adolescent girl. "They were all about love, lovers, sweethearts, persecuted
ladies fainting in lonely pavilions, postilions killed at every relay, horses
ridden to death on every page, sombre forests, heart-aches, vows, sobs, tears
and kisses, little boatrides by moonlight, nightingales in shady groves, gen-
tlemen brave as lions, gentle as lambs, virtuous as no one ever was, always
well-dressed and weeping like fountains."[48]

Here the melodramatic excess of popular romance is treated ironically as
seriality, conventionality, repetition; by turning narratives into lists, the narrator explicitly undermines and renders absurd the seductive lures of drama
and plot. Rather than embodying a meaningful organic whole, texts fragment
into a random juxtaposition of semantic units endlessly reiterated across
multiple locations. These stereotypical images of exoticism and escape will
form the basis of Emma's fantasies as an adult woman, as she seeks to render
her experiences meaningful by translating them into the literary codes of
romantic love. Yet she herself remains oblivious to their conventionality; for
her, they embody an absolute, an ideal plenitude against which is exposed the
paucity of the real. "And Emma tried to find out what one meant exactly in
life by the words *bliss, passion, ecstasy*, that had seemed to her so beautiful in
books."[49]

While some critics have taken as self-evident the debased nature of Emma's
readings as precursors of modern mass-market romances, others view her
behavior in a less judgmental light, perceiving a desire for transcendence
which possesses no other outlet. Thus Bersani notes that Emma's reading is
"the only spiritualizing impulse in her life," while Eric Gans points out that
in Flaubert's universe of infinite banality "Emma's longings produce the only
possible form of transcendence, the only possible religion."[50] Such statements link up to recent defenses of the utopian element in mass-culture texts
which suggest that even the most hackneyed forms do not simply reinforce
dominant ideological schemata but also express a moment of resistance
through a refusal of the status quo and a longing for a better world.[51]
Trapped within a sterile and narrow environment, her social options fore-
closed by the fact of her sex, Emma can only voice her dissatisfaction through
the texts that she reads.

As Rosemary Lloyd points out, these texts are in fact more varied than
critics have often acknowledged, including diverse works by Balzac, Sir

Walter Scott, and Eugène Sue alongside unnamed works of popular romantic fiction, engravings, and women's magazines.[52] The crucial issue, however, is surely not what Emma reads, but *how* she reads; her consumption of texts is such as to effectively erase any meaningful aesthetic differences between them. In this sense, *Madame Bovary* is less about the corrupting effects of novels per se than about the dangers of particular ways of reading. As the previous quotation indicates, Emma distills fiction into a random array of tableaux, a chain of unconnected images and stereotypes that are both highly particular—lagoons, Swiss chalets, Scottish cottages—and infinitely suggestive. Her reading, as Carla Peterson notes, thereby involves an extended process of morcellation and fragmentation, whereby particular literary works are reduced to nothing more than isolated segments of plot and models for imitation.[53] In this ascription of semiotic density and mystical plenitude to decontextualized, free-floating images, Emma uncannily anticipates the modalities of twentieth-century forms of mass-media culture and lifestyle advertising as adumbrated in recent theories of "the society of the spectacle."

In other words, Emma does not read as Flaubert wishes his own novel to be read. If the author seeks to destabilize the reader's expectations through meticulous composition and a carefully wrought opacity of style, Emma in turn transforms style into content by denying the mediating authority of literary form. She reads literally, and out of pure self-interest, searching only for specular images with which she can identify. Aesthetic value is reduced to emotional use-value; literature serves merely as a means to stimulate sentimental and erotic fantasies. Desperate to escape the stultifying constraints of the provinces, Emma turns to writing for depictions of the glamor and romance which her own life conspicuously lacks. "She subscribed to 'la Corbeille,' a ladies' magazine, and the 'Sylphe des Salons.' She devoured, without skipping a word, all the accounts of first nights, races and soirées . . . In Eugène Sue she studied descriptions of furniture; she read Balzac and George Sand, seeking in them imaginary satisfactions for her own desires."[54]

Thus Emma's desire for aesthetic transcendence is itself relativized in the novel by its unmediated relationship to women's emotional and sensual impulses; her yearning for the sublime is sentimental rather than monumental. This motif is already evident in Emma's youthful interest in the trappings of religion, which is characterized by an inability to distinguish between the complexities of spiritual aspiration and the shallowness of sensual pleasure. "This nature," writes Flaubert, "that had loved the church for the sake of the flowers, and music for the words of the songs, and literature for the passions that it excites, rebelled against the mysteries of faith as it had rebelled against discipline, as something alien to her constitution."[55] The

instrumental appropriation of cultural forms as a means of gratifying immediate subjective need is presented as a hallmark of Emma's character: "she
had to gain some personal profit from things and she rejected as useless
whatever did not contribute to the immediate satisfaction of her heart's
desires—being of a temperament more sentimental than artistic, looking for
emotions, not landscapes."[56] Here Emma functions as an emblem not simply
of "bourgeois sensibility," as Nathaniel Wing argues, but also of *feminine*
sensibility, as suggested in the yoking of the vocabulary of profit and utility
with that of affect and sentimentality.[57] As a result, her romanticism is
depicted as being of a debased kind, rooted in immediate emotional cravings
and corporeal desires, lacking any authentic impulse toward spirituality or
self-transcendence. Just as Emma loves church as a young girl because of the
flowers, so her pleasure in literature is based only on the "passions it excites."

The implicit norm being evoked here is a Kantian ideal of disinterestedness, which locates aesthetic judgment outside all utilitarian considerations
and sensual impulses. The work of art is to be valued as an end in itself,
separate from the contingent desires and needs of particular subjects. Something of this Kantian formulation can be glimpsed in Flaubert's own literary
credo, his fetishization of *impassibilité*, clarity, and stylistic perfection, as
expressed in his dream of creating "un livre sur rien." This notion of the
strict separation of art and life has of course rarely remained uncontested, as
artists and writers have sought to reclaim art for ethical and political ends.
What is presented as distinctively feminine, however, is an aesthetics of
use-value rooted in sensual rather than cognitive interests. The distinction
between art and reality is collapsed not in order to achieve a better understanding of society and human nature (the usual justification of a realist
aesthetic), but as a means of facilitating a loss of self in the pleasures of the
text.

This feminine susceptibility to emotional identification and passionate
abandonment is explored in the episode depicting Emma's visit to the opera
at Rouen to see *Lucia di Lammermoor*. Immediately comparing the heroine's
fate to her own, she is stimulated to melancholy reflections on the pathos and
limitations of her own existence. Her attempts to retain a degree of critical
detachment during the performance are rapidly swept away by the acting,
and conflating the identity of the male lead with his role, she projects onto
him all the romantic yearnings that her own lovers have been unable to
fulfill. "She longed to run to his arms, to take refuge in his strength, as in the
incarnation of love itself, and to say to him, to cry out, 'Take me away! carry
me with you! let us leave! All my passion and all my dreams are yours!'"[58]
Emma projects herself onto the text only in order to abandon herself to it, in

a yearning for oceanic merging that seeks to efface the very boundaries of identity. Her increasingly frenzied eroticism is portrayed as both sexual and textual, exemplifying an inchoate desire to merge and become one with both the real and the fictional other.[59]

Such episodes are indicative of the narcissism characterizing woman's response to art: woman is the archetypal naive reader who is unable to distinguish between texts and life. The ubiquity of this *idée reçu* among the French intelligentsia of the period is evidenced in statements such as the following, from the journal of the Goncourt brothers. "This evening the Princess said: 'I enjoy only those novels of which I should have liked to be the heroine.' A perfect illustration of the standard by which women judge novels."[60] Unable to make the imaginative and intellectual leap required to appreciate great literature, female readers use texts as mirrors in which they simultaneously discover and reconfirm their own subjectivity. In her confusion of the spheres of the real and the imaginary, Emma Bovary is the prototype of the modern reader who dreams of becoming the heroine of her own romance. Women's yearning for or identification with the object of representation thereby disrupts the distancing frame that characterizes the authentic modality of aesthetic contemplation.[61]

Of course, in interpreting *Madame Bovary* as symptomatic of a particular ideology of femininity, I leave myself open to the accusation of reading like Emma herself, of revealing either willful blindness or involuntary stupidity vis-à-vis the complexities and indeterminacies of the literary artifact. A number of critics have argued that Flaubert's novel may appear to condemn Emma's vulgarity and narcissism, but that in fact it contains numerous *mises en abîme* which undermine any ostensible claims it appears to be making. Flaubert's own ambivalent identification with the feminine, as exemplified both in his letters and in the frequent indeterminacy of narrative perspective within the novel, is further cited in support of such a position. Identification does not, however, automatically negate, but may in fact underpin, sadistic distantiation, as I demonstrate in more detail in the next chapter. And while empathy and irony do indeed coexist in Flaubert's novel, as Dominick LaCapra suggests,[62] a feminist reader may be more struck by its irony than its empathy, particularly at those moments in the text when the narrator offers a relatively unambiguous assessment of Emma's ways of reading.

Furthermore, such arguments are often about something other than the (unexceptionable) claim that texts contain multiple meanings. Rather, the repeated insistence that *Madame Bovary* resists recuperation in terms of any identifiable ideological position serves to reify the aura of the artwork in predictable ways. It is of course precisely this claim which *is* the novel's

aesthetic ideology, embodied in the distinction between the authentic modernity of Flaubert's writing and the naiveté of Emma's reading. Critics who
claim that Flaubert's novel subverts this distinction by acknowledging its
own complicity with its object of critique merely reinscribe the same opposition at a higher level; this very self-consciousness now becomes the marker
of authentic literariness which distinguishes *Madame Bovary* from more
dogmatic and univocal texts. Such debates, as Bruce Robbins suggests, are
only partly about the text under discussion; they are also "a pious exercise in
disciplinary self-corroboration, a demonstration that the discipline of literary
criticism is justified in its distinctness and autonomy."[63] The repeated elevation of the signifier over the signified, of the complexities of form over the
trivialities of (feminine) content, thereby enacts a defense of literary professionalization as both an established canon and a particular set of reading
practices.

It is precisely this professionalized status of the literary which is negated by
the specter of a feminized aesthetics of consumption. In using literature as a
means to narcissistic gratification and loss of self, the female reader denies its
autonomy, collapsing the distinction between subject and object, self and
text. The text is consumed metaphorically by analogy with the literal consumption of objects such as food; it is used to satiate an appetite, incorpo-
rated, used up. This uncritical devouring of fiction is a disturbing and
threatening phenomenon because it negates the autonomy of the literary
artifact; lacking any reverence for the auratic status of the artwork, female
desire collapses existing forms of cultural distinction and differentiation and
hence negates the specificity and value of the aesthetic. Emma's reading
practice thus threatens to undermine the very basis on which Flaubert's own
personal and social identity is built.

This compulsive reading in turn engenders dissatisfaction with the real
world; seduced by the words on the printed page, female readers become
discontented with their own lives because they do not imitate the plot of the
novels that they so eagerly consume. Thus critics have commented on the
increasingly aggressive and "masculine" force of Emma's desire, as she seeks
to transform her real lover, Leon, into the ideal hero of her dreams. Romantic
fiction infuses women with exaggerated and unrealistic ideas which they may
consequently seek to put into practice. Here again *Madame Bovary* ironizes
yet also reinforces a long tradition of discourses about the dangerous effects
of novels on women, whose French history has recently been surveyed by
Jann Matlock. "The wife who becomes an 'addict' of the passion and drama
of the novels of Balzac, Sue, Dumas, Soulié and Sand will be tormented by
her desires—and she will torment the man who does not satisfy them. The

roman-feuilleton will make her bored, discontented with her duties and dreamy. She will become a *'folle du logis'* (crazywoman of the hearth), her mind twisted by the 'impassioned and romantic exaggerations of that evil literature.' Worse still, she will begin to live the novels she has read."[64]

This association of femininity with the drive toward dedifferentiation explains the association of woman with modern mass culture more generally. The purported inability of women to distinguish between art and life, their confusion of aesthetics and erotics, finds its counterpart in an expanding consumer culture which permeates and textualizes all aspects of everyday experience. Women's lack of aesthetic distancing, as exemplified in their voracious consumption of fiction, renders them particularly susceptible to the illusory promises and glamorous image repertoires disseminated by the marketplace. Finally, their propensity for romantic love renders them ideal subjects of a consumer culture propelled by indistinct longings and unsatisfied desires, by the constant striving to close the gap between real and imagined pleasures.

Thus though female desire is rooted in emotional and bodily needs, this desire is not viewed as an authentic space of libidinality outside social regulation. Rather, women's lack of distantiation and self-discipline merely intensifies their receptivity to the secondhand images circulating within the commodity culture; their very desire is inauthentic in its reproduction of the desire of the other. As the economic logic of modern consumption encourages emotional and erotic investment in the redemptive power of commodities, so in turn images of romantic love propagated within novels invoke and intensify the allure of glamorous and wealthy lifestyles. Thus the apparently distinct spheres of romance and money, feelings and economics, reveal themselves to be indissolubly connected in the female imagination. Flaubert writes of his heroine: "In her wistfulness, she confused the sensuous pleasures of luxury with the delights of the heart, elegance of manners with delicacy of sentiment."[65] *Madame Bovary* suggests that the scenario of a woman reading a book—a conventional representation of the private female self—in fact symbolizes the social production of desiring subjectivity within modernity. The romantic and sentimental longings ascribed to women, rather than being a remnant of a historically outmoded structure of feeling, emerge as the key element in the operation of modern consumer culture.

Complicating Consumption

In her critical engagement with entrenched attitudes toward fashion and consumption, Elizabeth Wilson describes their typical underlying tenets as follows. "Consumerism becomes a compulsive form of behaviour, over which we have little conscious control. According to this puritanical view, we are squeezed between the imperatives of the market and the urges of an unconscious whose desires are warped and invalidated by the culture in which we live."[66] My discussion has explored some of the reasons why the image of the woman-as-consumer has been such a powerful presence in this dystopian vision of modernity. As a result of the gender division of labor, it was primarily women who were exposed to the "imperatives of the market," as exemplified in the selling techniques of advertisers and retailers. At the same time, women's long-standing association with nature and primordial desire helped to promote an identification of consumerism with feminine impulsiveness and irrationality. Given a prevalent equation of bourgeois masculinity with reason and self-restraint, it was above all through the representation of the consuming woman that writers criticized the vulgar materialism brought about by capitalist development.

Yet if the figure of woman provided a vehicle for expressing ambivalent responses to the social and economic transformations brought about by modernity, it is also true that the critique of capitalism provided an alibi for the expression of misogynistic attitudes toward women. The gendering of consumption, in other words, remains central to any assessment of its sociocultural significance. Whereas Marxism tends to interpret the consuming woman as simply the necessary by-product of a capitalist economy increasingly oriented toward the stimulation of consumer demand, such accounts fail to account for the particular and contradictory social meanings invested in *female* desire.[67] Yet to affirm such desire as authentically resistive of a symbolic order based on patriarchal repression is to ignore the ways in which consumer capitalism itself undermines such a logic of repression in its production of an endlessly desiring subject. Both functionalist accounts of cultural practices in terms of a unicausal economic model and feminist nostalgia for a space of pure resistance need to be replaced by reflection on points of contradiction as well as correspondence between capitalist and patriarchal logics.

The political implications of middle-class women's alignment with consumption are by no means straightforward in this regard. Some writers have argued that the rise of consumerism had a potentially democratizing effect in affirming the abstract equality of individuals in their status as consumers. Although it clearly failed to address, and indeed obscured, real economic inequalities between social groups, consumer culture nevertheless helped to break down fixed and seemingly natural hierarchies which assigned those groups a fixed place in the social order by sanctioning the legitimacy of individual desire.[68] This view relates to the Marxist understanding of capitalism as enacting a radical and potentially liberating dissolution of traditional and organic social bonds. The modern monetary economy exemplifies a logic of abstract equivalence within which inequality is increasingly seen to derive from quantitative degrees of wealth rather than from immutable and God-given hierarchical differences.

Such arguments are potentially useful in coming to grips with the phenomenon of female consumerism. Clearly, no neat, watertight distinction can be made between the desire for material goods and the desire for economic and political power, and the interpellation of middle-class women as consumers in the late nineteenth century undoubtedly bore a significant relationship to their rising expectations and their increasingly vocal political demands. Indeed, one can posit complex interdependences between the growth of a consumer economy and the development of women's public freedoms, even though nineteenth-century feminists themselves often challenged the image of femininity examined in this chapter by developing an alternative model of the rational female consumer.[69] William R. Leach, for example, observing the interconnections between early American feminism and the emergence of a culture of consumption, writes:

> In those early, nearly euphoric days of consumer capitalism, textured so much by the department store, many women thought they had discovered a more exciting, more appealing life, freedom remade within a consumer matrix. Their participation in consumer experience challenged and subverted that complex of qualities traditionally known as feminine—dependence, passivity, religious piety, domestic inwardness, sexual purity, and maternal nurture. Mass consumer culture presented to women a new definition of gender that carved out a space for individual expression similar to men's and that stood in tension with the older definition passed on to them.[70]

Such an account provides a useful corrective to traditional denunciations of consumerism by addressing its potentially liberating dimensions, albeit for a minority of women. Yet it also overemphasizes the equalizing logic of modernity and underestimates the influence and persistence of noneconomic forms of social differentiation, of which gender and race are the two most obvious examples.[71] The figure of the modern consumer, a disembodied and abstract category within the discourse of economic theorists of the time, was in fact layered with symbolic meanings which often renaturalized rather than denaturalized gender distinctions.

In this regard, the texts I have discussed possess an ambiguous significance from a feminist perspective. Foregrounding the aesthetic and erotic, as well as economic, dimensions of consumption, these novels suggestively explore the complex interrelations between socioeconomic change and the emergence of new forms of gendered subjectivity. Commodities are revealed not simply as material objects but as complex symbolic artifacts whose social meanings derive from the unfocused dissatisfaction and indistinct longings characteristic of modern experience. Yet the literary representation of consuming femininity also enunciates the anxieties of an economically marginal intelligentsia confronted by an encroaching commercialism and materialism. The addressing of middle-class women as consumers leads to a new prominence of icons of femininity in the public domain, and a concomitant emphasis on sensuousness, luxury, and emotional gratification as features of modern life. Such a feminization of the public sphere was clearly threatening to bourgeois men, whose psychic and social identity had been formed through an ethos of self-restraint and a repudiation of womanly feelings and whose professional status was based on an at-best ambivalent relationship to the marketplace. Thus fears of an uncontrollable female desire converge with a pessimistic view of the hedonistic excess engendered by capitalist expansion to create a dystopian vision of the all-consuming woman.

Such an explanation may help to account for male discomfort with consumption without the assumption that such a feminization of modernity was liberating for women in any straightforward way. As I have indicated, the rise of consumerism was linked to growing public freedoms for middle-class women in the latter half of the nineteenth century; more generally, the "democratization of luxury" made available new kinds of experience, enjoyment, and material objects unimaginable for the vast majority of individuals in the premodern world. The individualization of desire promoted by capitalist consumerism thus made it possible for women to articulate needs and wants in defiance of traditional patriarchal prohibitions, even as the department store offered a new and intoxicating public space beyond the walls of the familial home. Yet this relative degree of empowerment also went hand in hand with the emergence of new constraining influences on gendered identity. Not only did consumer culture subject women to norms of eroticized femininity that encouraged constant practices of self-surveillance, but it provided a conduit through which heterogeneous forms of desire could often be deflected and channeled into the imperative to buy ever more commodities. Even as it exemplified the erosion of certain traditional constraints upon desiring femininity, the culture of modernity also brought with it new, if less visible, networks of social control.

4

Masking Masculinity:
The Feminization of Writing

Since femininity is associated with masquerade, masquerade—the figurative, textuality, etc.—comes to seem feminine. Femininity would thus appear to have lost its terrors, to have settled, like magic dust, over the terrain of culture generally, and in the process to have transformed masculinity itself.

Tania Modleski, *Feminism without Women: Culture and Criticism in a "Postfeminist" Age*

Not all male artists and intellectuals were to react negatively to the prospect of an aestheticized and feminized modernity. On the contrary, for many of those alienated and disaffected from the dominant norms of middle-class masculinity, such a scenario offered the hope of a radical alternative to prevailing forces of positivism, progress ideology, and the sovereignty of the reality principle. Thus an imaginary identification with the feminine emerged as a key stratagem in the literary avant-garde's subversion of sexual and textual norms. This refusal of traditional models of masculinity took the form of a self-conscious textualism which defined itself in opposition to the prevailing conventions of realist representation, turning toward a decadent aesthetic of surface, style, and parody that was explicitly coded as both "feminine" and "modern." Loosening itself from the body of woman, femininity was to become a governing metaphor in the fin-de-siècle crisis of literary representation, linked to an aesthetic definition of modernity that emphasized, with Nietzsche, the undecidability and opacity of language and the omnipresence of desire.

Clearly, the extent of this crisis in masculinity should not be exaggerated. The transgressive gestures of the avant-garde were by definition limited to a small, if visible and influential, group that was by no means representative of writers as a whole, let alone of the broader cultivated public. By calling into question dominant ideals of manliness, however, this group aimed at the very heart of bourgeois modes of self-understanding. The separation of spheres, exemplified in the complementary opposition of industrious masculinity and nurturing femininity, was a central symbolic mechanism in the reproduction of dominant value systems. In undermining such distinctions, the feminized male became a provocative emblem of the contemporary crisis of values and the much proclaimed decadence of modern life. Masculinity, it seemed, could no longer be taken for granted as a stable, unitary, and self-evident reality.[1]

The feminization of the texts of the male avant-garde was of course only one of the ways in which gender identities were being contested during the period. The late nineteenth century saw feminist movements in various European countries becoming increasingly vocal in their demands that women be allowed access to the public sphere. Indeed, the aesthete was often linked to the New Woman in the discourses of the period, as dual focal points of contemporary anxiety about the rapidly changing nature of gender roles.[2] Yet it would be unwise to assume that this early modernist appropriation of the feminine was necessarily in sympathy with the aims of feminism. On the contrary, I will suggest, its appropriation of an aesthetic of parody and performance in fact reinscribes more insistently those gender hierarchies which are ostensibly being called into question. In at least some of the texts of early modernism, the resistive power of feminine artifice is predicated upon a radical disavowal of and dissociation from the "natural" body of woman.

I will pursue this argument through a comparative reading of three well-known texts of the period: J. K. Huysmans's *Against the Grain* (1884), Oscar Wilde's *Picture of Dorian Gray* (1891), and *Venus in Furs* (1870) by Leopold von Sacher-Masoch.[3] By linking together these works from different national traditions, my argument inevitably glosses over significant cultural variations affecting their particular conditions of production and reception. The aestheticism of Vienna, for example, diverged in certain key respects from that of Paris and of London; its cultural politics was more quietistic and utopian in form and less obviously linked to an openly oppositional agenda.[4] My primary concern in this chapter, however, is to examine the recurring configurations of the aesthetic, the feminine, and the modern within the European fin de siècle, a phenomenon which was itself shaped by processes of literary contamination and reciprocal influence across national borders. Oscar Wilde's interest in and appropriation of the texts of French decadence is well documented; Sacher-Masoch's influence on French culture in the 1870s and 1880s has, however, been hardly addressed by literary historians. In fact, until recently Sacher-Masoch's work has been almost completely

ignored by literary critics and has been read primarily for its clinical significance as the Ur-text of masochistic pathology.

The recent upsurge of interest in Sacher-Masoch is at least partly due to
the dissemination of the influential reading of *Venus in Furs* by Gilles Deleuze
and its appropriation by feminist scholars, particularly in the realm of film
theory.[5] The figure of the masochistic, feminized, male subject has become a
key focus for feminists increasingly interested in analyzing the construction
of alternative, nonphallic, masculinities; here, of course, there have been both
productive interactions and critical tensions with contemporary theories of
gay male subjectivity. In this sense, my choice of the work of Sacher-Masoch,
and indeed of Wilde and Huysmans, is by no means arbitrary, but is shaped
by my simultaneous interest in and reservations about this new feminist
focus on the feminized male. Although I am sympathetic to a project which
seeks to break down the chimera of a unified, monolithic masculinity by
exploring its alternative and perverse manifestations, feminist affirmations of
these deviant masculinities sometimes move overhastily from the domain of
the psychic to the political without any developed account of the interme-
diate and historically contingent zones of sociocultural determination. In
other words, to assume that a male identification with the feminine is *necessarily* subversive of patriarchal privilege may be to assume too much.

It is against this contemporary theoretical background that I seek to
address the history and politics of feminized masculinity in relation to the
social hierarchies of late-nineteenth-century European culture. Thus the texts
that I discuss bear witness to the artist's sense of alienation from dominant
social structures and his own class identity, articulating a "counterdiscourse"
of symbolic resistance to prevailing definitions of bourgeois masculinity.[6] Yet
they also reveal his enmeshment within an emerging commodity culture,
which provides an important precondition for his own strategies of stylistic
differentiation and self-conscious aestheticism. Through its emphasis on the
ambiguous and shifting qualities of both gender and sexuality, this feminized
counterdiscourse connected with elite homosexual subcultures of the fin de
siècle, enabling covert representations of homosexual identity and the articulation of same-sex desire. Yet my reading simultaneously relativizes the
adversarial status of these texts of early modernism by uncovering a mysogynistic strain that is intimately connected to, rather than at odds with, the
espousal of a self-reflexive and parodistic aesthetic. The fin-de-siècle cult of
art and artifice thus points to a complex array of alignments and contradictions between the structures of gender, class, sexuality, and commodity culture which both enabled and constrained the contestatory nature of its textual
politics.

The Feminized Male

The conception of the male artist as in some sense a feminine figure is already well established in the works of early Romanticism. The Romantic cult of genius celebrated an ideal of transgressive masculinity while simultaneously endowing the male artist with qualities of sensitivity, intuition, and emotional empathy characteristically seen as the province of women.[7] Thus the domains of science and art were increasingly differentiated in terms of a gender symbolism derived from the opposition of private and public spheres; the aesthetic realm was codified as feminine by contrast with the purported objectivity and rationality of a scientific world-view. In turn, the identification of masculinity with middle-class norms of industry, rationality, and self-restraint meant that the male artist was frequently perceived as an androgynous figure because of his continuing alliance with the sensuous and the beautiful. The aesthetic realm came to be seen as a privileged zone for exploring the complexities and ambiguities of gender identification.

The reemergence of this notion of the feminized artist in the context of fin-de-siècle movements such as symbolism, decadence, and aestheticism reveals, however, an important shift in register. Whereas in sentimental and early Romantic literature the male fascination with the feminine is associated with an expressive aesthetic, providing a vehicle for the cultivation and articulation of feeling, later manifestations of this motif emphasize very different qualities of parody, style, and artifice. Femininity is now appropriated by the male artist as emblematic of the modern, rather than as standing in opposition to it. This interpretive shift brings with it a reconceptualization of the feminine as epitomizing artifice rather than authenticity, simulation and illusion rather than the authentic voice of the heart. In this new guise, femininity is increasingly appropriated as a cipher for the very self-reflexivity and self-referentiality of poetic language itself.

An important precondition for this feminization of the aesthetic was the aestheticization of woman, exemplified, as already noted, by the phenomenon of conspicuous consumption and the increasing importance placed upon fashion, appearance, and display. Elaborate regimes of grooming, adornment, posture, and self-presentation that had previously been the province of an aristocratic elite were gradually to become part of the everyday practice of modern femininity. In the writings of Baudelaire, for example, one finds a repeated fascination with the artificiality of modern women, their reliance upon cosmetics, jewelry, and costume as a means of creating the illusion of beauty and of generating desire.[8] In becoming identified with such conventionalized signifiers, femininity loosened itself from its moorings in the natural body; as an ensemble of signs, it lent itself to appropriation and imitation by the male aesthete. Through its very artificiality, femininity was to become the privileged marker of the instability and mobility of modern gender identity.

The rhetoric of decadence was also to play a key role in the cultural formation of the feminized male, signaling both a generalized sense of exhaustion, of being at the end of an epoch, and a specific aesthetic emphasis on style as the supreme value. On the one hand, writers such as Max Nordau drew upon contemporary medical and scientific findings to develop an influential thesis of cultural degeneration which depicted modern civilization as being gradually sapped of its virility and strength.[9] On the other hand, the literary avant-garde appropriated many of the same metaphors of decadence and degeneration as a means of affirming their disaffection from bourgeois ideals of progress through a deliberate cult of the perverse and the artifical. Thus just as nineteenth-century ideals of progress, heroism, and national identity became identified with a somatic norm of healthy masculinity, so the motif of the feminized male offered a provocative refusal of such ideals. While contemporary reviewers criticized *The Picture of Dorian Gray* for its unmanliness and "effeminate frivolity,"[10] self-identified decadents were wont to agree that "man is growing more refined, more feminine, more divine."[11] For their supporters, the very modernity of aestheticism and decadence lay paradoxically in a proclamation of the exhaustion of the modern, a refusal of complacent bourgeois ideals of reason, progress, and industrious masculinity through a defiant celebration of the deviant.

This sensibility is clearly evident in the texts of Wilde, Huysmans, and Sacher-Masoch, whose protagonists are all identified with a love of artifice, excess, and everything that is unnatural. Significantly, in each text the hero is an aristocrat and thus situated outside the cycle of production and the ethos of bourgeois achievement, defining himself in the words of Severin, the hero of *Venus in Furs,* as "nothing but a dilettante ... an amateur in life."[12] Renouncing the struggle for active self-realization in the world, the aesthete is languid and passive, possessing traits usually associated with women, such as vanity, hypersensitivity, and a love of fashion and ornamentation. Spending much of his time in an interior, private space codified as feminine rather than in the public sphere of work and politics, he devotes himself to the cultivation of style and the appreciation of life as an aesthetic phenomenon. It is significant that neither Dorian Gray, nor Jean des Esseintes, nor Severin defines himself as an artist; the romantic myth of the creative genius has become exhausted and aesthetic pleasure is now located in the exercise of taste through the collection and enjoyment of beautiful objects. Given the association of femininity with consumption examined previously, this emphasis on the pleasures of consuming rather than producing accentuates the feminized status of the aesthete. So too does his fascination with the decorative as well as the "high" arts; the exercise of style manifests itself in a delight in the details of decor and costume, and the evocation of elaborately furnished interiors and glamorous fashions plays an important part in all three texts. Such decorative concerns were of course more usually associated with the middle-class woman, who, while being denied the possibility of creating great art, was encouraged to exercise her aesthetic sense in the decoration of herself and the intimate interior of the bourgeois household.[13]

The prototype being evoked here is clearly that of the dandy, described by Ellen Moers as a "creature perfect in externals and careless of anything belong the surface, a man solely dedicated to his own perfection through a ritual of taste."[14] Originating in the understated elegance of the legendary Beau Brummel, the mystique of dandyism was to assume a new importance in the context of fin-de-siècle decadence and its self-conscious celebration of form over content. An aristocrat of style, the dandy is acutely aware of the semiotic significance of the most minute details of clothing and behavior. Devoting himself to the production of the self as an aesthetic artifact, he is the ultimate representative of fashion, the embodiment of what Wilde, following Baudelaire, calls the "absolute modernity of beauty."[15] Like women and like the work of art, the dandy can thus be perceived as quite useless; exalting appearance over essence, decoration over function, he voices a protest against the tyranny of the utilitarian and the instrumental.

Thus a recurring trait of the feminized male is his transformation of everyday life into an aesthetic project, his tireless attention to the minutiae of lifestyle as performance. *Against the Grain,* for example, details the artistic experiments of the jaded aristocrat des Esseintes, the last scion of a family marked by a progressive "effemination" of its male members. Huysmans's protagonist abandons Parisian society to pursue the solitary cultivation of refined and artificial pleasures in an isolated and exquisitely fashioned retreat. Descriptions of his collections of esoteric and exotic *objets d'art,* his fastidious discriminations among colors, fabrics, and styles of furnishings, and his elaborate sensual experiments with liqueurs and perfumes constitute almost the entire body of the text. In *The Picture of Dorian Gray,* Wilde depicts the elegant aesthetes of English high society, for whom "life itself was the first, the greatest, of the arts,"[16] and who share des Esseintes's contempt for vulgar bourgeois social norms. Striking languid poses in fashionable London drawing rooms, Wilde's characters devote themselves to a single-minded cult of pure beauty and a meticulous pursuit of style. The dandy's transformation of the self into a work of art is graphically realized in the figure of Dorian, who takes on the qualities of his own portrait; enclosed within an invisible frame which separates him from the continuum of history, he is frozen into an image of static and unchanging physical perfection. "An excessively developed aestheticism" is also the defining characteristic of the hero of *Venus in Furs*,[17] and it causes him to flee the banality of modern society and devote himself to the worship of the ideal as embodied in the imperious Countess Wanda. Severin is both feminized and infantilized in his role as slave; whipped and humiliated by his mistress, he must listen to her repeated taunt that he is "not a man." Sacher-Masoch's text depicts the ritualistic enactment of an elaborately staged and costumed erotic drama; life is transformed into art by means of a highly stylized and deliberately anachronistic relationship between mistress and servant which constantly comments on its own status as theatrical performance.

Commodity Aesthetics and the Narcissistic Text

The narcissistic dimension of the feminized male is epitomized most clearly in the figure of Dorian Gray, whose androgynous qualities are repeatedly invoked in references to his scarlet lips, golden hair, and eternal youth. If, as Rachel Bowlby suggests, Dorian's yearning to retain the flawless and ageless qualities of his own portrait uncannily pre-empts the narcissistic fantasies inspired by the dream world of contemporary advertising, this yearning also accentuates his feminized status, given that it is above all images of women which circulate in commodity culture as objects of identification and desire.[18] Moreover, Dorian's preoccupation with his own portrait carries broader resonances as an allegory of the construction of identity in the sphere of representation. Dorian begins to develop a sense of self-consciousness only after viewing his own idealized image as painted by his friend the artist Basil Hallward: "A look of joy came into his eyes, as if he had recognized himself for the first time ... The sense of his own beauty came on him like a revelation."[19] As Ed Cohen argues in a reading of this scene which draws implicitly upon the Lacanian theory of the mirror stage: "looking on his completed portrait for the first time, Dorian encounters himself as reflected in the 'magical mirror' of Basil's desire. This image organizes the disparate perceptions of his body into an apparently self-contained whole and reorients Dorian in relation both to his own identity and to his social context."[20]

The point here, then, is that the "feminine" narcissism of Dorian, as exemplified in his fascination with his appearance and with a self-image generated by the desire of another, relates to a more general emphasis in the novel on the textual mediation of identity. The figure of Dorian Gray is in fact explicitly defined as a product of various textual influences—Basil's painting, an "evil book," Henry Wotton's aphorisms—and Wilde's text constantly plays with the distinction between original and copy, the real Dorian and the imitation. Just as identity is revealed as artifice, so too it is rendered indeterminate and unstable, undermining Romantic notions of authentic interiority and the organic subject. "Is insincerity such a terrible thing? I think not. It is merely a method by which we can multiply our personalities."[21] While *Dorian Gray* calls into question the meaningfulness of the distinction between original and reproduction, des Esseintes aspires to a completely artificial existence, in which experience can be translated into style. In his secluded retreat, the austere beauty of a monastery cell can be simulated through a skillful combination of fabrics and furnishings without the necessity for either physical hardship or religious conviction. A judicious selection of images, smells, and objects persuasively replicates the various sensations of a maritime voyage in his own dining room, rendering any need for actual travel obsolete. For Huysmans's hero, techniques of illusion and artifice made possible through the combination of aesthetic sophistication and technological expertise have conspired to render nature itself a mere anachronism.

Thus the blurring of gender roles evident in the texts under discussion forms part of a more general questioning of the authentic self within a culture increasingly shaped by the logic of technological reproduction and commodity aesthetics. On the one hand, the aesthete seeks to differentiate himself from the dull mediocrity of modern society by taking refuge in the solitary cultivation of the arcane and the exotic. His cult of extreme individualism takes the form of an aristocratic and idiosyncratic promotion of personal style at the expense of public and social interaction. This motif receives its most graphic expression in des Esseintes's solipsistic withdrawal into ever smaller arenas: modernity is equated no longer with the topography of public space but rather with a psychological and spatial self-enclosure that offers a refuge from the encroaching banalities of mass society. The exterior explorations of the flâneur give way to the interior explorations of the collector, who ranges mentally across space and time in the contemplation of his heterogeneous accumulation of artifacts and *objets d'art*—described by

Walter Benjamin as the phantasmagorias of the interior.[22] Yet temporal and spatial difference are curiously neutralized and decontextualized through the synchrony of the nonsynchronous, as the texts and objects of past cultures and exotic traditions are appropriated by the aesthete to serve as markers of stylistic differentiation through which he signals his own uniqueness. For des Esseintes, as for Dorian Gray, history has become a museum of eclectic and random artifacts that narcissistically mirrors his own fantasies and preoccupations.

Yet this very concern with the semiotics of style also reveals the aesthete's continuing dependency on the commodity culture against which he appears to position himself. The search for ever more arcane objects not yet trivialized by mass reproduction echoes the same cult of novelty which propels the logic of capitalist consumerism; the loftiest notion of cultural superiority still depends on the vulgar act of shopping.[23] As Rosalind Williams points out, the elite consumer, like his more humble counterpart, is always on the run; restlessly searching for the magical object that will endow him with the desired self-image and status, he is constantly engaged in a defensive and reactive response to the banalization of the commodity by the mass market. Thus the aesthete's attempt to create a uniquely individual style reveals his inevitable reliance upon the very categories of evaluation against which he ostensibly pits himself. Similarly, while he affects a disdain for modern industrial and technological processes, these same processes form the taken-for-granted preconditions of his own pursuit of distinction and refined pleasures.

At a more general level, the fin-de-siècle preoccupation with style and appearance itself reflects an expanding aestheticization of everyday life, a mediation of experience through the consumption of images and commodities which renders any appeal to a true self merely another fiction. As Henry Wotton compellingly concludes, "being natural is simply a pose."[24] The aesthete's recognition of the artificiality of identity, in other words, derives from a context in which mass-produced signs, objects, and commodities constitute increasingly significant yet unstable markers of subjectivity and social status. Thus the growing self-differentiation of the aesthetic sphere in the late nineteenth century should not be read as a definitive rupture with a purely instrumentalized and rationalized social world. Rather, early modernism exists on a continuum with a more general textualization of the social; the authority of nature is exposed as nothing but art, reality as mere simulation, as everyday life takes on ever more of the characteristics of imaginative representation. While railing against the vulgar manifestations of this new industrial and consumer culture, the artistic avant-gardes of the fin de siècle were simultaneously fascinated by the new power of image, text, and spectacle, a power which is both affirmed and questioned in the stylistic innovations of their writing.

Thus the flattening out of sociohistorical reality into an assemblage of surfaces and images is actualized in the creation of formal structures that are spatial rather than temporal, as literature seeks to approach the condition of painting. Paintings and mirrors are in fact thematically important in all three texts under discussion, paradigmatic instances of the two-dimensional stasis to which each work aspires. Gilles Deleuze, for example, describes the formal logic of *Venus in Furs* as follows: "the woman torturer freezes into postures that identify her with a statue, a painting or a photograph. She suspends her gestures in the act of bringing down the whip or removing her furs; her movement is arrested as she turns to look at herself in a mirror."[25] Shaped by a dreamlike logic of association—dreams in fact play a crucial role in the text—*Venus in Furs* simulates in its own episodic structure the paintings and images to which it frequently refers, images described as uncanny, fantastic, and completely lacking in historical character. This vagueness of geographical and temporal location reveals the true locus of the text as the imagination of the fantasizing subject, resulting in a ritualistic and self-referential repetition of the ever-same images of the cruel woman. Here, as in *Against the Grain*, description takes precedence over narration, developmental plot gives way to a sometimes claustrophobic sense of immobility and ahistoricity. The topography of aestheticism is that of the framed space, depicted as simultaneously liberating, by providing a degree of distantiation from the social, and imprisoning, by locking the hero into narcissistic self-contemplation.

The abandonment of organic narrative and the features of realist aesthetics leads to a self-reflexive preoccupation with the surface of language, with the grain and texture of the word. *Against the Grain*, for example, can be seen as one of the first modernist novels, a text that is, notoriously, without a plot. Structured around fetishistic, quasi-pornographic descriptions of works of art, bibelots, and interior furnishings, the style of the text, in spite of its avowed disdain for the commercial, is reminiscent of nothing other than the lavish prose of a consumer catalogue. Huysmans's fascination with the materiality of language, which is at one point likened to a decaying carcass, at another compared to the qualities of precious metals, enamels, and jewels, manifests itself in the form of a self-consciously decadent style of sinuous distortions and exotic references which aspires to this same quality of material opacity. Similarly, the formulaic quality of Sacher-Masoch's style, its reliance on cliché and stereotype, causes language to become solidified and unreal and hence to undermine any putative referential dimension.[26] *Dorian*

Gray remains closest to the conventions of realist narrative and Victorian melodrama, yet here too an acute linguistic self-consciousness manifests itself in elaborate and ornamental descriptions, in parodies and borrowings from such texts as *Against the Grain* and Walter Pater's *Studies in the History of the Renaissance,* and above all in the aphorisms and paradoxes strewn through the text that implicitly subvert its ostensible moral ending.[27] Language itself becomes a marker of fashion, a signifier of dandyism; literary style is turned into an object of ostentatious display that is flaunted for its own sake rather than being subordinated to any representational function. All three of the texts replicate both structurally and stylistically the preference for form over substance, for style over history, that is characteristic of their heroes. They thereby anticipate stylistic practices of parody, fragmentation, and aesthetic self-consciousness that will become defining features of the later texts of high modernism.

Textuality and Homosexuality

The topos of the feminine, it can be argued, thus serves a specific function in the counterdiscourse of late-nineteenth-century aestheticism, signaling a formal as well as a thematic refusal of an entire cluster of values associated with the ideology of bourgeois masculinity: the narrative of history as progress, the valorization of function over form, the sovereignty of the reality principle. From an antinaturalist standpoint, the category of gender, as one of the central terms of social and symbolic organization, provides a key terrain on which to challenge the authority of dominant definitions of the real. Feminine traits, in being adopted by a man, are defamiliarized, placed in quotation marks, revealed as free-floating signifiers rather than natural, God-given, and immutable traits. Defamiliarization through quotation in an incongruous context is of course the defining characteristic of parody, and the relationship between parody and male femininity here assumes the form of a dialectical interdependence. If the hero's preoccupation with style, quotation, and linguistic play is linked to his femininity, so in turn his mimicry of femininity confirms the authority of a parodistic world-view. The feminized male deconstructs conventional oppositions between the modern, bourgeois man and the natural, domestic woman: he is male, yet does not represent masculine values of rationality, utility, and progress; feminine, yet profoundly unnatural. His femininity thus signifies an unsettling of automatized perceptions of gender, whether hailed as subversive or condemned as pathological, whereas the same traits in a woman merely serve to confirm her incapacity to escape her natural condition. Richard von Krafft-Ebing, for example, claimed that masochism could only be seen as a true perversion in men, for nature had given to women "an instinctive inclination to voluntary subordination."[28] The semiotic significance of feminine traits, in other words, is fundamentally altered through their appropriation by the male aesthete.

It is not only gender, however, but also the notion of a natural sexuality that is questioned in these texts, as they explore a variety of sexual roles and options: male masochism, homosexuality, transvestism, voyeurism, and fetishism. Des Esseintes, for example, reminisces dreamily about a previous romantic attraction to a sturdy American acrobat called Miss Urania, an erotic attraction that derives from his perception of her latent masculinity. In the grips of this desire, "he presently arrived at the conclusion that, on his side, he was himself getting nearer and nearer the female type"; and he becomes increasingly infatuated with Miss Urania, "craving for her as an anaemic young girl will for some great, rough Hercules whose arms can crush her to a jelly in their embrace."[29] This desire to be dominated by a strong and powerful woman is associated with the thrill of perversity, the defiant exploration of unnatural and artifical pleasures. The Romantic yearning for an unmediated libidinal bliss beyond symbolization is radically undermined in these late works of early modernism; desire, rather than being repressed by the constraints of the symbolic order, is seen to be constituted through it. This aestheticization of the erotic is particularly apparent in *Venus in Furs*, where sexual desire is generated and mediated through diverse forms of textuality: letters, contracts, books, paintings, statues, and elaborate theatrical rituals. In his suggestive reading of Sacher-Masoch's work, Deleuze has established a number of links between the formal logic of his texts and their defining theme of male passivity and masochism. The text's fetishistic fixation on furs and costumes and its ritualized representation of static erotic tableaux derive from the pleasure of suspense, waiting, and disavowal in the masochistic fantasy, which, as Deleuze convincingly shows, differs fundamentally from sadism in its self-conscious and contemplative aestheticism.

My primary focus here is on the gendering of writing as feminine rather than its links to perverse sexuality, an issue I consider in more detail in the final chapter. It should be noted, however, that recent work in gay studies has contributed to a major reevaluation of the politics of style in the fin de siècle, a period usually seen as central to the formation of modern homosexual identities. Much of this work calls into question the established Marxist view of aestheticism as an apolitical flight from society by emphasizing its potentially resistive implications in the arena of sexual politics. Rather than being interpreted as an epiphenomenal consequence of the onward march of capital, aesthetic and stylistic practices are redefined as an important symbolic mechanism of resistance in the construction of subcultural identities. Richard Dellamora, for example, provides a detailed examination of the links between male homosexuality and aestheticism within the literary subcultures of nineteenth-century England, claiming that writers such as Hopkins and Swinburne attempted "to use the practice of poetry to create an aesthetic-cultural space in which men could contest conventional gender coding while expressing the worth of male-male desire."[30] The domain of the aesthetic was a seductive one precisely because it allowed for the expression of certain forms of homosexual feeling, albeit in indirect and disguised form, that could not be publicly expressed elsewhere.

From a present-day perspective, the affinities and parallels between the self-conscious aesthetic sensibility of early modernism and the social articulation of modern homosexuality appear striking. Aestheticism's denial of a natural self, and hence of a natural sexuality, provided a strategically valuable perspective for those who did not conform to dominant heterosexual norms. Its disdain for moral categories and neutralization of taboos engendered a potential point of resistance to the proliferating ethical and medical imperatives which sought to define and regulate the parameters of healthy male sexuality. Moreover, the fin-de-siècle preoccupation with beauty and appearance made it possible to eroticize masculinity by transforming it into spectacle in previously unavailable ways. The male body was repositioned as a source of visual pleasure and an object of desire at the same time as it was being revealed as a highly coded and artificial construct. The stylization and theatricality of aestheticism, exemplified through a living of life "in quotation marks," was thus to become a defining feature of a "camp" sensibility associated with the homosexual lifestyle of urban elites of the fin de siècle.[31]

It was of course in the figure of Oscar Wilde that the dandy and the homosexual were to become most visibly combined; by the time of his conviction for homosexuality Wilde had become the paradigmatic example of emerging public definitions of sexual deviance.[32] Although early critical discussions of homosexuality in *The Picture of Dorian Gray* mined the text for signs of socially conditioned guilt and self-hatred, more recent readings have moved beyond such a psychobiographical frame to situate the aesthetic self-consciousness of the work in relation to the ambiguous contemporary positioning of the homosexual. Thus Ed Cohen argues, "In *The Picture of Dorian Gray*, Wilde problematized representation per se to move athwart the historical limitations that define male homosexuality as 'unnameable,' therefore creating one of the most lasting icons of male homoerotic desire."[33] Jonathan Dollimore mounts a stronger claim for Wilde as a postmodernist *avant la lettre* whose anti-essentialist focus on surface and style allowed for an exploration of forms of fluid, decentered identity and desire that scandalized the culture of his time. For Dollimore, Wilde's "transgressive aesthetic" is intimately related to his transgressive sexuality, constituting a radical subversion of mystifying ideals of the authentic and natural self.[34]

Dollimore's focus on the liberating aspects of Wilde's parodistic aesthetic coexists, however, with a recognition of its links to a historical condition of sexual marginality and discrimination. Impersonation and disguise were often obligatory techniques of survival for the late-nineteenth-century homosexual rather than simply markers of adherence to a fashionable aesthetic philosophy. For those forced to adopt strategies of subterfuge to conceal a sexuality that was defined as both immoral and illegal, performance was often a daily imperative rather than a playful choice. Seen in this light, Wilde's celebration of artifice and the pleasures of the mask become a question of making a virtue out of a grim necessity. Neil Bartlett writes, "London in 1895 had no conception of a man being 'naturally homosexual.' A man who loved other men could only be described as an invert, an inversion of something else, a pervert, an exotic, a disease, a victim, a variation."[35] Adopting and reversing traditional hierarchies, the homosexual aesthete self-consciously sought to legitimate those qualities for which he had traditionally been condemned.

In spite of their suggestive affinities, moreover, aestheticism and male homosexuality constituted overlapping subcultural formations rather than identical domains. Not all aesthetes were homosexual; conversely, the effeminate aristocratic dandy was only one of the ways in which homosexuality was represented and represented itself in the fin de siècle. Another influential tradition, for example, portrayed male same-sex desire in very different terms through an appeal to a neoclassical ideal of heroic virility. Thus in Germany, the fin de siècle saw the emergence of all-male youth communities that explicitly refused the decadence of modernity, affirming an ideal of natural erotic manliness and celebrating the beauty of the naked, active, athletic body.[36] Sexology, moreover, was to provide a dominant framework for conceptualizing sexual "inversion" that depicted homosexuality as an innate and determined condition over which the individual had little control. In this context, as Dollimore notes in his discussion of André Gide, the appeal to a natural and inescapable sexual identity became an increasingly common stratagem in the legitimation of same-sex desire; essentialism and the appeal to biological determination could serve a historically progressive function in the defense of marginal identities.[37]

As even these few examples make clear, to hail irony, aestheticism, and masquerade as the defining features of a gay sensibility is problematic because it conflates sexual preference with a historically overdetermined and culturally specific set of practices. Such a move merely reinscribes the authenticity that it appears to undermine in ascribing to the homosexual a necessary allegiance to a "camp" aesthetic of artifice and excess.[38] An affinity with an aesthetics of performance and masquerade was itself significantly overdetermined by class privilege in the late nineteenth century; the composition of self through stylistic display and glamorous lifestyles was an option available only to a minority. Thus the dandy's ironic exposure of the eroticism and the arbitrariness of the commodity was itself a function of spending power and a social status marked by the "psychopathology of affluence."[39] In other words, as recent theorists have pointed out, it is misleading to interpret the culture of aestheticism as the coming-into-being of a true homosexual self. Rather, it may be more useful to analyze its historical particularity, showing how depictions of same-sex desire in late-nineteenth-century literature both drew upon and challenged the alternative definitions that were being formed elsewhere, for example in the legal and medical discourses of the period.[40]

The Abominable Woman

Having explored some of the affinities between the figure of the dandy-aesthete and the crisis of linguistic representation associated with the birth of literary modernism, I now wish to turn my attention to the not unproblematic relationship between "woman" and "the feminine" that structures these affinities. I have argued that parodistic techniques and embedded references to illusion, simulation, and masquerade in *Venus in Furs*, *Against the Grain*, and *The Picture of Dorian Gray* serve to destabilize and disrupt a series of oppositions, including the fundamental dichotomy of sexual difference. Yet this very strategy of subversion can in turn be shown to contain a powerful investment in the creation and maintenance of new boundaries, evidenced in the remarkably similar logics of exclusion operating in all three of these texts.

Here the notion of vulgarity reveals its symbolic centrality, as the epitome of everything that aestheticism is not. Its actuality is powerfully affirmed in the very act of its negation: Wilde's languid Henry Wotton, for example, reflects wearily upon "an age so limited and vulgar as our own" and expresses his own profound distaste for "vulgar realism in literature."[41] Severin in *Venus in Furs* describes his own extreme sense of revulsion at "everything base, common and ugly."[42] Des Esseintes condemns "the vulgar reality of actual, prosaic facts"[43] and defines his aesthetic preferences in explicit opposition to the coarseness of popular taste. Vulgarity assumes an array of diverse and complexly interwoven meanings in these various contexts; it references the realm of the material—nature, matter, brute fact—but also the realm of popular (that is, nonelite) culture, the coarse, unrefined, tawdry life of ordinary individuals. These two meanings are not of course unrelated; from the standpoint of the aesthete the vulgarity of the masses is closely tied to their immediate, sensory apprehension of the world and their natural closeness to the body.[44]

Thus the aesthete's very subversion of taken-for-granted distinctions both presumes and reinforces a primary division between the refined and the vulgar, who are by definition incapable of this kind of shifting ironic sensibility. This meta-distinction is in other words simultaneously aesthetic and political; it affirms the superiority of a particular interpretive mode (self-conscious, anti-utilitarian, ironic) that is in turn inflected by class and gender interests. The aesthete may be seen as voicing a heroic protest against the hypocrisy and rigidity of bourgeois culture; viewed from another angle, however, this act of negation bespeaks an aristocratic disdain toward everyone who does not form part of this same bohemian elite. As Andreas Huyssen has argued, this "everyone" has often been gendered feminine in the texts of male modernism; women and the masses merge as twin symbols of the democratizing mediocrity of modern life, embodying a murky threat to the precarious status and identity of the artist.[45]

Thus the aesthete's playful subversion of gender norms and adoption of feminine traits paradoxically reinforce his distance from and superiority to women, whose nature renders them incapable of this kind of free-floating semiotic mobility and aesthetic sophistication. Gender as well as class hierarchies are maintained and reinforced through a fastidious differentiation and classification of styles of consumption. Rachel Bowlby suggests that the fin-de-siècle aesthete foreshadows the replacement of the ascetic bourgeois individual of early capitalism by a feminized and narcissistic subject engendered by twentieth-century mass culture.[46] Yet at the same time great pains are taken to define this feminized aesthete in explicit opposition to the prototype of the vulgar female consumer. Des Esseintes, for example, is no longer able to gain pleasure from certain objects, such as particular kinds of flowers or jewels, which have become sullied by their association with feminine middle-class taste. In his consumption of literature, Huysmans's hero, "whose mind was naturally sophisticated and unsentimental,"[47] is unable to tolerate the works of women writers, whose "wretched prattlings" are couched in a style of nauseating triviality.[48] If the aesthete and dandy shares with women his identity as consumer, it becomes imperative for him to signal his superiority of taste and the qualitative difference of his own aesthetic response. As A. E. Carter has pointed out, decadence differs most significantly from the Romantic tradition in its enactment of a *dual* negation, its condemnation not only of a tawdry modern urban culture but also of the nostalgic yearning for an idyll of unmediated nature.[49] In this pessimistic vision, women come to stand for the most despised aspects of both culture *and* nature, exemplifying the crass vulgarity and emptiness of modern bourgeois society as well as an uncontrolled passion and excessive emotionality that is deeply repugnant to the disengaged stance of the male aesthete.

Thus the dandy, in pursuit of uniqueness through the narcissistic cult of self, sees women as exemplifying the uniformity and standardization of modern life which he most abhors. In a characteristically sour mood of melancholic reflection, des Esseintes recalls his encounters with the prostitutes and bar-girls of the Latin Quarter: "all, like so many automata wound up at the same time with the same key, uttered in the same tone the same invitations, lavished the same smiles, talked in the same silly phrases, indulged in the same absurd reflexions."[50] Such phrases conjure up the motif of the mechanical woman noted earlier; compressed together within the confines of narrow city streets, the working prostitutes of Paris appear indistinguishable to the passing flâneur, an array of identical, mass-produced, mechanical dolls exemplifying the logic of serial reproduction. Romance and passion have themselves become routinized, transformed into a standardized series of gestures and expressions automatically performed by the disciplined female body. In a similar manner, Dorian Gray explains his passion for Sybil Vane by contrasting the glamour of the actress with the mundane, transparent, and predictable qualities of ordinary women: "they are limited to their century. No glamour ever transfigures them. One knows their minds as easily as one knows their bonnets. One can always find them. There is no mystery in any of them . . . They have their stereotyped smile, and their fashionable manner. They are quite obvious."[51] In both these examples, the superficiality and interchangeability of women symbolizes an abstract identity and an economy of the same, an all-pervasive disenchantment of the world in which feminine sexuality, like art, has been deprived of its redemptive aura, contaminated by the rationalization of everyday life.

Yet while such descriptions emphasize the mechanical, depersonalized, and ultimately soulless quality of modern femininity, the dandy simultaneously views women as embodying the innate folly of their sex, an instinctual irrationality and natural inclination to emotional excess. Wilde's Henry Wotton and Dorian Gray, for example, make frequent jibes about a tiresome sentimentality associated with women, their subjection to overwhelming feelings they are unable to control. "Women . . . lived on their emotions. They

only thought of their emotions."[52] Wilde's novel repeatedly identifies wom-
en—as opposed to "the feminine"—with the uninhibited expression of an
excessive and stifling love. This equation of the female sex with the domain
of instinctual and even atavistic emotion is obediently echoed by the heroine
of *Venus in Furs*: "In spite of all the advances of civilization, woman has
remained as she was the day Nature's hands shaped her . . . Man, even when
he is selfish or wicked, lives by principles; woman only obeys her feelings."[53]
Severin's reminiscences of his youth reaffirm this association of women with
excessive emotion that pervades the textual logic of *Venus in Furs*: "When I
first began to think about love, it seemed to my raw adolescent's eyes particularly crude and vulgar; I avoided all contact with the fair sex."[54]

The aesthete thus explicitly defines his identity in opposition to all such
womanly inclinations to instinctual passion. Dorian Gray, for example, articulates his desire for self-sufficiency and control over his own feelings in the
following words: "a man who is master of himself can end a sorrow as easily
as he can invent a pleasure. I don't want to be at the mercy of my emotions.
I want to use them, to enjoy them, and to dominate them."[55] In this yearning
for self-domination through self-discipline, aestheticism clearly reveals its
underlying similarity with the rationalist and ascetic world-view against
which it ostensibly defines itself. Thus Henry Wotton's purely aesthetic
appreciation of life is compared, in its disinterestedness and detachment, to
the experimental method of science and the dissecting gaze of the surgeon.
"He had been always enthralled by the methods of natural science, but the
ordinary subject-matter of that science had seemed to him trivial and of no
import. And so he had begun by vivisecting himself, as he had ended by
vivisecting others . . . What matter what the cost was? One could never pay
too high a price for any sensation."[56] Here aestheticism reveals its integral
connections with naturalism, as exemplified in a shared reliance on an overarching trope of experimentation. In a similar fashion, des Esseintes positions himself as an ironic and dispassionate observer, not only of his own
inner psychological processes but of the lives of others, which are revealed
under his weary scrutiny to be nothing more than badly plotted and cliché-
ridden works of art.

In this context, Baudelaire's assertion that the artist "stems only from
himself"[57] can be read as symptomatic of an ideal of self-sufficient individualism that is defiantly affirmed in the detached sensibility of the aesthete. In
the act of self-creation, the dandy denies his dependency on others, in particular on the figure of the mother, the woman that he most abhors and
fears.[58] This dread of emotional ties as embodying a potential threat to
autonomous selfhood also incorporates anxieties about sexuality and the

body; a sublimating impulse is apparent in the fantasy of transcending the constraints of a body associated with putrefaction and decay. The aesthete denies the reality of his own biological and physiological determination and seeks to overcome the base appetites of the flesh. The theme is clearly evident in *Against the Grain,* where, as Rodolphe Gasché notes, des Esseintes lives against nature as a means of transcending nature, in order "to achieve a purity independent from the senses, and, thus, a life of spirituality exclusively concerned with simulacra of nature in the shape of artefacts, memories or essences."[59] A similar desire to escape the limitations of the material body reveals itself in the aestheticization of Dorian Gray, his transformation into an unblemished icon which defies—if only temporarily—the "hideousness of age" and the reality of his own mortal condition. Sacher-Masoch's apparently erotic text is also paradoxically preoccupied with asceticism, aspiring to the ideal through the spiritualization of the senses and the transcendence of the flesh. The fascination with the trappings of religious ritual evident in all three works is symptomatic in this context of a deeper allegiance to a Christian conception of nature as fundamentally base and corrupt, with art now taking on a sublimating function previously ascribed to religion.[60]

In this context, the female body comes to function as a primary symbolic site for confronting and controlling the threat of an unruly nature. If the dandy-aesthete embodies an aspiration to the ideal, then woman, according to the dualisms of nineteenth-century thought, represents materiality and corporeality, or the "triumph of matter over mind."[61] The purported neutrality of scientific discourse, feminists have argued, is frequently freighted with metaphorical references to the subjugation of a feminized nature; and the disinterested contemplation of the world as an aesthetic phenomenon is marked by a similar subtext of repressed violence and revenge. One commentator's telling description of des Esseintes's aestheticism as a "violation of nature," indicating a consuming desire to "thwart, chastise and finally *humiliate* nature," hints at the psychosexual aggression underlying the persistent association of women and nature in late-nineteenth-century writing.[62] Charles Bernheimer has argued that an obsessive fear of the female body lies at the heart of Huysmans's work, revealing a profound castration anxiety in the recurring association of female sexuality with pervasive corruption and decay. Huysmans's preoccupation with artifice in terms of both the style and the content of his writing can in turn be related to this anxiety; the creation and manipulation of simulacra offers the illusion of control, operating as a form of sublimation in its denial of the organic, that is, of the material body of woman.[63]

Here one can note the repeatedly fetishistic impulse informing aestheticism's textualization of the female body. Again it is in the texts of Baudelaire that one can find some of the first explicit acknowledgments of the importance of clothing, jewelery, and cosmetics in deflecting and disguising the horror of female nudity. The overt fetishism of Venus in Furs similarly bears witness to the "sex-appeal of the inorganic," in Walter Benjamin's luminous phrase;[64] the materiality of the naked female body is erased in order to relocate erotic excitement in an exotic apparatus of whips, furs, and elaborate costumes. The idealization of the "cold, cruel beloved" requires her decorporealization, given her status as symbol of the divine law. This function of the cruel woman in relation to the male aspiration to transcendence through martyrdom is made explicit in the biblical epigraph at the beginning of Venus in Furs: "The Lord hath smitten him by the hand of a woman."[65] In the dreamlike structure of Sacher-Masoch's text, the body of the dominatrix frequently blurs into the image of a white statue made of marble or stone, offering a clear example of what Christine Buci-Glucksmann describes as "the masculine desire to immobilize, to petrify the feminine body."[66]

Thus a symptomatic double strategy of projection and denial manifests itself with particular clarity in Sacher-Masoch's text. First, woman is identified with the primitive, uncontrollable forces of nature: "she is like a wild animal, faithful or faithless, kindly or cruel, depending on the impulse that rules her."[67] Woman is nothing but body, symbolizing the unruly excess of an unconscious and undisciplined subjectivity. Yet at the same time, woman is aestheticized, and the threat of the natural is thus negated by being turned into art; the female body is transformed into a visually pleasing play of surfaces and textures under the scrutiny of the male gaze. Whereas Venus in Furs freezes woman into the form of a painting or statue, Dorian Gray and Henry Wotton's textualization of the actress Sybil Vane takes the form of reducing her to a collection of dramatic performances, a series of roles acknowledged to be more real than the performer herself. Hence, Wotton serenely concludes, "the girl never really lived, and so she has never really died."[68]

It might be objected that such an aestheticization is hardly surprising within the context of modernism's valorization of artifice and masquerade. In being portrayed as actresses, images, and works of art, women, like the dandy, simply serve to illustrate the general theme of the pervasive textualization of modern bodies. The crucial point, however, is that women, unlike the dandy, lack the ironic self-consciousness which their presence inspires in others. They embody artifice naively, as it were, without being able to raise it to the level of philosophical reflection: women, Wotton concludes, "are charmingly artificial, but they have no sense of art."[69] This aperçu is emphatically vindicated in an episode of *Dorian Gray* which underscores this profound aesthetic naiveté of the female subject. Having become infatuated with the actress Sybil Vane after seeing her in a variety of roles, Dorian Gray is half aware that his passion is inspired by the androgynous charm of her performances rather than by any interest in the history and identity of the performer. Sybil herself, by contrast, on learning of his adulation, responds by losing all interest in her acting, which she now decries as false and illusory, and reverts to a sentimental aesthetic of romantic love grounded in a naive belief in the authentic subject. As a result, of course, her aura of desirability is immediately eradicated and Dorian's abandonment of her and her subsequent suicide provide an appropriately melodramatic ending. So too, des Esseintes's hopes of experiments in erotic perversity with the athletic Miss Urania end in disappointment when, unlike the male aesthete, she reveals herself unable to transgress the limits of her own gender. "He had pictured the pretty American athlete to be as stolid and brutal as the strong man at a fair, but her stupidity, alas! was purely feminine in its nature ... all the childish weaknesses of a woman were there in full force; she had all the love of chatter and finery that marks the sex specially given up to trivialities; any such thing as a transmutation of masculine ideas into her feminine person was a pure figment of the imagination."[70]

Women's association with performance thus does not signal any deeper commitment to or comprehension of a parodistic vision; women are "sphinxes without secrets" in the words of Wilde, their enigmatic aura purely superficial, exemplifying conventionality without aesthetic self-consciousness. Wanda in *Venus in Furs* is the woman who comes closest to attaining the ironic detachment of the aesthete in acting the part of the cruel mistress and fulfilling Severin's yearning for a woman who will dominate him "in a serene and fully conscious manner."[71] Yet she too continually slips out of her role and needs to be guided and educated by him into the appropriate requirements of her part. Thus, while the text apparently places the male in the role of subordinate and victim, it is his desire, as Deleuze points out, which controls the structure of the fantasy; the cruel woman functions as his double or reflection who speaks the words he wishes to hear.[72] *Venus in Furs* undoubtedly mocks the traditional iconography of patriarchal law in its imaginative reformulation of the erotics of power; yet its representation of the feminized, masochistic subject ultimately reaffirms an androcentric world-view and an established hierarchy of the sexes. The writer's adoration of the deviant despotic woman denies her agency and self-consciousness in the very process of idealizing her; women can function only as the Other of a male subject, a stimulus to his own pursuit of the ideal.

Against Nature?

In one of his more notorious statements, Baudelaire writes, "Woman is *natural,* that is to say abominable. Also, she is always vulgar, that is to say the contrary of the dandy."[73] I have suggested that the trope of the feminine in certain key texts of early modernism compulsively reenacts this pervasive horror of woman. A parodic subversion of gender norms reveals a persistent identification of women with vulgarity, nature, and the tyranny of the body, allowing the aesthete to define his own identity in opposition to these same attributes. The aesthete's performance of femininity is depicted as authentically modern precisely because of its self-conscious transcendence of the constraints of corporeality and natural sexual identity within which woman remains imprisoned. Thus while challenging the ideal of a phallic, unified, repressed masculinity, the cult of aestheticism contains a mysogynistic dimension that is closely linked to, rather than dissolved by, its antirepresentationalism and antinaturalism.

In this context, there emerges a significant web of affinities between the seemingly antithetical discourses of Enlightenment modernity and aesthetic modernism. The Enlightenment narrative is one of increasing liberation from the constraints of material determination through the power of instrumental reason and the subjugation of nature. This naive faith in the redemptive power of rationality and science is often counterposed in contemporary theory to textualist models of the linguistic construction of identity. Yet my argument suggests that the self-consciously literary texts of early modernism reveal profound similarities with the ideology of modern rationalism in their shared vision of overcoming the constraints of physiological determination and dissolving the power of sexual difference. Reducing the body to a free-floating play of signs and codes, aestheticism, like science, positions itself as being against (female) nature.[74]

In a recent book, Charles Bernheimer tackles this question of the connections between gender and early modernism, arguing that "from the mid-nineteenth century to the beginning of the twentieth, modernism obsessionally and anxiously displays its innovative desire by fragmenting and disfiguring the female sexual body, epitomized in male fantasy by the prostitute."[75] Developing arguments not unlike my own, Bernheimer shows that the modernist shift toward a self-conscious textuality, often hailed as aesthetically and politically subversive, was in fact predicated upon a concerted repression of woman/nature/the organic. In the works of nineteenth-century aesthetes and early modernists, gender difference is reduced to a purely rhetorical signifier; while appearing to offer "a liberating release from the reductive biologism of the essentialist plot," this move offers an equally questionable denial and displacement of the sexed female body.[76]

The gender politics of early modernism is not perhaps as unilaterally negative as Bernheimer's narrative suggests; there remains, for example, the question of women's own appropriation of an aesthetics of cross-dressing and performance in the fin de siècle, an issue I consider in more detail in the final chapter. In our own time, moreover, the destabilization of nature and the subversion of gender binaries have emerged as key concerns of many female as well as male writers, as evidenced in the proliferation of various forms of feminist poststructuralism. Many of the insights about the plasticity and ambiguity of gender identity first explored in the texts of early modernism are currently being deployed, elaborated, and redefined in the turn toward the performative within feminist theory itself. Antinaturalism, in other words, does not automatically signify antifeminism, even if some of the more textualist forms of contemporary feminist theory are less than fully convincing in terms of their explanatory and analytical power.

Nevertheless, a feminist hermeneutics of suspicion may well be in order in the face of the by now routine invocations of the destabilizing power of a feminine textuality. In recent years, such invocations have infiltrated the domain of philosophy as well as literature in the recurring deployment of the motif of "becoming woman" as a trope for the crisis of Western philosophical thought. In a trenchant critique of this intellectual tactic as manifested in the writings of Jacques Derrida and Deleuze and Guattari, Rosa Braidotti argues that such a mystification of the feminine as indeterminacy, oscillation, a play of veils and simulacra, is highly problematic in its concomitant denial of the reality of sexual difference and its avowed hostility to feminism.[77] I would suggest that this gesture does not in fact deny sexual difference so much as reinscribe it in the form of hierarchical relationship. The male theorist's fantasy of "becoming woman" is defined and valorized in opposition to the naiveté of feminist struggles for social change; accused of either vulgar essentialism or phallic identification, real women are, it appears, incapable of "becoming woman."

Without wishing to exaggerate the similarities between very different intellectual and political contexts, one might note that this strategy appears to enact an uncanny repetition of the dandy's affirmation of his own "feminine" semiotic and sexual mobility at the expense of women. Given the acknowledged debt of much contemporary French theory to the founding texts of literary modernism, such parallels are not, perhaps, completely surprising. They are addressed in a recent argument by Charles Bernheimer that explores the remarkably similar technologies of gender underpinning Derrida's representation of woman as the force of indeterminacy and the dandy's valorization of the figural over the natural, the undecidable over the referent. More generally, Tania Modleski has cautioned against premature feminist enthusiasm for male appropriations of feminine textuality, suggesting that such an alliance with the figural may coexist with undisguised expressions of anxiety and hostility to women.[78] To dematerialize the "natural" by insisting upon the totalizing power of the textual may thus be to echo rather than challenge a long-standing aesthetic tradition which has sought transcendence through a denial and erasure of the female body.

5

Love, God, and the Orient:
Reading the Popular Sublime

Women, of course, have a privileged (or fatal) relationship with
the sentimental. From the point of view of literary modernism,
sentimentality was both a past to be outgrown and a present
tendency to be despised. The gendered character of this condemnation seemed natural; women writers were entangled in sensibility . . . even the best might not altogether escape this romantic
indulgence in emotion and sublimity.

Suzanne Clark, *Sentimental Modernism: Women Writers
and the Revolution of the Word*

The English writer Marie Corelli, "the queen of bestsellers," was said to
be the most famous and highly paid novelist of her generation. *The Sorrows
of Satan* sold more copies on first publication than any previous English
novel, and many of her other books sold in the hundreds of thousands,
effortlessly outstripping the works of other popular writers of the day. Corelli
was a unique figure in the history of English publishing: no previous novelist
had ever secured such vast audiences or wielded so much power. As one of
her biographers writes in a hyperbolic but not inaccurate formulation,
"While Queen Victoria was alive, Miss Corelli was the second most famous
Englishwoman in the world; afterwards, there was no one to approach her."[1]
Spurning the fashion for literary realism, her novels offered fantasies of
escape and transfiguration, depicting glamorous and mysterious imaginary
worlds far removed from the everyday lives of her readers. This skillful
blending of romance, religiosity, and exoticism spoke to the needs and desires
of a vast contemporary public that spanned class boundaries; Corelli's dev-
otees included such eminent figures as Gladstone, Tennyson, and Queen
Victoria as well as the many thousands of ordinary readers who flocked to
her public appearances and avidly awaited the publication of each new novel.
Corelli herself helped to fuel this adulation through her expertise in the field

of publicity, cultivating a mystique of authorship which helped to establish her as a major international celebrity. Popular literary success was becoming increasingly linked to skillful marketing strategies and the manufacture of a glamorous and visible public personality.

The accolades bestowed upon Corelli were not, however, echoed in the responses of professional critics and reviewers. On the contrary, her novels were given such disparaging notices that she ultimately refused to send out review copies to the press, without any apparent loss of sales. In this regard, Corelli's career offers a striking example of the widening gap between serious literature and popular fiction that was coming into force at the end of the nineteenth century. Of course, Corelli was not the first writer to have enjoyed commercial success without accompanying critical acclaim, but never had the contrast between the rewards of capital and cultural capital seemed quite so dramatic. The more books she sold, the more, it seemed, she was vilified by the literary press. Some reviewers grudgingly conceded the value of her writing as a "supreme example of a popular style," but others went so far as to accuse her of hysteria and erotic degeneracy, describing her as a social menace.[2] Corelli's faults, it appeared, were many: vulgarity, sensationalism, self-aggrandizement, an inflated imagination, lack of restraint, and, above all, an incurably commonplace mind. The general tenor of critical opinion during her lifetime and afterward is well encapsulated in the frosty tone of *The Spectator:* "Marie Corelli was a woman of deplorable talent who imagined that she was a genius, and was accepted as a genius by a public to whose commonplace sentimentalities and prejudices she gave a glamorous setting and an impressive scale."[3]

It should not be assumed that Corelli herself was a quiescent bystander in this clash between the values of the literary intelligentsia and those of low- and middle-brow taste. On the contrary, she repeatedly represented herself as a writer of genius instinctively attuned to the hearts and souls of the English people and hence loftily indifferent to the envious carpings of a coterie of snobbish intellectuals. At the same time, however, she was quick to detect personal slights in any references to herself or her work, constantly threatening to sue anyone whose opinion contradicted her own. Such public and acrimonious responses merely served to intensify her notoriety and celebrity status, so that the experience of reading Corelli's novels became indissolubly linked to the circulation of her name and the auratic qualities with which it became invested. The public visibility of her writing, combined with her personal elusiveness and notorious reluctance to be interviewed or photographed, contributed to the gradual creation of a legend.[4]

Issues of gender were well to the forefront in this vituperative clash of taste cultures, evident in the numerous and often highly pejorative references to Corelli's sex by reviewers and critics. Much of Victorian literature had retained an overt fidelity to moral ideas, subordinating its use of realistic techniques to an overarching idealist and often didactic vision that was explicitly linked to the values of middle-class femininity.[5] By the end of the nineteenth century, however, the precepts of naturalism were gradually taking hold, and a belief in the spiritual and moral function of art began to cede ground to an aggressively modern realism concerned to record unflinchingly the details of a blemished social reality. At the same time, previously value-neutral terms such as "sentimental," "melodramatic," and "romantic" acquired increasingly negative, feminine, and old-fashioned connotations as labels for those texts which sought refuge from the critical understanding of reality in the form of beautiful illusions and exaggerated displays of feeling. Thus while women gained a significant hold on the literary marketplace, the aesthetic qualities associated with femininity were simultaneously downgraded and trivialized. "Sentiment and emotiveness were reduced in significance to 'sentimentality' and exaggeration, domestic detail counted as trivia, melodramatic utopianism as escapist fantasy and this total complex devalued by association with a 'feminised' popular culture."[6]

In this chapter, I wish to pursue this cluster of themes—escapism, fantasy, melodrama, sentimentality—as an important aspect of women's popular fiction and of modern culture more generally. The typical classification of such fiction as realist, because it is not concerned with subverting literary conventions and hence clearly not modernist, fails to do justice to its frequently utopian and quasi-transcendental aspirations, as exemplified in a gesturing toward an ineffable domain beyond the constraints of a mundane material reality. Corelli's fiction provides an ideal basis for such a discussion because it is so centrally concerned—both thematically and formally—with the invocation of elsewhere, with the imaginative and often hyperbolic representation of a "higher" world. It is also this aspect of her work which has received most criticism from those who detect only hackneyed inauthenticity and pretentiousness in such exalted references. Q. D. Leavis, for example, suggests that Corelli's novels

> have aroused such torrents of enthusiasm because they excite in the ordinary person an emotional activity for which there is no scope in his life. These novels will all be found to make play with the key words of the emotional vocabulary which provoke the vague warm surges of feeling associated with religion and religion substitutes—e.g. life, death, love, good, evil, sin, home, mother, noble, gallant, purity, honour. These responses can be touched off with a dangerous ease—every self-aware person finds that he

has to train himself from adolescence in withstanding them—and there is evidently a vast public that derives great pleasure from reacting in this way. This vocabulary as used by bestsellers is not quite the everyday one; it is analogous to a suit of Sunday clothes, carrying with it a sense of larger issues; it gives the reader a feeling of being helped, of being in touch with ideals.[7]

It is these idealist and emotionally charged dimensions of Corelli's fiction—disinvested of Leavis's own patronizing tone—which I wish to explore in more depth as part of a broader consideration of the relationship between gender, mass culture, and modernity.

There already exists, of course, an established vocabulary within critical theory for discussing the romantic and escapist tendencies in modern popular fiction. The word "kitsch," first coined in the 1870s as a term for cheap, rapidly produced works of art, has come to serve as a generic label for the conciliatory dimensions of mass culture. The aesthetic inadequacy that is seen to characterize kitsch arises out of a perceived incongruity between its aspiration to a transcendent religious or aesthetic ideal and its concrete manifestation as a modern, cheap, mass-produced commodity. Kitsch is thus "short-order charisma," "the miniature attempting to signify the gigantic," finding its ultimate expression in such mawkish, mass-produced objects as the Mona Lisa ashtray or the fluorescent statue of the Virgin Mary.[8] It is often seen as synonymous with sentimentality, encouraging a wallowing in sugary romanticism and unrestrained emotion that is antithetical to the ironical and critical stance of the avant-garde. Kitsch is thus explicitly feminized, linked to assumptions about the necessarily spurious and superficial nature of any appeals to the emotions in popular culture; women's romance fiction, for example, is repeatedly cited in the critical literature as the ultimate in literary kitsch.[9] Furthermore, kitsch is identified as old-fashioned and retrogressive in its invocation of romantic or religious ideals, circumventing the newness of modernity in favor of a "debased Romanticism" grounded in a conservative longing for past traditions and aesthetic conventions. According to Hermann Broch, it is nothing other than "an escape into the idyll of history, where set conventions are still valid . . . Kitsch is the simplest and most direct way of soothing this nostalgia."[10] Thus while kitsch is quintessentially modern in terms of its technical reproducibility, it is also antimodern in its aesthetic conservatism, its appeal to "old-fashioned" feelings, and its reliance on outmoded convention. Finally, kitsch is seen as regressive in a personal as well as a historical sense, catering to an infantile desire to flee from the complexities of reality into a predictable fantasy world of immediate and unobstructed gratification. In this context, discussions of the psychological functions of popular culture are frequently linked to assumptions about the inevitable naiveté and emotional immaturity of its audience.

Since all these assumptions are also prominent in the critical reception of Corelli's work, it might appear logical to approach her fiction via the concept of kitsch. Yet there are obvious problems with the term, given its peremptory conflation of the cheapness and availability of modern, mass-produced objects and texts with sweeping value judgments about their necessarily inauthentic and unethical status. The search for the ideal, eagerly endorsed by critics when expressed in difficult works of modern high art or organic forms of preindustrial folk culture, is redefined as nothing more than falseness, self-deception, and banal escapism when manifested in popular, mass-produced texts. Such summary evaluations seem highly dubious in their sweeping and unreflecting universalization of the norms of a sociologically specific taste culture. The aesthetic inadequacy that is identified as an integral feature of kitsch surely needs to be linked to the critic's own training in particular techniques of cultural discrimination rather than being designated a self-evident feature of the object itself.[11]

The category of kitsch is, in other words, too heavily laden with pejorative connotations to serve a useful function in coming to grips with women's popular fiction. I have opted instead for an alternative formulation—that of the popular sublime—as a means of addressing some of the same questions in a less predetermined fashion. By using this term, I aim to highlight the significance of the aspiration to the transcendent, exalted, and ineffable as a central impetus of modern mass culture. Of course, the category of the sublime brings with it its own specific chain of associations, so that my use of the term in the present context may appear doubly perverse. First of all, the sublime has notoriously been seen as a masculine form (in contrast to the feminine domain of the beautiful); furthermore, in our own time the sublime is typically identified with the avant-garde critique of representation rather than with conventional mass-market forms. Jean-François Lyotard's positioning of the sublime at the heart of his aesthetics and politics is symptomatic of the contemporary fascination with the sublime as an index of the unrepresentable, as that which exists beyond prevailing discourses, conventions, and systems of meaning.[12] Thus by relocating the term in the context of a study of women's popular fiction, I do violence to its prevailing meanings in two ways.

Nevertheless, such a relocation is by no means as arbitrary as it may appear, in that the history of the sublime reveals a number of connections to a feminine sensibility that have been obscured by the canonical pre-eminence of the writings of Burke and Kant. The identification of the sublime with fear and terror, for example, characterizes only one part of its varied history; at other moments it has been associated with a more general emotionalism, rapture, and loss of self that have historically been gendered feminine rather than masculine. This is not necessarily to concur with Patricia Yaeger's plea for an autonomous female sublime, but merely to note that literary representations of the aspiration to infinitude, transcendence, and boundlessness assume a much wider variety of forms than has usually been acknowledged in the critical literature.[13] Such motifs may occur, for example, within traditionally feminine genres of romance and melodrama in their depiction of an insignificant self dwarfed by the vastness of excessive, violent, and turbulent emotion. Indeed, Ann Cvetkovich suggests that the sublime may in fact be nothing more than the culturally prestigious version of a structuring of affect that can also be found within the feminized and devalued forms of melodrama, sentimental writing, and sensationalist fiction.[14]

Furthermore, the usual critical containment of the sublime within a high culture tradition stretching from Romantic poetry to the twentieth-century avant-garde has served to obscure the centrality of sublime imagery and vocabulary in many of the texts of modern mass culture. Such popular genres as the Western and science fiction, for example, rely heavily upon the archetypal sublimity of the solitary subject confronted with the enigmatic boundlessness of nature, while in forms such as the popular romance transcendent yearnings are more frequently expressed in the vocabulary of ecstatic passion and oceanic surrender. By deploying the notion of the popular sublime, then, I seek to address this paradoxical and perhaps oxymoronic relationship between the ineffable and its popular modes of representation. As Celeste Olalquiaga writes in her discussion of religious kitsch, such forms seek to familiarize the ungraspable, to materialize the transcendent, thereby setting up a field of tension between the otherworldiness they invoke and its depiction through familar and established conventions.[15]

My use of the term "sublime" is thus intended to include all those representations which contain some form of "aspiration of the human mind towards the infinite,"[16] which invoke a sense of rapture, transport, or self-transcendence that is linked to a perception of the ineffable and otherworldly. In the context of Corelli's fiction, this effect is achieved through the combination of a formal register of melodramatic intensity with a thematic focus on the transcendence of quotidian reality and the material world. The pervasiveness of such idealist and utopian motifs in popular fiction further undermines the narrative of modernity as growing disenchantment by drawing attention to the ineluctable power of escapist fantasy and a longing for the ideal. A romantic yearning for the ineffable, rather than exemplifying a conservative and anachronistic throwback to an earlier epoch, as writers on kitsch often imply, emerges as a key element of the modern and a central aspect of mass culture's interpellation of femininity.

Furthermore, the politics of escapist forms is more complex than many critics have allowed, in that their negation of the everyday may hold a powerful appeal for disenfranchised groups. Naomi Schor suggests that idealism may offer a meaningful representational mode to those who do not enjoy the privileges of subjecthood in reality, and who thus refuse to reproduce mimetically an existing social order.[17] Such a claim is potentially relevant in understanding Corelli's ornate visions of the remote past, the exotic Orient, and mysterious spirit worlds. This is not to imply that her fiction is to be read as resistive or oppositional in any straightforward way; on the contrary, I hope to indicate some of the problems underlying any such automatic equation of the popular with the transgressive. Nevertheless, in seeking to make sense of her phenomenal success, it becomes necessary to disinvest such terms as "sentimental," "romantic," and "escapist" of their pejorative connotations in order to attempt a more nuanced investigation of their significance and function.

Melodrama and Modernity

The critical terminologies of both realistic and modernist aesthetics are patently inadequate in coming to grips with the distinctive features of Corelli's fiction. Her writing is concerned neither with mimetic fidelity and accuracy of representation nor with ironic techniques of self-reflexivity and play. Indeed, Corelli explicitly defined her own work in opposition to writers such as Zola and the naturalist school, whose work she regarded as both cause and symptom of a wide-ranging moral malaise afflicting contemporary society. Against the materialism and scientism of such writers, she pitted her own idealism: the purpose of literature is not to show things as they are, but as they should be, to express "beautiful thoughts in beautiful language." Her aesthetic is simultaneously sentimental, moral, and didactic, seeking to capture emotional intensities and spiritual essences rather than to record the contingent details of contemporary social life.

Peter Brooks's discussion of melodrama provides a helpful framework for making sense of such a mode of literary representation. Having originated in the eighteenth century as a form of popular theater that combined music with verse, melodrama gradually came to encompass a range of dramatic and novelistic forms that were characterized by moral polarities, implausible plots, and rhetorical exaggeration. Melodrama is thus defined less by a distinctive narrative or thematic logic than by a mode of aesthetic presentation which can recur across a variety of different texts. Brooks defines the typical features of this mode as follows: "the indulgence of strong emotionalism; moral polarization and schematization; extreme states of being, situations, actions; overt villainy, persecution of the good, and final reward of virtue, inflated and extravagant expression; dark plottings, suspense, breathtaking peripety."[18] Melodrama's rhetoric, in other words, is one of extremes, of hyperbole, sensationalism, and exaggeration.

Such a description accurately characterizes the distinctive features of Corelli's textual world. Her novels are best described as moral fables, which organize textual meaning and events in order to demonstrate triumphantly the overarching presence of a guiding spiritual principle. The key focus is the dramatization of ethical and emotional conflict rather than the particularities of social relations; actions and character are invariably schematized according to an overarching Manichean dualism of good versus evil. The structure of a Corelli novel typically relies upon a chain of dramatic confrontations, rapid changes of fortune, implausible coincidences and exotic tableaux, concluding in a suspense-filled denouement. Figures are often allegorical and emblematic, embodying quintessential aspects of human nature rather than psychologically individuated characters. The body bespeaks the qualities of the soul, or in some cases cunningly conceals it; in either case the moral status of the characters is unambiguously announced to the reader. To this end, characters frequently proclaim aloud their own essence, like the society heroine of *The Sorrows of Satan:* "I am a contaminated creature, trained to perfection in the lax morals and prurient literature of my day."[19] As Brooks points out, such acts of definition are central to the melodramatic imagination, as characters explicitly voice their moral judgments of themselves, others, and the world. "They proffer to one another, and to us, a clear figuration of their souls, they name without embarrassment eternal verities. Nothing is *under*stood, all is *over*stated."[20]

Corelli's first major success, *The Sorrows of Satan,* is a powerful example of this form of aesthetic presentation. The novel is narrated by Geoffrey Tempest, an idealistic and impoverished writer who suddenly finds himself fabulously wealthy after inheriting a mysterious bequest. He simultaneously acquires the friendship of the charismatic and enigmatic Prince Rimanez, who undertakes to act as his guide to high society as Tempest launches himself into a new life of wealth and celebrity. It is made clear to the reader from the start that Rimanez is none other than Satan himself, hoping to corrupt Tempest's soul by exposing him to the materialism, cynicism, and hypocrisy of the English ruling classes. The hero's progress is framed in terms of a series of moral dualisms; choosing the path of indolence over work, of social success over integrity, of money over art, of sexuality over spirituality, he sinks ever more deeply into the mire of immorality. In a final surrealistic denouement on the open seas, Rimanez reveals his true identity to Tempest while accusing him of the chief crime of the age, "Sensual Egotism." Tempest's ultimate repentance ensures his redemption and the chance to begin life anew in more modest circumstances, but the novel itself concludes on an ironic and pessimistic note, with a description of Rimanez entering the Houses of Parliament arm in arm with a well-known politician.

Summarized in this manner, the didactic logic of the novel as a modern pilgrim's progress is obvious enough. Its social criticism is couched in the language of moral and spiritual absolutes; the ruling classes are attacked not because of their economic or political exploitation of others, but because they exemplify the worst extremes of sin and iniquity. Corelli's unremittingly negative polemic depicts high society as a form of hell on earth, a lurid emblem of modern decadence, lasciviousness, and corruption, peopled by villains and hypocrites. Yet one is also struck by the author's evident and intense fascination with the life of luxury that is under attack. Much of the text consists of extensive and detailed descriptions of the extravagant furnishings, expensive clothes, and lavish entertainments of the immoral rich, dwelling exhaustively on the very lifestyles it claims to condemn. Here, as elsewhere in Corelli's work, a professed belief in the ethical superiority of a frugal and modest life is combined with a distinct lack of interest in depicting it in novelistic form.

In this context, Corelli's fiction offers a significant departure from the prevailing tradition of domestic melodrama that is often seen as the quintessentially nineteenth-century feminine genre, foreshadowing the centrality of glamorous locales and conspicuous consumption to much of twentieth-century popular culture. Whereas the domestic novel typically focused on the minutiae of everyday life in the private sphere, preaching the values of feminine modesty and restraint, Corelli sets many of her novels in exotic and sumptuous locations. These texts typically reveal a symptomatic clash between a traditional petit bourgeois ethos of self-discipline, restraint, and "knowing one's place" and the new vistas of hedonism, wealth, and consumerism that were opening up in late Victorian England. As a self-made woman from a lower-middle-class background, her childhood painfully scarred by the stigma of illegitimacy, Corelli was uniquely placed to experience conflicting emotions of *ressentiment*, desire, and a painful sense of exclusion vis-à-vis the English upper classes. This is a theme taken up by all her biographers, who note her overpowering sense of social inferiority about

her own class position. The creation of "Marie Corelli" out of Minnie Mackay
was a key stratagem in her lifelong and largely unsuccessful attempts to
establish herself within English high society through the invention of a mys-
teriously exotic aristocratic heritage.[21]

This simultaneous longing for and hostility to the lifestyle of the English
upper classes forms a pervasive motif in Corelli's work. Brian Masters refers
to the centrality of envy in her novels, commenting that "all her books
vibrate with the pain of the underprivileged."[22] The comment is a perceptive
one, although marred by Master's own unfortunate antagonism toward his
subject. Here Carolyn Steedman's discussion of a "politics of envy" can
provide a more helpful way of coming to grips with the complex intersection
of class and gender politics in popular fantasy. Seeking to understand, rather
than condemn, her own working-class mother's yearning for glamorous
material objects—a house, a fashionable coat—Steedman reads such a
yearning as part of a more general "structure of feeling," a symbolic expression of the desire to transcend the limits of a constrained and impoverished
life. She writes, "by allowing this envy entry into political understanding, the
proper struggles of people in a state of dispossession to gain their inheritance
might be seen not as sordid and mindless greed for the things of the market
place, but attempts to alter a world that has produced in them states of
unfulfilled desire."[23] I have already explored the possibility that the pleasures
of consumerism may hold a particular allure for women, given that female
fantasies of self-transformation have historically been closely linked to the
charismatic power of the commodity. In the context of class relations, one
can further speculate that Corelli's novels served a complicated array of
psychological and social functions for their working-class and lower-middle-
class readers. On the one hand, by reading such novels they could indulge
vicariously in those sumptuous commodities, glamorous environments, and
aristocratic lifestyles which otherwise remained beyond their reach, partaking
in an imaginary experience of luxury and pleasure. On the other hand, the
framing of such depictions by a rhetoric of moral condemnation sanctioned
their own class position, allowing them to gain comfort from the affirmation
of their modest way of life as ethically superior to that of the idle and
immoral rich.

As realistic accounts of the social world, such fictions are obviously inadequate, but it is equally clear that their primary literary and ethical concerns
lie elsewhere. Peter Brooks suggests that melodrama needs to be seen as a
distinctively modern attempt to dramatize spiritual meaning in the absence
of an overarching notion of the sacred: "melodrama becomes the principal
mode for uncovering, demonstrating and making operative the essential

moral universe in a post-sacred era."[24] Refusing to accept that the world is drained of transcendence, melodrama relocates the spiritual at the level of the personal, endowing individual characters with auratic significance as representatives of moral absolutes. Through the heightened expressivism and emotionalism of melodrama, the particular is transfigured into the universal; the form constantly gestures toward an ineffable horizon of meaning in its struggle to transcend the limitations of the material world.

The language of melodrama bears witness to this yearning for metaphysical plenitude in its reliance on exaggeration, hyperbole, repetition. Brooks notes that the "desire to express all seems a fundamental characteristic of the melodramatic mode."[25] Such a desire is clearly evident in the works of Corelli, which strain to their utmost to express the inexpressible. Her primary technique is hyperbole, piling one adjective and metaphor onto another in the struggle to achieve an effect of grandiose sublimity. Exclamation marks, italics, dashes, and other typographical devices are regularly deployed to convey a sense of the insufficiency of words and to intensify the emotional effect communicated to the reader. Corelli's vocabulary is self-consciously archaic, aspiring to a biblical or epic quality, with exalted references to God, truth, love, and heaven investing the most minor descriptive or narrative detail with profound symbolic significance. Through such rhetorical effects Corelli seeks to convey the awe-inspiring presence of the absolute, even as the very excess of her rhetoric indicates that this presence is not as self-evident as she might wish.

It is this linguistic effusiveness, described by *The Times* as a "feminine redundancy of adjectives," which was frequently seized upon by journalists and critics as evidence of Corelli's lack of literary substance.[26] Her crime was that of writing too much, of unleashing a flood of excessive and unrestrained emotion onto the printed page. It is striking how often the same words recur in descriptions of the author and her work: hysterical, undisciplined, immature, emotionally unstable, illogical, adolescent, sentimental. Desmond MacCarthy commented in the *Sunday Times:* "whatever she wrote gushed unchecked and uncensored from the burning centre of her desires at the moment."[27] Similarly, her most recent biographer attributes to Corelli a process of quasi-instinctual and unconscious creativity:

It is a lush, verbose, diffuse style, wildly exaggerated, exuberant, exotic and colourful. Epithets tumble over each other without discrimination. The writer gives the impression of never having corrected a line, but on the contrary heaped elaboration upon an already crowded canvas. She does not pare, select, revise; her enthusiasm splurges forth like a burst dam. She is hysterical and is not afraid to scream. The maxim "nothing succeeds like excess" would suit her well. She writes in top gear all the way, as if her novels were intended to be printed in capital letters. She has no sense of proportion, no feeling of restraint.[28]

In such commentaries Corelli's fiction is framed as the uncontrolled and irrational outpourings of a hysterical female subject. Governed by the pleasure rather than the reality principle, her writing is the ultimate surrender to a regressive emotionality unchecked by considerations of reason or art.

Yet it is not just those hostile to melodrama who perceive it to bear an unmediated relationship to powerful unconscious emotions. Brooks, for example, claims that melodrama exemplifies a victory over repression and a rejection of censorship, as the forces of desire burst through the constraints of the reality principle. The excessive emotions articulated in melodrama he describes as almost overwhelming in their instinctual purity, evoking the grandiose emotional states associated with infantile narcissism.[29] Similar arguments can be encountered within the domain of film theory, where melodrama's preoccupation with intensities of feeling and stylistic excess has been linked to the domain of the maternal and pre-Oedipal as the expression of a repressed feminine voice that resists the regulatory restraints of realist narrative.[30] Yet to define popular forms such as melodrama as resistive in their liberation of previously repressed desires is to ignore the very shaping of such desires by the fantasmatic representations of mass culture. The refusal of realism can just as easily be allied to conservative ideological agendas and the inscription of normative ideals of femininity; within the domain of the sentimental and the melodramatic, as Suzanne Clarke points out, the transgressive may not be completely removed from the banal.[31]

Love and the Ideal

One of the defining features of Corelli's fiction is its overwhelming preoccupation with romantic love. Her novels can be described as hymns to the transcendental power of a grand passion that is seen as the prime mover and ultimate cause of historical and social processes. Rather than restricting feeling to the domain of the private, Corelli enlarges and elevates its scope to a world-historical significance. In an ironic reversal of male-defined hierarchies, the political and the public are transformed into epiphenomena of the personal and emotional, now redefined as the primary and sovereign dimensions of reality. Through the power of romantic love, individuals are raised to a spiritual plane of ineffable plenitude beyond the trivial constraints of human history.

One of Corelli's seemingly more political works, *Temporal Power* (1902), illustrates this theme very clearly. The novel is set in an imaginary country, its hero an ineffectual monarch whose troubled reign and apparent tolerance of corruption has engendered extensive political unrest. The text moves between descriptions of events at the court and the nearby town, where the members of a secret society are plotting to assassinate the king and bring down the government. At a crucial point in the plot, however, one of the leading agitators turns out to be the king himself in disguise, who has infiltrated the revolutionary movement in order to uncover the real views of the people and introduce social reforms. Discovering that their political enemy is their personal friend, the socialist revolutionaries are robbed of an opponent, and political antagonisms are effortlessly smoothed over through a serene affirmation of the underlying identity of royal and popular interests. "I have played two parts at once,—Revolutionist and King! But both parts are after all but two sides of the same nature."[32]

On its publication, Corelli's novel was read by some critics as a political allegory commenting on contemporary individuals and current events. Yet the sociopolitical stance of the novel—which could be described as monarchist and quasi-feudalist—is of secondary importance in a story crucially indebted to the standard devices of the melodramatic repertoire: improbable disguises, secret societies, faithful retainers, foundlings saved from the sea, and so on. In fact, the weight of much of the text lies on a variety of romantic subplots, including an unconsummated passion between the disguised king and Lotys, a mysterious and charismatic revolutionary and woman of the people. The ultimate theme of the novel is the superficiality and insignificance of political conflicts and temporal power compared with the overpowering force of love. While the social contradictions in the text are easily resolved, romantic love engenders passionate conflict and intense despair, culminating in grand tragedy with the death of both Lotys and the king. Thus the novel concludes by counterposing the insignificance of politics to the eternal verities of love and death. "The glory of Empire,—the splendour of Sovereignty,—the pride and panoply of Temporal Power! How infinitely trivial seemed all these compared with the mighty force of a resistless love!"[33]

This invocation of the sublime nature of romantic passion simultaneously reaffirms it as women's distinctive domain. Drawing on many of the conventional understandings of Victorian femininity, Corelli's fiction frequently contrasts men's base sexual desires with women's moral virtue and freedom from such lowly impulses of the flesh. Women's propensity for romance is thereby linked to their elevated spiritual status and their striving for the ideal; through the transfiguring power of selfless love they transcend the materiality within which men remain embedded. One of Corelli's novels makes this point explicitly:

> For, as a rule, men do not understand love. They understand desire, amounting sometimes to merciless covetousness for what they cannot get— this is a leading natural characteristic of the masculine nature—but Love— love that endures silently and faithfully through the stress of trouble and the passing of years—love which sacrifices everything to the beloved and never changes or falters—this is a divine passion which seldom or never sanctifies and inspires the life of a man. Women are not made of such base material; their love invariably springs first from the Ideal, not the Sensual, and if afterwards it develops into the sensual, it is through the rough and coarsening touch of man alone.[34]

This view of the radical incompatibility of masculine and feminine spheres is a recurring theme in Corelli's fiction; man and woman confront each other as alien beings, shaped by radically divergent and conflicting needs and desires. Rejecting any notion of the equality or identity of the sexes, her novels sanctify women's moral purity and passionlessness as an indication of their spiritual superiority to the male sex. They thereby enact a negotiation with dominant ideologies not unlike that which Janice Radway identifies in present-day popular romance fiction. The familiar binary oppositions of public versus private, sex versus love, remain essentially unchallenged, but within the constraints of this overarching structure, the devaluation of women is reversed in order to proclaim them and their interests triumphant.[35]

As in the present-day romance novel, however, it is only a certain kind of femininity that receives textual approbation. Those women who fail the test of sexual innocence and moral purity are vehemently condemned according to a dualistic schema which pits female virtue against vice. In *The Sorrows of Satan*, for example, the emblematic figures of two women serve to symbolize the moral choices facing the hero. On the one side is the glamorous Sibyl Elton, representing the decadence and corruption of high society; on the other, the innocent and unspoiled writer Mavis Clare: "the one sensual, the other spiritual,—the one base and vicious in desire, the other pure-souled and aspiring to noblest ends."[36] Such evaluative juxtapositions are common in Corelli's diatribes against the moral decline of English society. Much of her wrath is specifically directed to the figure of the sexually liberated and sophisticated New Woman, as diverse aspects of modern femininity, from smoking to low-cut gowns to the reading of French novels, are subjected to outraged condemnation. A new sexual liberalism is seen to have the paradoxical effect of desexualizing women; in entering the modern world, they surrender their special claims on moral authority by becoming like men. Corelli repeatedly insists by contrast that women can retain their special status and their nobler nature only by refusing to adopt such practices and by continuing to be as different from men as possible.[37]

This view of women's moral mission is linked to an overt antagonism toward many aspects of the feminist agenda; Corelli has often been classified as part of the late-nineteenth-century backlash against feminism. Like other prominent anti-suffragette campaigners, such as Mrs. Humphry Ward and Eliza Lynn Linton, she was convinced that women's primary power lay behind the scenes, in their ability to sway the minds and hearts of men.

> What does Accursed Eve want with a vote? If she is so unhappy, so ugly, so repulsive, so deformed in mind and manners as to have no influence at all on any creature of the male sex whatever, neither father, nor brother, nor uncle, nor cousin, nor lover, nor husband, nor friend—would the opinion of such an one be of any consequence, or her vote of any value? ... Speaking personally as a woman, I have no politics and want none. I only want the British Empire to be first and foremost in everything.[38]

In this polemical and openly contradictory statement, Corelli denies women any political identity except as defined through their familial or sexual connection to men. Her opposition to the suffragette movement relies upon a highly idealized evocation of women's influence within the domestic realm, invoking a mystified vision of feminine power prevailing behind the throne. In many of her essays, she stages a determined defense of the virtuous wife and mother against contemporary challenges to the stability of gender identity; Corelli could experience little kinship with the violent struggles of the suffragettes, whose behavior she saw as violating the sacred qualities and traditional powers of femininity. Indeed, her own public persona was very much that of a "womanly" woman, involving the performance of an often exaggerated masquerade of femininity.[39]

And yet, the representation of gender relations in Corelli's novels is more ambivalent than the above statements might indicate. Not only does her own fiction reveal a conspicuous lack of interest in depicting the idylls of home life, but her female characters frequently engage in passionate tirades against male power and the tyranny of marriage rather than placidly accepting their natural feminine role. In *Temporal Power*, for example, the queen exclaims, "All women's lives must be martyred to the laws made by men—or so it seems to me—I cannot expect to escape from the general doom apportioned to my sex ... I have never loved any man, because from my very childhood

I have hated and feared all men!"[40] Similar passages recur throughout
Corelli's novels, which contain numerous instances of forceful, angry, and
frustrated women railing against men's egoism and failure to recognize
women's abilities and achievements. Her novels reveal a profound emotional
ambivalence in their representation of gender relations, oscillating between
recurring expressions of anger, frustration, and resentment toward the male
sex and a yearning for oceanic dissolution of the self in an ecstatic merging
of souls.

In spite of Corelli's avowals of moral purity, moreover, her books were
banned by a number of libraries for their purported vulgarity and sensationalism. While avoiding any actual reference to sexual activity, her hyperbolic
descriptions of the intensities of romantic love were clearly far too suggestive
for some readers. Rather than being individuated figures, her characters are
textual ciphers compulsively driven by overwhelming yearnings and oceanic
passions. Their thoughts and feelings are etched on the body, expressed in the
form of elemental somatic sensations: limbs stiffen, blood freezes, lips
tremble, senses swoon. Ann Cvetkovich refers to the mid-century maternal
melodrama (East Lynne) as both producing and regulating feeling in its
distinction between the appropriate disciplined emotion of bourgeois femininity and a hysterical, excessively sentimental excess associated with the
aristocracy.[41] This distinction is much less clear in Corelli's fiction, where
both male and female characters are buffeted by waves of powerful and
uncontrollable emotion. The religious and moral framework of her novels
often serves not to modulate but rather to intensify this rhapsodic fervor, as
evidenced in the ecstatic and highly wrought tone of Corelli's novelistic
depiction of the death of Christ, Barabbas.

In this context Brian Masters makes an interesting reference to the "gen-
eralised voluptuousness" characterizing Corelli's depictions of women, as
opposed to her sketchy and perfunctory descriptions of men, commenting in
particular upon her "full-blown celebration of the female."[42] In fact, Corelli's
most intimate and lifelong relationship was with another woman, her live-in
companion and devoted friend, Bertha Vyver, a relationship either ignored
or trivialized by the various biographers who have presented her as an isolated and sexually frustrated spinster. This is not to imply that Corelli was a
lesbian at the level of self-identification; given her well-publicized attitudes
toward various sexual and moral issues of the day, it seems likely that she
would have rejected such a categorization with vehement indignation. Nevertheless, Corelli's detailed and intensely wrought descriptions of languid
tresses, shining orbs, and heaving bosoms acquire a more complex and
suggestive array of meanings when read against this background of intimate

female friendship, highlighting a pervasive and intense romanticization of femininity within her work. Corelli's frequent choice of a male hero and point of view in her novels may also be significant in this regard, in allowing her greater narrative license to explore the erotically thrilling dimensions of feminine beauty than would otherwise have been possible.

Unlike the standard plots of heterosexual romance, moreover, Corelli's novels often culminate in tragedy and death. The conciliatory fiction of a love that can overcome all obstacles is abjured in favor of a pessimistic and fatalistic vision of the sexes as separated by an eternal chasm of antagonism and misunderstanding. Her heroines are only rarely integrated into the sphere of domesticity and a reassuring idyll of motherhood and family; they remain aberrant, marginal, awkwardly positioned in relation to the social structures within which they find themselves. To point this out is not to uncover a proto-feminist message hidden within Corelli's texts, but merely to suggest that they articulate a persistent if inchoate dissatisfaction with the ideal of heterosexual romance that they simultaneously seek to invoke.

This simultaneous investment in and dissatisfaction with the ideology of romantic love is juxtaposed in Corelli's fiction to a pursuit of other paths to self-transcendence. I have already referred to her lavish descriptions of glamorous lifestyles and commodities as promising an imaginary escape from the mundane constraints of feminine domesticity. Other texts offer more openly fantastic representations of otherworldliness in their invocation of the religious and the exotic sublime. In the rest of this chapter, I will consider the significance of spiritualism and orientalism as two intertwining themes within the realm of late-nineteenth-century popular fiction. Paradoxically, what renders such novels distinctively modern is their characteristic antimodernism, their creation of irridescent and seductive dream-worlds free of the humdrum constraints of historical contingency. The "magical fictions" of romantic fantasy should be seen less as an abandonment of the secularized, disenchanted perspective of modernity than as another recurring dimension within the modern itself.[43] Within the restless and dissatisfied consciousness that seems so central to modern experience, redemption is always located *elsewhere.*

Out of This World

To the present-day reader, one of the most striking features of Corelli's fiction is its focus on supernatural and spiritual forces as a means to the transfiguration and transcendence of a debased social and material reality. Many of her novels are peopled by enigmatic emissaries from other worlds—

angels, spirit guides, and demons—whose presence acts as a dramatic reminder of the sacred mysteries lying behind the facade of empirically verifiable phenomena. The familiar vocabulary and symbolism of orthodox Christianity is fused with Eastern doctrines of reincarnation and soul migration as well as with the rhetoric of late-nineteenth-century science to create a distinctively modern cosmological vision. Such metaphysical imaginings were by no means unique to Corelli's work; rather, the late-nineteenth-century reaction to the limits of a positivist world-view expressed itself in a widespread fascination with the powers of the occult and a literary turn toward the supernatural and the fantastic.[44] The numerous letters that poured in from grateful readers testified to Corelli's success in fashioning a contemporary synthesis of scientific knowledge and religious mysticism that had mass appeal.

Peter Brooks notes that melodrama arises out of the irrevocable loss of the sacred, representing "both the urge towards resacrilization and the impossibility of conceiving sacrilization other than in personal terms,"[45] but his argument overlooks the recurring attempts throughout the nineteenth and twentieth centuries to counter this loss through the creation of new metaphysical systems. Sweeping descriptions of modernity as an epoch of all-pervasive secularization and disenchantment underestimate both the persistence of traditional forms of belief and the new spiritual and religious cosmologies which arose in response to the crisis of established religion. To equate modern consciousness with the atheistic or agonistic values of a minority of nineteenth-century intellectuals is to bypass the much more ambivalent attitudes of the majority of men and women, for whom spirituality remained an urgently contemporary issue rather than an outmoded concern. The impact and consequences of secularization were uneven and contradictory rather than uniform; thus, for many, an acceptance of the claims of modern science and reason could coexist—however uneasily—with an equally firm belief in supernatural forces and moral absolutes.[46]

The vogue for new forms of religious experience reached a peak in the various cults which flourished in both Europe and America in the latter half of the nineteenth century. Spiritualism was one of the most influential of these movements; its democratic insistence that anyone had the potential to commune with the spirit world appealed to a wide spectrum of individuals across different social classes. Theosophy, another well-known cult of the period, based itself on the study of mystic ancient texts and counted a number of prominent and charismatic women among its members.[47] What these and many other religious cults of the period shared in common was a rejection of a mechanistic and rationalistic world-view, accompanied by the conviction that established churches could not provide adequate answers to the contemporary crisis of faith. In their confident affirmation of a benevolent divine will and an overarching cosmic purpose, they were thus able to offer an alternative to encroaching post-Darwinian conceptions of a seemingly random universe drained of moral and spiritual meaning. Yet while rejecting many of the tenets of Western rationalism, the religious cults of the fin de siècle frequently appealed to the language of science to legitimate their own doctrines. Spiritualists, for example, drew extensively on materialist arguments to prove the ultimate reality of a spirit world, hoping thereby to reconcile modes of scientific knowledge with extant religious traditions.[48] The supernatural was thereby naturalized, as references to atoms, ectoplasm, electromagnetism, and various other forces and substances were used to substantiate the language of faith and revelation. Through such means, spiritualists and psychic researchers sought to demonstrate the modernity and up-to-dateness of their methods and concerns as part of the mainstream of contemporary thought.

Corelli explicitly distanced herself from the excesses of the spiritualist movement; yet her own writing is profoundly shaped by many of its assumptions. In the introduction to her first novel, *A Romance of Two Worlds*, for example, Corelli defines her project as bringing the "light of Science" to bear upon the New Testament in order to offer scientific proof of the existence of the Divine. The novel recounts the initiation of a young female concert pianist into the occult wisdom of a mysterious sage named Helobias, a descendant of the wise men of the East and founder of "an electric theory of Christianity." Corelli's heroine is not only cured of a debilitating illness, but ultimately finds herself able to leave her body and travel through the universe with the accompaniment of an ethereal spirit-guide. After visiting various worlds within the solar system, she is ultimately granted a glimpse of the center of the universe, the home of God. The discourse of religious mysticism and revelation is interspersed in the novel with the language of early science fiction: descriptions of ecstatic visions and mystic symbols are juxtaposed to rationalistic explanation of the physical operation of electric forces. In later novels such as *Ardath* and *The Soul of Lilith*, Corelli was to repeat this mixture of science, Christianity, and quasi-theosophical mysticism to wide and enthusiastic acclaim.

Such invocations of the spiritual world in Corelli's novels provide a dramatic contrast to the religious fiction that had served as staple reading matter for many working and middle-class women during the nineteenth century. Spirituality is no longer harnessed to the ritualistic performance of mundane duties and a fatalistic acceptance of women's limited sphere; rather, it offers a means of breaking open the walls of an imprisoning domesticity through the exploration of imaginary worlds. Corelli's fantastic representations of astral forms traveling freely through the universe offered images of feminine freedom and mobility, providing a radical alternative to the narrow fictional spaces within which female characters had often been confined. Her heroines experience exalted visions that transcend the limits of everyday consciousness; their ardent religiosity expresses itself in a loss of self that blends the ecstatic with the erotic. When coupled with a fierce polemic against institutionalized and hierarchical forms of Christianity, such descriptions of transfiguration and *jouissance* must have been appealing to women dissatisfied with the limited horizons of their own social world. In Corelli's fiction, women gain access to a traditionally masculine discourse of the religious sublime.

Women were in fact to play a central role in many religious cults of the period, acquiring a power and prominence that was denied them in the patriarchal structures of the traditional churches. Spiritualism in particular became a highly feminized movement; offering a form of religious experience free of male mediation, it provided an outlet for many women's dissatisfaction with established religions. In fact, the purported attributes of femininity—impressionability, sensitivity, passivity—were deemed the ideal qualities of a medium, whose success depended on her ability to surrender their identity and become the instrument of others. The alibi of the seance thus allowed women to transgress flagrantly prevailing gender norms; passivity and the renunciation of self, stereotypical attributes of the Victorian middle-class woman, became a means of tacitly acquiring authority and power. As a result, spiritualism bore a complicated relationship to issues of gender politics and "the woman question," with which it was often associated. Like feminism, spiritualism contained within its ranks a number of highly visible and often flamboyant women; celebrating female spiritual authority, it offered women possibilities for attention, opportunity, and status denied elsewhere. By gesturing toward a mysterious other world, spiritualism revealed the limitations of the present one; her trancelike state permitted the female medium to defy traditional constraints on female behavior and public speech by abrogating responsibility for her own actions and words. Yet this circumvention of gender norms rarely took the form of a direct attack on the status quo. On the contrary, spiritualism granted women a privileged status as mediums only in order to reaffirm the connection between femininity, passivity, and the renunciation of self. As a cultural arena riddled with social and sexual tensions, it thus both undermined and reinforced Victorian conceptions of womanhood.[49]

A similar ambivalence is evident in the representation of feminine religiosity in *A Romance of Two Worlds*. Corelli's novel draws on and reworks a recurring fantasy of an indestructible and immutable body able to transcend the limitations of earthly corporeality. Rejecting traditional associations of femininity and confinement, it depicts the heroine soaring into the upper reaches of the cosmos and traveling through an "unexplored wilderness of spheres," thereby invoking a limitless territory of ever-expanding spiritual horizons. Woman is explicitly identified with the quest for absolute knowledge and the search for the divine. There is a remarkable confidence—not to mention grandiosity—in Corelli's depiction of her heroine's insights into the mysteries of the universe and her own immortality.

> I gazed upon countless solar systems, that like wheels within wheels revolved with such rapidity that they seemed all one wheel. I saw planets whirl around and around with breathless swiftness, like glittering balls flung through the air ... a marvellous procession of indescribable wonders sweeping on for ever in circles, grand, huge and immeasurable. And as I watched the superb pageant, I was not startled or confused ... I could scarcely perceive the Earth from whence I had come—so tiny a speck was it—nothing but a mere pin's point in the burning whirl of immensities. I felt, however, perfectly conscious of a superior force in myself to all these enormous forces around me—I knew without needing any explanation that I was formed of an indestructible essence, and that were all these stars and systems suddenly to end in one fell burst of brilliant horror, I should still exist—I should know and remember and feel—should be able to watch the birth of a new Universe and take my part in its growth and design.[50]

On encountering this rapturous language of religious revelation, it is startling to realize that it is a young woman who is being granted such a God's-eye view of the meanings and workings of the universe. As the heroine herself acknowledges, "a plunge into the unseen world is surely a bold step for a woman."[51] Such an ecstatic apprehension of the sublimity of creation can be read as spirited defiance of traditional constraints on Victorian femininity, whose access to spiritual truth was usually depicted in a much more modest and deferential fashion. By depicting her heroine as a bold seeker after knowledge, Corelli aims to bestow grandeur and authority to women's spiritual quest. Yet such ecstatic visions of heightened religiosity also reveal a distaste for the imprisoning constraints of the flesh that is less easily reconciled with a proto-feminist impulse. The quest for religious knowledge is accompanied by a profound discomfort with the sensual and material body that reinscribes women's traditional connection with modesty, chastity, and sexual purity. In fact, in spite of its innovative themes, the novel ultimately reaffirms a vision of the demure and self-denying woman whose access to sacred knowledge is directed and controlled by the charismatic male teacher. The spiritual boldness of the heroine does not translate itself into any external challenge to the subordinate social positioning of women.

The Exotic Sublime

The appeal to Eastern philosophy, religion, and culture played a key role in the fin-de-siècle reaction to the values of Western materialism. While Victorian scientists were demonstrating the evolutionary inferiority of non-Western cultures, many religious cults of the period explicitly reversed this hierarchy of value, elevating the East to a position of spiritual superiority vis-à-vis a declining West. The writings of nineteenth-century anthropologists and linguists had helped to popularize the doctrines of Buddhism, Hinduism, and Islam, while archaeological discoveries sparked a profound and long-lasting fascination with Egyptian religion and culture. The attraction of such traditions was self-evident; they provided alternatives to Western systems of rationality and materialism that were already imbued with an aura of venerable wisdom and sacred authority. Imagined as an atemporal space of eternal truth, the Orient provided a source of authentic spirituality against which the progress-oriented and materialist impulses of the West could be judged and found wanting.[52]

In spite of their idealization of the East, however, the occult religions that sprang up in England shared with the rhetoric of imperialism a common reliance on metaphors of exploration, emigration, conquest, and colonization. The desire to escape the constraints of Western culture expressed itself in fantasies of exploring new, uncharted realms, whether actual or metaphysical; the spirit world was yet another territory to conquer, another enticing frontier. The metaphorical parallels between the spirit world and the Orient as twin zones of enigmatic otherness were, moreover, reaffirmed through a more immediate connection; the East was perceived as a realm where mystical unknown forces still held sway. Numerous novels and stories by H. Rider Haggard, Rudyard Kipling, and other writers of the period situated lurid descriptions of supernatural or paranormal events in the exotic outposts of Empire, as a liminal zone not yet fully bound by the laws of Enlightenment modernity.[53]

By and large, recent critical discussions have tended to equate the literature of imperialism with the adventure narrative describing the white man's journey into the exotic interior. In this paean to rugged white masculinity, the racial other is typically feminized as a dark continent to be penetrated and subjugated; ideologies of race and gender come together in the linking of woman and the primitive as twin symbols of atavistic and irrational forces. The pre-eminence of this adventure plot in both factual and fictional representations of non-Western cultures has caused some critics to consider the ideologies of colonialism and femininity as in some sense antithetical. In her illuminating discussion of nineteenth-century women travelers, for example, Sara Mills refers to the fundamental tensions and conflicts between discourses of imperialism and prevailing notions of English womanhood.[54] This contradiction is only in evidence, however, if such discourses are assumed to be coterminous with a quintessentially masculine narrative of sexual and colonial conquest. Yet there exists another equally influential cultural tradition of imagining non-Western cultures as exotic zones of spiritual plenitude and erotic transfiguration. Instead of affirming the hegemony of modern civilization over less developed territories, this latter motif privileges those very territories as a redemptive refuge from an overbearing modernity.[55] This kind of romantic exoticism connects more directly to dominant cultural fashionings of Western femininity and forms a pervasive, as yet hardly analyzed, trope within a wide range of nineteenth-century women's texts. If, as Patrick Brantlinger argues, "Africa, India, and the other dark places of the earth become a terrain upon which the political unconscious of imperialism maps its own desires, its own fantastic longitudes and latitudes,"[56] such fantasies of racial and cultural otherness are clearly gendered in significant ways. To analyze white women's entanglement in the project of colonialism is to address this question of the nature of *their* psychic investment in representations of the exotic.

A number of Corelli's texts are set in locations such as Egypt, India, and the biblical lands, providing an exemplary illustration of the operation of feminine orientalism in the domain of popular romance. The author's choice of such settings did not derive from first-hand experience, as in the writings of those nineteenth-century female explorers who sought to record faithfully the details of their adventurous encounters with alien cultures. On the contrary, Corelli frankly acknowledged her exotic settings as the product of fantasy, exclaiming, "on the magic carpet of the imagination one can go anywhere."[57] The mysterious East is transparently an imaginary landscape, a signifer of mysterious alterity which provides an alibi for the exploration of particular erotic scenarios. Thus in Corelli's novels a double stratagem is deployed; romance is exoticized at the same time as the exotic is rendered romantic. The Orient functions as a fantasmic realm for the enactment of highly charged libidinal dramas; positioned outside history and modernity, it allows for the expression of a pure and elemental masculinity and femininity that is no longer possible in the sterile and decadent West. Against sultry stage sets of palm trees, lagoons, and pyramids, men and women revert to a primitive condition, magnetically drawn together by extremities of passion and desire in an eternal pattern of domination and submission.

In Corelli's novel *Ziska*, first published in 1897, this deployment of the Orient as a signifier of the exotic and erotic sublime is clearly in evidence. Set in Cairo, where fashionable high society has fled to escape the European winter, the novel opens with a series of satirical references to the "blandly-smiling, white-helmeted, sun-spectacled perspiring horde of Cook's 'cheap trippers.'"[58] The banality of Western tourism is counterposed to the sublimity of the real Egypt, "the mystic land of the old Gods," where lie buried "profound enigmas of the supernatural—labyrinths of wonder, terror and mystery."[59] This theme of occult orientalism is pursued in the novel's description of the passion of a French painter, Armand Gervase, for the glamorous and enigmatic Russian princess Ziska. In spite of their European origins, both characters are described as looking like Arabs "of the purest caste and highest breeding."[60] This affinity is accentuated when Gervase and Ziska both appear in Egyptian costume for a fancy-dress ball, causing one of the other characters to exclaim in astonishment, "Born in Egypt; born *of* Egypt. Pure Eastern! There is nothing Western about you."[61]

Described by its publisher as a "supernatural thriller," *Ziska* combines elements of the heterosexual romance plot with melodramatic devices from the repertoire of popular Egyptology. Gervase's instant and inexplicable passion for Ziska brings him under her spell, engendering an intense struggle for power between them. Meanwhile, it is only Dr. Maxwell Dean, a visiting archaeologist, who realizes that Gervase is in fact the reincarnated spirit of an ancient Egyptian warrior, Araxes, drawn inexorably to the dancing girl Ziska, whom he loved, abandoned, and finally murdered in his previous life. The climax of the narrative takes place in the gold-laden sarcophagus room of an Egyptian pyramid, as Ziska confronts the man who once destroyed her and seeks to wreak her terrible revenge. Simultaneously, Gervase is dramatically awakened to his true identity and to the eternal laws governing human destiny: "he recognised himself as Araxes—always the same Soul passing through a myriad changes—and all the links of his past and present were suddenly welded together in one unbroken chain, stretching over thousands of years."[62] The novel ends with Cairo society gossiping over the mysterious disappearance of the two lovers, while a moldering corpse lies stretched out on the golden floor in the darkness of the Great Pyramid.

In this highly melodramatic narrative, the pretext of oriental occultism—of simultaneous geographical, temporal, and cultural displacement—allows Corelli a significant imaginative license in her character construction. The exotic Armand embodies an ideal of dominant male sexuality untrammeled by the restraining imperatives of morality or any chivalrous respect for femininity: "men were originally barbarians, and always looked upon women as toys or slaves; the barbaric taint is not out of us yet, I assure you—at any rate, it is not out of me. I am a pure savage."[63] The figure of the "noble Arab" thus comes to represent a charismatic, potent virility that is defined in opposition to the effeteness and passivity of the late-nineteenth-century European male. He offers the promise of a primitive yet perverse eroticism far removed from any regulatory notion of sex as marital and procreative duty. This figure of the masterful male whose intense sexual power is linked to his non-Western origins was to become a prominent feature of women's popular culture with the later success of *The Sheik* and numerous other "desert romances" of the 1920s. In such texts, the fictional scenario of masculine domination gains much of its power from the erotic frisson engendered by ethnic and racial difference and the cultural taboo against miscegenation. Within the carefully staged script of the masochistic fantasy, the stereotype of the oriental despot thus provides a textual alibi sanctioning the heroine's surrender to sexual pleasure without individual responsibility or moral guilt. For white women as for white men, it seems that the exotic is intimately linked to the erotic, as racial and cultural difference is woven into the very heart of sexual fantasy.[64]

In the figure of Ziska, furthermore, a demure ideal of English womanhood is replaced by the fin-de-siècle figure of the exotic-sadistic femme fatale. A symbol of seductive evil and passionate cruelty, Ziska bears obvious similarities to the heroine of Rider Haggard's *She,* published some years earlier. As an archetype of female monstrosity, she is associated both with the animalistic (tigress, spider, snake) and with the uncanny realm of death, burial, and the supernatural. I have already indicated some of the more problematic dimensions of this feminine icon, yet her pervasive presence in popular fiction indicates her potential appeal to female as well as male readers. As a cultural stereotype, the femme fatale may well have appeared more attractive to some women than alternative formulaic images of virtuous domestic womanhood or the "sexless" feminist virago; combining authority and vigor with intense sexual power, she imperiously expresses her disdain for the world and values of men.[65]

Corelli's novel thus draws on a long-standing Western tradition of representing the East as a space far removed from the constraints of social and sexual regulation, a domain of the monumental and exotic sublime. While this theme has received much attention from contemporary critics, their usual focus upon such figures as Flaubert and Baudelaire often makes it seem as if orientalism were the exclusive province of a small group of French bohemian artists and intellectuals. As Flaubert's own writings make clear, however, the myth of the Orient was a recurring and powerful presence in the popular imagination throughout the nineteenth century; the logics of imperialist expansion generated an inexhaustible supply of references to and representations of cultural otherness. The exotic sublime became an increasingly pervasive theme in a diversity of texts—advertising, popular fiction, early cinema—and formed a frequent centerpiece of the great commercial and trade exhibitions which proliferated in the latter half of the century, where the wandering visitor could easily stumble across an Arab tent, a Japanese farm, or an oriental bazaar.[66] The yearning to be "somewhere, out of this world," rather than characterizing the uniquely alienated consciousness of the marginal Romantic artist, emerges as a ubiquitous theme in the packaging of the Orient as an imaginary spectacle for the ordinary Western consumer. Exoticism was to become central not just to modernist art works but to many of the texts and genres of mass culture; the nostalgic representation of the enigmatic and primitive other became a central part of the shaping of modern cosmopolitan sensibility.

Ziska thus offers one interesting example of the feminization of the Orient in romantic fantasy; women's potential dissatisfaction with aspects of their everyday lives is both addressed and allayed through erotically charged representations of racial and cultural otherness. At the same time, however, this is a difference that is not really a difference. The "Egyptian" protagonists of the novel—Armand and Ziska—while marked by a certain veneer of glamorous exoticism, are effectively indistinguishable in their manner, behavior, and modes of speech from the characters of any other Corelli novel. While ostensibly deferring to the superior wisdom of the East, *Ziska* is ultimately peopled by white men and women in oriental drag. As in other popular texts, such as *The Sheik* and *Tarzan*, which toy with the reality of racial difference only to finally uncover the reassuringly European origins of the hero, the unfamiliar is invoked only to be rendered surprisingly familiar. Denied their own specificity and history, the diverse cultures of the non-Western world are reduced to emblems of an exotic, yet easily consumable "foreignness." Perhaps inevitably, the idealization of the East simply affirms the defining power of the imperializing gaze, as cultural otherness is reduced to its function as a corrective to Western ills and a mirror to the European self.[67] The exotic sublime promises women a temporary escape from the mundanity of the everyday; yet this very nostalgia for redemption from the limits of modernity reinscribes the hegemonic centrality of the European perspective that it simultaneously seeks to escape.

The Politics of the Popular

As cultural studies has distanced itself from the Left pessimism of the Frankfurt School in order to explore the resistive potential of popular forms, an enormously successful, yet critically disdained, writer such as Corelli has been redeemed as a topic for analysis. The immensity of her sales, the fact that her works were banned from libraries because of their vulgar sensationalism, and the misogynistic condescension with which she was treated by the literary establishment render her an ideal candidate for rediscovery. The negative associations adhering to such epithets as "vulgar," "sentimental," and "sensationalist" can thus be reversed in order to set into motion a counter-reading which affirms the subversive power of fantasy, pleasure, and carnivalesque excess. In such an account, the feminine and the popular blur together as twin markers of opposition to the overbearing logic of patriarchal prohibition, restraint, and law.

My interest in Corelli derives at least partly from the fact that her work effectively renders such a reading impossible; it cannot be easily recuperated into a critical apparatus which simply equates the popular with the radical. To make such a point is not to deny the debt which my own analysis owes to the above-mentioned paradigm shift. Traditionally, popular fiction has come under fire from both the Right and the Left; read by conservatives as an ominous sign of the lowering of cultural and moral standards, it has also been condemned by the Left for its reactionary inscription of dominant bourgeois ideologies. In the recent past, such accounts have given way to new critical methodologies which have explored the semiotic and intertextual complexities of popular texts in order to give a more nuanced account of their aesthetic and political significance. My discussion has clearly benefited from the less judgmental analyses and modes of apprehension made possible by such an altered perspective.

The rehabilitation of the popular text as an object worthy of analysis may, however, slide into a rhapsodic hymn to its subversive powers. Such a move reiterates many of the well-rehearsed problems within feminist theory, whereby an identity politics which identifies female gender as a guarantor of resistance insists on finding evidence of buried feminism within every text written by a woman. This kind of strategy can be detected in two influential studies of nineteenth-century women's popular fiction, by Nina Baym and Jane Tompkins, many of whose analytical insights I have found useful, but whose conclusions I do not ultimately share. Noting the marginal status accorded such fiction within the established American literary canon, Baym and Tompkins seek to reverse these negative judgments in order to reassert the importance of sentiment, melodrama, and sensationalism as key aspects of women's popular culture.[68] My disagreement here relates not to the careful acts of literary contextualization undertaken by these critics, but to the implicit assumption that such a contextualization thereby serves to render women's writing immune to critique. Although there may be some strategic value for feminists in affirming the value of such writing, its feminine or popular status does not act as a guarantor of either its authenticity or its transcendence of power relations.

Thus in the present case, the fact that Corelli was a woman who was treated with often appalling misogyny by a male-dominated literary establishment has clearly contributed to my interest in her work. Yet this interest cannot be extended to a reading of her texts as the literary expression of an oppositional feminine culture, a move which reinscribes the more dubious tenets of subculture theory in its appeal to a unified collectivity of resistive subjects. On the contrary, a contemporary perspective that is even slightly conscious of hierarchies of class and race as well as gender cannot help finding many aspects of nineteenth-century women's popular writing deeply problematic. Here I find myself in agreement with Ann Cvetkovich's questioning of the widespread assumption that the noncanonical text must be legitimated as subversive in order to be considered worthy of study.[69] In particular, the pervasive romanticization of popular texts as in some sense directly rooted in an affective and libidinal reality is in urgent need of reappraisal. If it is unsatisfactory to condemn mass culture because of its retrogressive aesthetic and emotional qualities, it is equally dubious, as Cvetkovich argues, simply to "reverse the relation between affective intensity and political value, seeing the emotions produced by mass culture as evidence of transgressive impulses, as the germ of desire for social transformation or as signs of dissatisfaction with oppressive social structures."[70]

Rather than either reproducing or heroically resisting a univocal dominant ideology, popular fiction can more usefully be read as comprising a variety of ideological strands that cohere to or contradict each other in diverse ways. My own analysis has sought to elaborate some of these conflicting ideologies, fantasies, and modes of literary representation which inhabit the popular as well as the elite text. In the case of Corelli, for example, a melodramatic rhetoric of excessive "feminine" sentimentality and hyperbolic emotion intermingles with a rigid sexual moralism and frequent expressions of disapproval of and hostility to women. A democratic defense of the ordinary person and the authority of popular taste coexists with an explicit snobbery, a petit bourgeois nostalgia for feudal authority and a bland denial of social inequalities; according to Corelli, it is only the lazy who remain poor. Passionate indictments of the hierarchical and elitist structures of institutions such as church and government are juxtaposed to fervent expressions of religious dogmatism, an explicit anti-Semitism, and a defense of the glory of Empire. Such interconnecting and conflicting ideological perspectives make it impossible to separate out an autonomous "women's culture," revealing how deeply women's texts are enmeshed within wide-ranging structures of race and class as well as gender inequality. Similarly, they unsettle any simple equation of the popular with the transgressive by revealing the constitution of popular fiction through a tangle of conservative and oppositional, naturalizing and critical discourses.

My own discussion has concentrated upon the ambiguous politics of the popular sublime. I have suggested that the utopian gesturing toward an ineffable otherness can be seen as a critical response to irresolvable tensions within the social; the pursuit of the ideal thereby partakes of a logic of displacement which distances authentic meaning from the realm of the quotidian in order to situate it in a remote and unattainable domain. Yet such escapist fantasies may also be imbued with nostalgic archetypes and conservative affirmations of the eternal verities of sexual and racial otherness which are less easily reconciled with any form of resistive impulse. In particular, the intellectual's fantasy of the essentially sensory, immediate, and "carnivalesque" qualities of the popular is significantly undermined by the success of a writer such as Corelli, whose works are saturated with appeals to moral, ethical, and spiritual absolutes. Rather than articulating an authentic corporeality that threatens the regulatory principles of class and gender hierarchy, her writing reveals a feminine and petit bourgeois adherence to morality and religion that was derided as quaintly old-fashioned by many male cultural legislators of the period.

Yet Corelli's fiction also suggests the limitations of a reading which seeks to anchor textual meaning too rigidly in a specific class or gender position. My own discussion has sought to establish some points of connection between Corelli's own social positioning and the ideological and aesthetic features of her work, connections which shaped not only the act of production but also that of reception. Thus critics constantly framed their discussion of Corelli's fiction around questions of class and gender; reviews often contained sneering references to the author and her readers, who were described as possessing the mentality of a milliner's apprentice, a nursemaid, a superior barmaid, a haberdasher's assistant, or a "poetically minded shop-

girl." Yet Corelli's readership, as I indicated earlier, was not in fact so neatly
stratified; it included men as well as women, and members of the middle and
upper classes as well as the working class. Affiliation with an increasingly
educated and professionalized literary intelligentsia, rather than socioeconomic status alone, seemed to be the crucial factor in determining whether
one abhorred Corelli rather than adored her. Part of her success—and here
she again foreshadows later developments in popular culture—lay in her
ability to create forms of fantasy that could cut across class and gender
barriers. Rather than constructing mimetic accounts of the social world
linked organically to a particular class or gender experience, she created
opulent dreams of transfiguration that could lock into the imaginative worlds
of individuals from diverse social groups.

In one of the few feminist references to Corelli that I have managed to
discover, Patricia Stubbs writes: "Marie Corelli was a popular and extremely
successful writer. Her crude simplifications of contemporary ideology very
largely account for this success, and a reading of her work, though it requires
stamina, does reveal dominant social and political assumptions in a particularly clear way."[71] One of my concerns has been to question this view of
popular fiction as simply a transparent vehicle for a pre-existent ideology as
well as an inverse reading of the popular as a necessarily resistive force.
Rather, I suggest, we need to take more seriously the distinctive and determining, rather than simply determined, nature of generic forms such as
romance and melodrama in shaping the culture of modernity. In its gesturing toward a displaced sphere of ineffable plenitude, the popular sublime
articulates a powerfully charged zone of fantasy and enchantment within the
modern itself. If its characteristic form is that of nostalgia, then it is a
homesickness, as Sainte-Beuve notes in his reading of *Madame Bovary,* for an
unknown country.[72]

6

Visions of the New:
Feminist Discourses of
Evolution and Revolution

Modernity, femininity, evolution ... were brought together in
suffrage argument to defend the natural and inevitable development of a new type of modern femininity ... To her critics the
modern woman was a symptom of the social decline she helped to
precipitate ... to her champions, she was not unwomanly, but
womanly in a new and developing way.

> Lisa Tickner, *The Spectacle of Women: Imagery of the*
> *Suffrage Campaign, 1907–1914*

Women's affinity with the temporal dynamics of the modern was to
vary significantly in the fin de siècle, shaped as much by their particular
ideological affiliations as their material and social circumstances. If some
sought refuge in a nostalgic traditionalism or exoticism, others were to seize
eagerly on the transformative promise embedded in the idea of modernity as
constant change. Thus first-wave feminism encouraged many women to
identify themselves as historical subjects and to present themselves as liberatory agents of the new. In this chapter, I aim to elaborate the apprehension
of temporality shaping the emergence of a politicized women's culture in
late-nineteenth-century England. How did feminists imagine the shape and
contours of historical time and their own positioning as women in relation
to large-scale social processes? What was the nature of their investment in
notions of evolutionary and revolutionary change? Through an analysis of
the narratives and philosophies of history underpinning early feminist discourse, I hope to uncover its particular inflections of the cultural "time-text"
of modernity and in turn to offer a reassessment of the gender politics of
historical thought.[1]

The culture of the fin de siècle was marked by the rhetoric of novelty, innovation, and futurity. The sense of an ending engendered by the perception of a century drawing to a close also brought with it the consciousness of a new beginning; motifs of degeneration and decadence were often juxtaposed to appeals to the future and invocations of a radiant new dawn. Such rhetorical genuflections to the transfigurative power of the new linked together a range of texts often driven by very different political agendas and contextual concerns. In countries such as Germany, France, and Scandinavia, the term "modern" became a rallying slogan of almost irresistible drawing power, while in England the idea of the new conveyed a similar sense of urgency and heightened expectancy, of being poised on an epochal threshold. The New Theatre, the New Art, the New Psychology, the New Politics, the New Fiction, the New Woman, the New Spirit; these and similar terms were regularly deployed to signal an exhilarating sense of liberation from the tyranny of the past, a leaving behind of outmoded and irrelevant values and traditions through the espousal of a radical modernity.[2]

In this imagining of the future, femininity played a central part. The changing economic, legal, and cultural status of women encouraged a sense among many that it was they, above all, who epitomized the changing nature of modern life and the spirit of the new. Numerous writers focused on the fashionable if controversial topic of the woman question as the seemingly stable ideological edifice of the Victorian marriage ideal began to crumble. The sound of the door slamming as Nora left her husband and children at the end of Ibsen's *A Doll's House* reverberated across national borders, exciting feverish speculation about the specter of feminism that was haunting Europe. In England, women were themselves heavily involved in the cultural production of narratives of women's emancipation; the last twenty years of the century saw an unprecedented upsurge of activity on the part of female novelists who self-consciously addressed the problems facing their sex. These were new novels about New Women, a term coined in 1894 which rapidly acquired popular currency as a label for the energetic and independent woman struggling against the constraints of Victorian norms of femininity. Numerous novels of the 1880s and 1890s, many of them by female writers, offered detailed and sexually candid depictions of women's unhappy experiences of marriage and their struggles to find alternative paths to fulfillment through work or higher education.[3]

Within the constraints of a predominantly realist format, however, most of these novels could offer only a pessimistic conclusion. Typically, the heroine's rebellion fails, her longing for emancipation frustrated by the social and sexual realities of her time. Other genres of writing such as the utopian novel and the political essay offered a more hospitable framework for inspiratory and programmatic writing, inviting the imaginative projection of alternative scenarios. Katherine Stern, for example, has uncovered the existence of a popular genre of suffragette fantasy in the late nineteenth century which offered wildly varying speculations about the nature of women's lives in a future post-feminist world.[4] Such forms were increasingly attractive to those interested in the modern less as an existing reality than as a promise whose benefits for women had yet to materialize, for whom the meaning of history lay less in its past than in its as yet unrealized future. Feminist discourse here acquired a performative and prophetic function, seeking to bring into exist- ence through its own writing that political community to which it aspired.

This proliferation of texts of female emancipation was itself closely related to the increasing political and cultural presence of the women's movement. Although feminism had gained a number of notable victories throughout the Victorian period, it was in the late nineteenth and early twentieth centuries that it came to impress itself inexorably on the public consciousness as a major and above all as a *modern* political movement, a significant force for social change. Rather than a unified and cohesive body, feminists comprised a fractured collectivity of groups and webs of affiliation marked by disagree- ment as much as by consensus. A central issue which united most of them was the struggle for the vote, even though many suffragettes possessed a far-reaching vision in which the acquisition of suffrage was seen as only one step in a radical transformation of Western culture. In these diverse contexts, the resonant associations of the modern and the new were to play a central part in the self-representation of the women's movement and the symbolic politics of suffragette activism. The feminists of the period explicitly espoused what can be described as a quintessentially modern time awareness; in cre- ating their vision of the present and the future, they affirmed a sense of history as chronological development and as embodying a linear, irreversible flow of time.[5] For many women, such an experience of historicity was a dramatically new and exhilarating phenomenon that announced a dawning public intimation of the significance of women as political agents, as subjects of, rather than simply subject to, history.

The most common metaphors in the history of modern thought for describing processes of social change are undoubtedly those of revolution and evolution. Revolution, which originally conveyed the sense of a repetitive circular movement (the revolution of Fortune's wheel) gradually came to describe a decisive moment of rupture with the status quo and the inaugu- ration of a new order. The French Revolution is often seen as the exemplary historical moment in which this modern meaning of the word as an irrevo- cable break with tradition became established. In its political sense, revolution denotes the sudden and violent overthrow of an existing regime, but it simultaneously encompasses a wider and more general meaning of any process of radical and fundamental change. In both these contexts, it is typically opposed to the temporality of evolution, as an organic process of development or growth. The ascendancy of evolution as a dominant paradigm in nineteenth-century European thought was often accompanied by a strenuous repudiation of the unnatural forces that advocated radical change, as the disturbing spectacle of uncontrolled and chaotic transformation was replaced by a vision of history as the systematic unfolding of an inherent pattern. The appeal to evolutionary forces thus assumed continuity and connection rather than rupture with the past, its political correlate being that of piecemeal reform rather than violent change.[6]

These two metaphors of evolution and revolution permeated the field of nineteenth-century cultural representations, molding prevailing attitudes toward the modern as both historical period and normative project. Many present-day feminist historians and social theorists, however, continue to view these terms with suspicion as enshrining a fundamentally male-centered lineage of political modernity. An extant body of research on the revolutionary personality, for example, relies heavily upon an Oedipal model of generational conflict to explain political insurrection as a revolt against the tyranny of the imaginary father, taking for granted the inherent masculinity of political radicalism. Feminist research has tended to support this view, albeit from a more critical perspective, in its analyses of the masculine inflection of revolutionary discourse. Thus in the specific case of the French Revolution, the iconography of republicanism and the accompanying rhetoric of liberty, equality, and fraternity are viewed as having both echoed and reinforced an exclusion of women from the political process.[7] Similarly, as my previous discussion of Simmel indicated, nineteenth-century models of evolution sought to relegate women to an atemporal zone outside the path of historical development. Lorna Duffin has argued in this context that evolutionary theory was deliberately deployed to render women "prisoners of progress," serving the interests of conservative and antifeminist ideologies intent on keeping women within the home. Christine Crosby also describes Victorian notions of evolutionary history as quintessentially patriarchal in their definition of women as the "unhistorical other of history," noting that historical meta-narratives of this kind are necessarily hierarchical and exclusionary because they do violence to heterogeneity and otherness.[8]

Yet the demystifying critique of modern logics of temporality does not in itself explain their centrality to feminist discourse. References to evolution and revolution saturated the texts of fin-de-siècle feminist thought. Why, then, did women employ such terms and to what end? How did *they* imagine the laws and rhythms of historical time? Here my concern is less with the ultimate accuracy of either evolution or revolution as a description of the material achievements of first-wave feminism than with the metaphorical power of such terms as differing but interrelated temporal modalities through which feminists sought to articulate a sense of their own historical identity. As Peter Osborne writes, "'modernity' has a reality as a form of cultural self-consciousness, a lived experience of historical time, which cannot be denied, however one-sided it might be as a category of historical understanding."[9] It is the significance of this lived experience of historical time, of the intersection between the feminist activities and struggles of the fin de siècle and the modern temporalization of history as expressed in the valorization of futurity and the new, that guides the following discussion.

The hostile commentary which the suffragette movement attracted during its period of activism is a telling index of the disturbance generated by women's attempts to place themselves on the stage of world history. In fashioning their own modern meta-narratives, feminists were both drawing on and responding to an extensive cultural repertoire of mythologies of progress and degeneration. On the one hand, they agreed with prophets of decadence that society was becoming feminized, but simultaneously transformed this symptom of decline into a sign of advancement to a higher condition; on the other hand, they borrowed from established narratives of progress while rendering woman rather than man the dynamic subject of history. As feminists appropriated traditionally male-centered notions of evolution, revolution, equality, liberty, and citizenship in their fight for emancipation, the meanings of these terms shifted and resonated differently.

At the same time, of course, words are never completely free-floating and malleable, insofar as they bring with them a sedimented tradition of ideological usage. Even as feminists sought to refashion notions of history and progress for their own ends, they were influenced by the heritage that such terms brought in their wake. Thus the primarily middle-class members of the women's movement frequently presented themselves as an intellectual and political vanguard at the forefront of history. Within this scenario, women of other races and classes were often depicted as primitive and backward, yet to be awakened to the light of feminist consciousness. The strategic value of metaphors of evolution and revolution in helping some women to express a growing sense of their agency, historical purpose, and political radicalism cannot be separated from this more problematic inheritance of exclusion. Some women, it seemed, were clearly more modern than others.

Feminist Symbolic Politics

In recent years, feminist historians have turned their attention to the many facets of the first-wave women's movement, charting the various stages of the suffrage campaign as well as investigating numerous other arenas—educational, legal, medical—in which women fought for change and reform. Taking to task a condescending and frequently misogynistic tradition of historical writing on female suffrage, these revisionist critics argue for a serious reconsideration of the wide-reaching implications of early feminist activism, defined not simply as a struggle for the vote, but as a far-reaching and determined attempt to "redefine and recreate, by political means, the sexual culture of Britain."[10]

Increasingly, theorists are combining political with cultural analysis to read feminism as a form of "symbolic politics," that is, as a struggle for social change whose analytical and theoretical claims were indissolubly linked with specific metaphors and figures of representation.[11] Here feminist criticism connects with the "new cultural history," which has drawn attention to the import of symbolic practices such as language, imagery, clothing, gesture, and ritual in the maintenance and transformation of social relations. As Lynn Hunt suggests in her study of the French Revolution, such practices may play an integral part in the formation of political consciousness; rather than simply expressing an already constituted sphere of "real politics" grounded in the economy or the state, they may themselves operate as instruments of transformation, ways of reconstituting the social and political world. Thus one of the chief accomplishments of the French Revolution, according to Hunt, was its institution of a dramatically new kind of political culture.[12] In a similar vein, feminists are beginning to explore the "semiotics and somatics of woman's suffrage," in Jane Marcus's suggestive phrase, to read the history of feminism as an intervention in the realm of textual as well as political representation. Lisa Tickner's *The Spectacle of Women* remains one of the most impressive recent examples of such an approach, interweaving historical scholarship with textual analysis in its meticulous analysis of the iconography, displays, and discourses of the suffrage campaign.[13]

In this chapter, I offer a reading of feminist discourse that is indebted to the work of Tickner and Martha Vicinus as well as to the more recent work of Janet Lyon.[14] Throughout the late nineteenth century, and above all during the high point of suffrage activity between 1906 and 1914, the women's movement generated a deluge of texts about the "Woman Question," the catchall phrase that embraced a multiplicity of debates about the social, political, and sexual status of women. These texts included such genres as pamphlets, speeches, manifestos, autobiographies, scientific tracts, suffragette novels, and plays and petitions, not to mention the panoply of visual images—banners, posters, postcards, processions—detailed by Tickner. It was a period when women moved toward the center of public life and when there was a growing exultation, excitement, and sense of power on the part of many female reformers and activists.[15] Antisuffrage campaigners countered with an equally vigorous, wide-ranging, and polemical set of responses intended to expose the futility and absurdity of feminist demands. In this war of words, the issue of suffrage became for both sides a powerful, highly charged symbol of the wider feminist challenge to established institutions and patterns of male-female relations.

Although nonfictional forms of feminist discourse have received less attention from textual analysts than the New Woman novels of the period, they offer a rich and fruitful field for investigation. First of all, these are public texts in the most literal sense of the word, explicitly addressing themselves to a broad audience which they seek to persuade of the rightness of the feminist cause. They thereby invoke a symbolic gesture not only forward, but *outward*, equating women's freedom with an increasing conquest of public opinion as well as public space. As Martha Vicinus argues, "the most revolutionary aspect of the suffragette movement was precisely its insistence upon a female presence—even leadership—in male arenas"; one of the key ways of achieving this presence was by appropriating modes of writing and speaking that had previously been denied to women.[16] In the same way as suffragettes sought to break down established spatial hierarchies through a mass occupation of traditionally male space by women's bodies, suffragette discourse defiantly infiltrated a normatively masculine domain of political rhetoric and argument. Feminism's alliance with a specific temporalization of history was closely linked to its commitment to claiming the public sphere as both a symbolic and a material space for women.

Furthermore, political tracts and speeches are often infused with abstractions and metaphorical formulations, thereby exposing metaphysical tenets that may remain implicit in other genres of writing. Thus the historical-philosophical assumptions embedded in first-wave feminist thought are revealed with exemplary clarity in much of this literature. Its aim is not merely analytic and diagnostic, but prophetic and exhortative; it appeals to an imaginary future seen as synonymous with the triumph of a feminine principle. This dimly envisioned moment stands guarantor for the hopes of the present, a radiant *telos* that served as inspiratory motif and redemptive promise when the feminist movement was encountering its many setbacks in the painstaking struggle for social reform. A future-oriented temporality thus provided an overt structural principle for much of feminist discourse.

My corpus of relevant texts includes *The Awakening of Women* and *Woman and Labour,* two book-length treatises by Frances Swiney and Olive Schreiner respectively, as well as articles published in *Votes for Women,* the flagship journal of the Women's Social and Political Union. These articles were often verbatim transcripts of speeches by prominent activists; actively interpellating a feminist audience, they rely heavily on classical oratorical strategies to convey the urgency and authenticity of their demands. By contrast, *The Awakening of Women* and *Woman and Labour* offer encyclopedic surveys of the female condition and of women's position in nature, history, and society that adopt quite different narratorial stances and stylistic techniques. Here the authors are at pains to convey the objective nature of their own arguments through frequent references to scientific findings and by voicing, and then patiently refuting, the objections of imaginary opponents.

As instances of overtly politicized writing, nevertheless, these differing genres of discourse reveal a shared reliance on common rhetorical devices. A characteristic technique is the repeated invocation of a unitary "we" around which the claims of the text are organized. This "we" becomes the grammatical subject of programmatic statements, exhortations, and demands, articulating a communal solidarity which grounds and legitimates the author's speaking position. The stance is one of moral and ethical critique, uncovering the radical insufficiency of the present in order to counterpose it to an alternative scenario of female triumph and empowerment. In this gesture of denunciation, feminist discourse often relies on hyperbolic claims about the condition of all women and men and on a Manichean vocabulary which contrasts the moral high-mindedness of the speaker and her comrades with the iniquity of the government and opponents of female suffrage. Such linguistic maneuvers arose almost inevitably out of the political exigencies of feminist campaigns and the need to forge a distinctive and purposeful counter-identity. Women's own acts of disobedience, resistance, and protest were legitimated by framing them in terms of an overarching moral teleology. Polemical oppositions of good versus evil, right versus wrong, and innocence versus corruption were harnessed as incantatory devices to sustain women through the extended experiences of mockery, harassment, and violence—and in some instances, imprisonment and force-feeding—that regularly faced many of those campaigning for the vote. More generally, language performed a vital role in the creation of collective subjectivities, welding together individuals whose relationship to communal action was by no means self-evident, but was often—as in the case of Olive Schreiner—a fraught and ambivalent one. In the act of enunciation, a communality of female interests was affirmed and, even if only temporarily, made real.

In one sense, then, the feminist discourse of the period was primarily strategic, subordinating the various dimensions of communication to an analytic, and often overtly propagandistic, function in the diagnosis of social inequity. Paradoxically, however, this instrumental use of language to achieve determinate political goals was itself complexly interwoven with a highly aestheticized, richly metaphorical, and emotionally charged mode of address that sought to create shared identities, rituals, and symbols of meaning. As Tickner has emphasized, an integral part of the politics of the suffragette movement was its development of an extensive and highly elaborated culture, which included pageants, marches, costumes, and a rich repertoire of visual imagery. Feminist identities were forged not simply through the making of analytical truth claims—though the force and the far-reaching effects of those claims should not be denied—but also through forms of display, spectacle, and ritual. The aestheticization of politics, often interpreted as synonymous with the ideology of fascism, was in fact an integral part of the creation of a feminist presence in public life and its critical challenge to the givenness of gender hierarchy.

The specific addressee and the thematic content of the various strands of feminist discourse could in turn vary significantly, depending upon the contingencies of the moment. Tickner writes:

> In order to mobilise public opinion—beyond that of a handful of radicals— suffragists had to persuade the working as well as the middle classes, men as well as women, the unions and the labour movement as well as Tories, Free Traders, Home Rulers, Anglicans and Non-Conformists (there being in the end no such homogeneous entity as "public opinion"), that women's suffrage was a good and desirable thing by which the family and the whole social fabric might be strengthened, not destroyed. It has somehow to be understood as a very serious question that could also be treated lightheartedly if that was the way to open people's minds, and as a very large question that was in some respects a small and unimportant one. The vote had to be seen as the key to sweeping and entirely beneficial kinds of social reform, and at the same time as the simple correction of a historical and anomalous injustice drawing no unwanted consequences in its wake . . . All this could be argued and was; and understandably, suffrage propagandists cut their cloth according to the context in which they found themselves.[17]

This diversification of feminist positions was not, however, always as harmonious as such a description suggests, but often bore witness to serious disagreements over rhetorical and political strategy. Appeals to the public interest and the good of humanity embellished many feminist texts that depicted the emancipation of women as an inevitable stage in the development toward a higher level of civilization. The "we" of such discourse sought to be inclusive rather than exclusive, to minimize rather than exacerbate gender difference. Yet the emergence of the militant suffragette movement signaled an impatient response to the perceived limitations of this evolutionist perspective, leading to the formation of a vanguardist stance that explicitly defined itself in opposition to the public at large. Through rallying cries of resistance and martyrdom, the militant suffragettes created an oppositional feminine subculture that saw itself enacting a radical rupture with the norms and values of the present. In reading for metaphors of evolution and revolution, then, one can map out some of the key parameters of feminist discourse and disentangle its differing, if interlocking, political, philosophical, and temporal directions.

The Future Is Female

In writing their respective works on the Woman Question, Olive Schreiner and Frances Swiney were contributing to a genre that had become a respectable and established part of the intellectual culture of nineteenth-century Europe. Encyclopedic treatises on the development of man had become commonplace in a period eager to taxonomize and narrativize the course of human history. Increasingly, the figure of woman was subjected to the same intellectual scrutiny; writers delved into the history and etiology of sex roles, hoping perhaps that their findings might help to illuminate the turbulent condition of contemporary gender politics. August Bebel's *Woman in the Past, Present, and Future,* Eleanor Marx and Edward Aveling's *The Woman Question,* Friedrich Engels's *The Origins of the Family,* Havelock Ellis's *Man and Woman,* and Patrick Geddes and J. Arthur Thomson's *The Evolution of Sex* are only a few examples of the many learned volumes that scrutinized and anatomized the condition of femininity from a variety of political and methodological perspectives.

Evolutionary theory crucially affected the shape of this genre of writing, encouraging a magisterial vision that swept through history in a stately and synoptic fashion. One of the most distinctive features of the nineteenth-century treatise was a formal scaffolding that anchored temporal flux in an organically unfolding narrative driven by an inexorable causality. In this climactic emplotment of history, an omniscient and often overt narrator acts as an authoritative hermeneut, providing intellectual and moral clarification of the hidden meanings of surface phenomena. This sense of a confident and all-inclusive mastery of the totality of phenomena is accentuated by the range and breadth of many Victorian treatises; written at a time when disciplinary boundaries were less rigidly demarcated than they are today, these texts encompass and extrapolate results across fields as diverse as biology, psychology, sociology, and anthropology. Biological principles, for example, offered an intepretative mechanism for understanding the logic of social change, while scientific categories were in turn infused with teleological and often religious dimensions. Thus Darwin's theory of natural selection, which might appear to indicate the random and purposeless nature of human activity, was frequently refashioned to convey a view of history as purposeful and goal-directed, offering a secularized version of a Christian redemption narrative.[18]

As part of the prevailing intellectual currency of the time, evolutionary theories were regularly invoked to justify the necessity of women's place within the domestic sphere. Writers drew on entropic models to argue that the progress of society required the retarded development of women, who needed to conserve their energy for their vital role as mothers of the race. Herbert Spencer, for example, found evidence of a "somewhat earlier arrest of individual evolution in women than in men; necessitated by the reservation of vital power to meet the cost of reproduction."[19] Feminists thus clearly posed a threat to future development by calling into question the natural destiny of woman; any challenge to the established division of the sexes would lead not to further progress but to the inevitable decline of the race. For society "as a whole" to develop, women had to stay as they were. In other words, male advancement required female stasis.[20]

It is against such a background that feminists' own use of evolutionary narratives needs to be situated; enacting a negotiation with the prevailing intellectual vocabulary of the time, they sought to demonstrate not only the desirability but also the inevitability of women's emancipation. Feminists used many of the same arguments as their opponents, albeit to different ends; women's emancipation, they claimed, would further the course of evolution, while their containment within the home could only exacerbate social decline. Thus the alignment of the modern woman with a narrative of progress was a deliberate attempt to refute contemporary views of suffragettes as dangerous and unnatural figures whose activities posed a threat to the social fabric. Feminists frequently resorted to eugenic theories to insist that women's presence in education, the workplace, and the public realm would lead not to the depletion of the race, as conservatives feared, but rather to a population of healthier and more vigorous bodies.[21]

The positioning of women at the heart of evolutionary theory was nevertheless a provocative act because it disrupted the traditionally masculine lineage of teleological history. Both Schreiner and Swiney argued that women *as women* had a central and world-historical role to play in the development of the race; the position of women was the standard against which the progress of civilization was to be measured. Their particular concretizations of this argument reveal the diverse strands of feminist evolutionism. Schreiner's perspective is fundamentally sociological, while Swiney's is biological; Schreiner assumes the essential similarity of the sexes, while Swiney predicates her polarized vision of sexual difference on the evolutionary superiority of the female. Beyond these variations in content, however, both *Woman and Labour* and *The Awakening of Women* are indebted to a common organicist and evolutionary paradigm that directs their mode of argumentation, emplotment, and address. Rather than an analytical tool to be adopted or cast off at will, this paradigm was so deeply embedded in common-sense attitudes of the period as to be almost invisible, shaping the discourses of critics as well as of supporters of the status quo.

Olive Schreiner's *Woman and Labour,* a fragment of a much longer work which had occupied her since the 1880s, was published in 1911 with a dedication to the well-known suffragette Constance Lytton. After the immediate success of *The Story of an African Farm* in 1885, Schreiner had become acquainted with many of the prominent social reformers and free-thinkers of the period, such as Havelock Ellis, Eleanor Marx, Karl Pearson, and Edward Carpenter. Within this climate of intense political and philosophical exchange, the relationship between sex and evolution was a recurring and passionately debated theme whose ramifications extended across both intellectual and personal domains. Schreiner's own work on the woman question was an attempt, she informed Ellis, to write a paper that was purely scientific in principle and that would use the theory of evolution to elucidate sex problems.[22] The final version of *Woman and Labour* is a combined treatise and manifesto, intertwining sources from biology, sociology, anthropology, and history with a passionate demand for women's rights encapsulated in the recurring phrase "we take all labour as our province."

Schreiner begins by using the discourse of science to criticize science's own rigid polarization of the sexes. She counters Geddes and Thompson's notorious antifeminist assertion that "what was decided amongst the prehistoric *Protozoa* can not be annulled by act of parliament" by pointing to the radical diversity of natural phenomena, arguing that "sex relationships may assume almost any form on earth as the conditions of life vary."[23] Nature, rather than providing a prescriptive guide to social conduct and gender roles, takes on an almost infinite multiplicity of forms. At the same time, however, there is for Schreiner a meaningful pattern underlying this diversity, and it is here that evolutionary theory provides the schema for grasping the hidden laws of human development.

The category of labor, as the supreme marker of humanizing activity and individual agency, provides the key to situating women in history. Schreiner shares the Marxian emphasis on the primacy of work and production, yet shows little interest in exploring questions of capitalist economics. For the middle-class woman who is the focus of her study, production is defined as the primary means to self-production; labor is interpreted as dignified and socially useful toil rather than being identified with alienation and exploitation. Women's emancipation is fundamentally linked to their movement into the workplace; only then will they be freed from their "sex parasitism," Schreiner's scathing term for the powerless and passive nature of the modern feminine condition. This parasitism is seen as an inevitable result of long-term patterns of social change, as industry and technology slowly take the place of traditional feminine skills. Modernization thus promotes female inequality and powerlessness through the gradual disappearance of women's work and the decreasing value and status allotted to reproductive labor.

The by now familiar dichotomy between production and consumption structures the argument of *Woman and Labour*, crystallized in its elevation of a work ethic of manful exertion over the decadent lassitude of sex parasitism. Schreiner's views on the pervasiveness of female enervation and debilitation owe much to prevailing fin-de-siècle images of cultural decline; like Zola, she depicts female sexuality through recurring metaphors of corruption, contagion, and disease. Thus the kept woman, whether wife, mistress, or prostitute, is described as "the human female parasite—the most deadly microbe which can make its appearance on the surface of any social organism."[24] This disturbing image of female contamination is contrasted with Schreiner's own vision of the ideal woman as "active, virile and laborious." In its plea for female liberation, *Woman and Labour* reproduces a powerfully gendered cluster of metaphors which counterposes the laboring, healthy, and virile body to the insidious threat of passivity, femininity, and disease.

At the same time, Schreiner also describes history as enacting an inexorable movement toward ever greater equality and interdependence between modern men and women. Here feminism becomes symptomatic of a general world-historical trend, symbolizing a "great movement of the sexes toward each other, a movement towards common occupations, common interests, common ideals, and towards an emotional sympathy between the sexes more deeply founded and more indestructible than any the world has yet seen."[25] Like many other texts of the period, *Woman and Labour* thus interweaves differing and contradictory interpretations of the direction of history rather than inscribing a single and unambiguous meta-narrative. The motif of history as (feminine) decadence is juxtaposed to a competing narrative of progress which identifies the New Woman as an inspiratory symbol of modernity at the forefront of social change. Here Schreiner's optimistic vision presents feminism as a movement of world-historical significance sweeping across humanity that will lead to the creation of a new and better world.[26] The modern woman epitomizes a new spirit, refusing the dead weight of the past and the tyranny of the present in a quest for a more liberating and emancipated future. Thus Schreiner's text ends with the following words: "it is because so wide and gracious to us are the possibilities of the future; so impossible is a return to the past, so deadly is a passive acquiescence in the present, that to-day we are found everywhere raising our strange new cry—'Labour and the training that fits us for labour!'"[27]

On first reading Schreiner's text, one is struck by the frequency of its references to the modern and the new. From its opening pages, which address themselves to the readers of as yet unborn generations, it gestures boldly and restlessly outward toward a dimly envisioned and distant future. Unlike *The Story of an African Farm,* which is described by Elaine Showalter as depressing and claustrophobic in its narrow conception of women's potential,[28] *Woman and Labour* opens on up an expansive horizon of future possibilities, offering a programmatic and inspiratory account of women's developmental path. This effect is intensified by a visionary and messianic tone which overshadows the scientific pretensions of the text. Schreiner's style is repetitive, stylized, and incantatory, its stately rhythms and use of rhetorical questions, exhortation, and apostrophe endowing the text with a religious and prophetic quality. This straining toward the elemental authority of biblical or epic writing is accentuated by the recurring allegories and parables through which, Schreiner notes in her introduction, she sought to express the emotional dimensions of abstract thought.

Within such a context, the author's recourse to the imagery of the promised land is not unexpected. Schreiner repeatedly employs biblical metaphors to evoke a utopian future, a new paradise to which women of the present will lead future generations. The myth of the Garden of Eden is reconfigured as a future possibility rather than a past moment, as Schreiner sows her text with dreamlike images encapsulating a transcendent future of awakening into enlightenment and transfiguration.

The ancient Chaldean seer had a vision of a Garden of Eden which lay in a remote past. It was dreamed that man and woman once lived in joy and fellowship, till woman ate of the tree of knowledge and gave to man to eat; and that both were driven forth to wander, to toil in bitterness; because they had eaten of the fruit.

We also have our dream of a Garden: but it lies in a distant future. We dream that woman shall eat of the tree of knowledge together with man, and that side by side and hand close to hand, through ages of much toil and labour, they shall together raise about them an Eden nobler that any the Chaldean dreamed of; an Eden created by their own labour and made beautiful by their own fellowship.[29]

In this allegorical vision, labor is no longer the punishment that accompanies expulsion from paradise but the precondition for the creation of a new Eden. It is through the redeeming power of labor that women will enter modernity and shape its future directions, as Schreiner's text transposes the imaginary plenitude of the past into an authentic and liberated future of equality between the sexes that guarantees the ultimate meaning of history.

Like *Woman and Labour,* Frances Swiney's *The Awakening of Women* was much cited within the suffragette movement. First published in 1899, it was hailed by sympathetic reviewers as a "trumpet-call to all women," "the book of the age on the woman question," and as the "most rational, the most philosophical and the most earnest plea presented to the public, especially by a woman on behalf of her own sex, during the last quarter of a century."[30] Swiney was a prominent feminist lecturer and activist, the author of a number of influential books on sexuality, and a well-known theosophist and spiritualist. In *The Awakening of Women* she interweaves the vocabulary of Christianity and spiritualism with references to "research in biology, embryology, psychology and sociology" to put forward an extended case for the evolutionary superiority of woman. Drawing extensively on the work of such contemporaries as Havelock Ellis, Cesare Lombroso, August Bebel, Max Nordau, and Thompson and Geddes, she simultaneously reformulates or reverses many of their conclusions. In Swiney's radically dimorphous universe it is women who are revealed as the advanced sex, who bear on their bodies the unmistakable natural signs of the law of evolutionary progress.

Thus while Schreiner stresses the similar interests of men and women in all areas apart from reproduction, Frances Swiney depicts a world in which individuals are saturated by the difference of their biological sex. Nature, rather than history, is her primary reference point, and nature is read in this context as emphatically contradicting "the fallacy that woman is the inferior being."[31] Rather, Swiney argues, recent developments in embryology and biology have conclusively shown that man is in fact an undeveloped woman and that the male element was originally "an execrescence, a superfluity, a waste product of Nature."[32] Various forms of medical and biological evidence are adduced to support her point that woman is a higher organism than man; these include her greater hardiness and efficiency, her more developed sensory capacity, the superior adaptability of her organs, and her decreased susceptibility to insanity and atavism. Science, rather than being the enemy of feminism, becomes a central means of enlightening the modern woman as to the innate superiority of her sex.

Moving from the physiological to the cultural plane, Swiney tackles entrenched assumptions about the relative importance of sex roles in socialization, language, and the civilizing process. Delving into the remote past, she argues that women have historically been the inventors, disseminators, and conservers of language and the primary bearers of culture. "All the social and industrial development upon which modern civilisation rests is owing, to a great extent, to the inventive genius and crude expedients of primitive woman."[33] In a bold disavowal of the equation of civilization with masculinity, Swiney insists that it is women who possess a greater linguistic facility and a more refined aesthetic sensibility. While conceding that within a patriarchal world structure the artistic genius has almost invariably been male, she claims that it is nevertheless women who have borne the main responsibility for transmitting culture from one generation to the next. Furthermore, it is they who have always been to the fore in ethical progress, providing moral guidelines of idealism and altruism which have exercised a moderating force on man's more egotistic and intemperate nature.

Extrapolating from the past to the future, Swiney prophesies the gradual dawn of the women's era as an inevitable consequence of the underlying cosmic imperative for ever higher development. Her recasting of Darwinism in the vocabulary of spirituality and social purity campaigns results in the assertion that the evolutionary process is one of increasing victory over animal nature and instinctual desires. Women's spiritual proclivities render them natural leaders in all such future development, while men remain for the most part anchored in their material bodies and constrained by their primitive sexual impulses. Against the conventional identification of progress with masculinity, Swiney deftly maintains that modernization is synonymous with the feminization of the race and the increasing sovereignty of the female principle. Citing Havelock Ellis's claim that industrialization is feminizing men by rendering their physical strength obsolete, Swiney confidently concludes that "the matriarchal rule will be re-established, not on the crude and primitive lines of the pre-historic races, but in accordance with the unconscious evolution, physical, mental and spiritual, of mankind in general, which tends more and more towards the development of those virtues and characteristics that are essentially womanly."[34]

While efficiency and adaptability cause women to take a leading role in the advancement of society, men flounder helplessly in the mire of tradition, anachronistic figures whose characteristics and values are threatened with extinction. "Let not men assume the ridiculous attitude of so many Dames Partington, and strive vainly to keep back the incoming tide with worn-out brooms, composed of obsolete and discredited prejudices and barbarisms."[35] For Swiney, then, the future is indisputably female, whereas the dead weight of the past is embodied by men, clinging to increasingly outmoded virile values. Indeed, as they are gradually liberated from their sex obsessions, men will eventually become more and more like women. Femininity is portrayed as both the alpha and omega of the human condition, the universal standard against which the progress of civilization is to be measured. Just as organic life originates with the single mother cell, so the female element will again finally predominate, assuming its rightful and sovereign place in a future society.

Woman and Labour and *The Awakening of Women,* like other feminist texts of the period, thus firmly recenter modernity on the category of woman, creating alternative histories which openly contest evolutionary doxa and male-driven teleologies. Schreiner and Swiney's largely unquestioning acceptance of the givenness of racial hierarchy, however, constitutes the tacit background for their championing of a femininity that turns out to be exclusively white. The assumed inevitability of such a ranking of cultures reveals the pervasive influence of colonialist and eugenicist ideologies on even the more progressive perspectives of the period. Schreiner, for example, was actively involved through much of her life in anticolonialist struggles in South Africa and was personally committed to a campaign for multiracial suffrage.[36] Yet, as Nancy Stepan has shown, the model of an ascending ladder of racial types was so central to the period's cultural imaginings of non-Western societies as to be virtually ineradicable. Whether condemned as the embodiment of dark and destructive irrationality or idealized as a noble and innocent savage, the racial other occupied the bottom rung of the evolutionary ladder, represented a primitive closeness to origins that Western humanity no longer possessed.[37]

At the beginning of *Woman and Labour,* Schreiner sketches a portrait of the native Kaffir woman, whose fatalistic acceptance of her lot is contrasted to the European woman's expressions of dissent and protest. In Schreiner's historical account, the African indigene is placed outside history, a majestic symbol of timelessness and native suffering from which the white woman can distinguish her own commitment to modernity and progress. This ideology of primitivism is echoed in *The Story of an African Farm,* where the native Africans remain nameless, silent, and anonymous, identified only by the fact of their race or tribe, placed on a continuum with an exotic and alien landscape into which they imperceptibly merge. Schreiner goes on to ground her plea for female emancipation by explicitly distinguishing between sexual and racial hierarchy: the one, she implies, is natural and inescapable, while the other is not. Men and women evolve simultaneously and interdependently as two halves of one species, whereas there remains a vast gulf between "races and classes which are in totally different stages of evolution."[38] In other words, Schreiner's argument for sexual equality relies on the assumed necessity and inevitability of racial inequality, which guarantees the lack of intimate connection and understanding between different cultures and peoples.

The racial ideologies underpinning first-wave feminism are more immediately apparent in *The Awakening of Women,* which includes a survey by Swiney of the condition of women around the world. Unsurprisingly, geopolitical location is mapped directly onto a historical narrative of development to interpret African and Asian cultures as exemplifing the West's own forgotten past. The benighted condition of women in countries such as Turkey is contrasted with their situation in Europe and above all in the United States, the country which epitomizes the culminating point of women's striving toward unfettered development. Anglo-Saxon women, Swiney notes in a typical hyperbolic flourish, "have been the pioneers bearing the banner of progress into the Land of Promise; the advance guard opening out the way for weaker sisters to follow in their steps; they have been the initiators of all the principal women's movements; and to them the mothers and daughters of other nations have ever looked, and not in vain, for sympathy, encouragement and guidance."[39]

On encountering such rhetoric, it is tempting to interpret Western feminism as nothing more than another arm of the imperialist enterprise, defending the moral imperative of the civilizing mission. Yet Swiney's text also reveals a certain inchoate aspiration to female connection and coalition across nations and cultures alongside its largely unquestioned assumption of Western superiority. Her survey of the condition of women in countries outside Europe and America, however problematic from a present-day perspective, served at least to widen the horizon of her European readers by insisting upon the global dimensions of gender politics. Noting the recurrence of the unequal division of labor which transforms women into little more than beasts of burden across a variety of cultural contexts, Swiney pays tribute to their creative and aesthetic skills and their significant contribution to tribal and indigenous cultures. Moreover, her discussion of countries such as India, China, Turkey, and Persia, while often unabashedly orientalist in tone, acknowledges the existence of autonomous women's resistance movements rather than simply reproducing an established stereotype of Eastern feminine passivity.

The recurrence of eugenic and often overtly racist arguments in other parts of *The Awakening of Women* cannot, however, be granted the same degree of latitude. Swiney cites as evidence for the superiority of white women their distaste for sexual intercourse with the "lower races," invoking the specter of miscegenation to reinforce the view of white women as guardians of civilization and moral purity. Warnings of the dangers of half-castes and tainted blood form the basis of a plea for controlled racial hygiene and a condemnation of the Aryan male for his lack of self-restraint and willingness to have sexual relations with the "lowest females" of the most "degraded races."[40] Here non-Caucasian women are represented not simply as a backward group that needs to be awakened from slumber to political self-consciousness by the agency of others, but as a dangerous source of pollution and a threat to European racial stock. Vron Ware has recently commented on the historical use of an image of vulnerable white femininity to justify racist and imperialist politics in both America and Europe. This tradition is tacitly invoked in Swiney's text, which affirms the purity of the white woman through a contrast with a generalized and murky notion of female racial otherness. The body of the black woman was to become a cipher of pathological sexuality in the late nineteenth century, a perception encouraged by medical and biological discourses that decoded this body to reveal unmistakable indices of uncontrollable and deviant sexual desire.[41] Any notion of a common political identity or set of interests arising out of shared oppression as women disappears here behind the sexualization and pathologization of racial categories that permeated the culture of the fin de siècle.

Writing Revolution

In *The Awakening of Women* Swiney expresses her revulsion at the violent and bloody horrors of revolutionary politics. The French Revolution and the Paris Commune epitomize an era of "human vice, cruelty and blood guiltiness," in which, she concedes, women played a significant part. Nevertheless, Swiney insists, women are naturally more inclined toward an evolutionary path of progressive social change which shuns radical instability and cataclysmic transformation. By contrast, "man's ways are mostly revolutionary, instead of evolutionary, and therefrom arise the wars, discords and inequalities in the world."[42] *The Awakening of Women* frames its account of historical modalities in explicitly gendered terms: revolution is simultaneously stigmatized and depicted as masculine, whereas evolution is essentially feminine in form and homologous with the distinctive rhythms of the female psyche.

Other feminists of the period did not agree. The relative merits of evolutionary and revolutionary strategy constituted a question that exercised the minds of many of those involved in the suffragette movement and in particular the Women's Social and Political Union. Founded in 1903 by Emmeline and Christabel Pankhurst, the WSPU was to become a prime mover in the campaign for female suffrage, attracting extensive press coverage and inspiring thousands of previously apolitical women to join the cause. As well as engaging in numerous marches, meetings, and other public forums to present their case, the members of the WSPU gradually moved toward a wide-ranging and often spectacular campaign of militant activities. The spectrum of their actions ranged from disrupting politician's speeches to invading the Houses of Parliament, from chaining themselves to railings to engaging in the systematic destruction of property. They thereby helped to create some of the most powerful and highly charged images of modern femininity to circulate in the press and public consciousness. Representations of women struggling with police officers, breaking shop windows, and being force-fed in prison profoundly altered popular views of the relationship between women, politics, and violence.[43]

In this context of active civil disruption, the historical and temporal frame of feminist discourse urgently required refashioning. Militant feminist radicals were by no means opposed to the tenets of evolutionary theory, which appeared with some frequency in the pages of *Votes for Women*. Nevertheless, they were frustrated and impatient with a progress narrative which constantly deferred women's freedom to a far-distant future. Emmeline Pethick Lawrence, a leading figure of the WSPU and cofounder of *Votes for Women*, wrote in 1909: "It must be frankly recognised that the woman's movement today is a revolution. People do not like revolutions, but it must be remembered that it is those who check the process of *evolution* who are responsible for the *revolution*."[44] Here revolution is justified as the unavoidable response to an evolutionary narrative which has failed to fulfill its liberatory promise. Emmeline Pankurst also addressed this question in a speech delivered in New York in 1913. "You are saying, 'Woman Suffrage is sure to come; the emancipation of humanity is an evolutionary process, and how is it that some women, instead of trusting to that evolution, instead of educating the masses of people of their own country, instead of educating their own sex to prepare them for citizenship, how is it that these militant women are using violence and upsetting the business arrangements of the country in their undue impatience to attain their end?'"[45] Pankhurst answers her own rhetorical question with a vehement indictment of the immobility and conservatism of the English political system, which she contrasts to America's own proud revolutionary heritage. The need for women's revolt is justified by the need to break free of the shackles of the English past; "our revolution" is the only possible response to an illusory narrative of evolution.

This adoption of revolution as a guiding image of feminist activity brought with it not just connotations of violence, agitation, and extremity but a marked difference in temporal register. The idea of history as an organic continuation of an already existing process was replaced by the vocabulary of rupture, transformation, and discontinuity. Rather than gesturing hopefully toward a distant utopia, militant feminist discourse demanded the future *within* the present from a vanguardist standpoint that denounced the prison-house of the past and the tyranny of the present. The appeal to a revolutionary moment of rupture constituted a different conception of historical consciousness, in which radical newness became a marker of political value and guarantor of integrity. Here the polemical strategies of militant feminism overlapped with those of contemporary artistic avant-gardes such as Futurism and Vorticism, which sought a similarly violent negation of the old through the new, even though the relationship between these differing groups remained an uneasy and troubled one. A movement largely seen as "middle-class, middle-aged, reformist and feminine" began to appropriate metaphors of aggression, destruction, and violent transformation previously viewed as inimical to women, while also gaining much of its strength from the previous extended history of female public activism. It was in this sense, as Martha Vicinus notes, that the suffragettes constituted both a culmination of and a break with the Victorian women's movement.[46]

Like members of any radical organization, militant feminists sought to crystallize their distinctive identity through an inspiratory myth of origin. The narrative of long-term evolutionary change was replaced by an impassioned description of the founding moment of the revolutionary body, as a spontaneous process of self-creation almost *ex nihilo*. Emmeline Pethick Lawrence, for example, ascribes the genesis of modern feminism to Christabel Pankurst and Annie Kenney: "two women against the whole world—that was the beginning of this movement."[47] Emmeline Pankhurst recounts a similar founding myth of exemplary heroism that pits a few women against the

Goliath of the state: "we in Great Britain, on the eve of the General Election of 1905, a mere handful of us—why, you could almost count us on the fingers of both hands—set out on the wonderful adventure of forcing the strongest Government of modern times to give the women the vote."[48] Such statements conform to what Janet Lyon describes as a conventional motif of manifestoes and other forms of rhetorically charged political writing, the tendency to historicize a legendary point of crisis as the founding moment of a collective subject. As she notes, the construction of a "foreshortened, impassioned, and highly selective history chronicles the oppression leading to the present moment of rupture."[49] Previous constructions of the past are revised in order to center the struggles of the marginalized group, which creates its own etiology and history as part of its project of achieving collective recognition and cultural legitimation. In this unmaking and remaking of history, temporality is shaped according to a Manichean logic which reads past time as an inauthentic precursor of a redemptive future.[50]

Feminism's relationship to the past was also, however, more ambiguous than such a description suggests. If suffragettes dramatized their own sense of alienation from the givenness of tradition, they also viewed the past as a potential source of inspiration and symbolic strength. The self-identification of a political constituency as absolutely new could easily result in a sense of vulnerability and transience, encouraging a response which turned to the past to find in it a symptomatic foreshadowing and confirmation of present truths. Thus Olive Schreiner's paean to the New Woman, for example, simultaneously insists that she is not really new, but a descendant of the proud Teutonic warrior womanhood of ancient history. Similarly, suffragette iconography regularly resorted to images of female warriors drawn from history, allegory, and myth. Such figures as Boadicea, Athena, and above all Joan of Arc were proudly displayed on banners and posters as idealized symbols of feminine heroic power, bearing witness to a gynocentric tradition of militancy in the distant past.[51]

The suffragettes' invention of tradition also established an alternative connection to a modern lineage of radicalism that had begun in 1789 with the founding of democratic ideals of liberty, equality, and citizenship. The French Revolution was a key point of reference for feminists, who saw themselves as primary inheritors of the heroic mantle of oppositional struggle, retrieving the radical kernel within the Enlightenment project. A symptomatic statement in this regard is the young Rebecca West's description of Emmeline Pankhurst as "the last popular leader to act on inspiration derived from the principles of the French Revolution; she put her body and soul at the service of Liberty, Equality and Fraternity, and earned a triumph for them."[52] Similarly, parallels were often drawn between the feminist struggle to liberate women and the achievements of the American Revolution as a casting off of the yoke of slavery and racial bondage. Emmeline Pankhurst exclaimed to her American audience: "our hearts burn within us when we read the great mottoes which celebrate the liberty of your country; when we go to France and read the words liberty, fraternity and equality, don't you think that we appreciate the meaning of those words?"[53] Through such comparisons to the great liberatory struggles of the past, suffragettes characterized their own movement as a world-historical event of equal importance. Countering accusations of narrow self-interest, they depicted themselves as pursuing the cause of universal liberty, which would transform and benefit all of humanity. History thus dignified the meaning of individual and particular actions as the ultimate court of appeal which would provide final confirmation of the rightness of the feminist cause.[54]

This invocation of the revolutionary ideal frequently coincided with a heightened and hyperbolic use of language, as feminist discourse strove to simulate the intensified political activity to which it referred. The rhetorical vigor of much of this writing is directly related to its particular contexts of enunciation; as already noted, many of the articles published in *Votes for Women* were transcriptions of public speeches or exhortative editorial pieces addressed to an implied feminist reader. One of their main functions was thus to engender political cohesion and commitment through inspiratory, emotionally charged, and openly didactic messages. Seeking to minimize the degree of mediation between speaker and public, such texts aimed at communicative transparency, at conveying an authenticity and intensity of emotion that would engender intimate connection and sympathy in their audience. Feminist discourse became a form of textual mirror which reflected back to its readers a sense of collective identity grounded in a common purpose.

This status of feminist writing as injunction and advertisement encouraged particular modes of address, including the ritualized invocation of moral absolutes. Many of the articles in *Votes for Women* were straightforward accounts of recent political events or pragmatic discussions of policy issues, but others adopted a highly exhortative and high-flown rhetoric. A single quotation gives an adequate indication of the tenor of much of this writing. "This is a revolution. This is a war. But it is a revolution forced upon us. It is a war which we are called upon to wage in the name of liberty and justice. Let the heart of every woman in the movement be the heart of a hero and a warrior, then shall we fight unflinchingly to the very end, and shall forget the strain and the stress in the joy of the battle, which is bound to end in victory for the right."[55] In this excerpt are encapsulated many of the typical strategies of political rhetoric: repetition, abstraction, hyperbole, prophecy. The dramatization of political events through imagery of revolution and war is accompanied by a denial of individual responsibility and a heroization of an interpellated constitutency that is being compelled to act by the force of a higher good. The vocabulary of militarism divides the political spectrum into two conflicting and bitterly opposed camps, while the assumed support of providence leads to a prophetic affirmation of the inevitability of success for the righteous. Through the recurring deployment of the imperative, the future tense, and modal verbs such as "shall" and "must," readers are repeatedly invited to position themselves in relation to an as yet unrealized but inevitable and glorious destiny.

Such techniques of persuasion and justification can of course be found in many examples of political discourse, but they gained a particular significance in relation to the middle-class Englishwomen who were the primary authors and addressees of this militant rhetoric. In defiance of popular opinion, including that of many sympathetic contemporaries, they boldly insisted that women could be revolutionaries. In doing so, they found themselves confronted with the inevitable tension between the masculine coding of the revolutionary subject and the characteristic traits of femininity. To be a revolutionary woman was thus to risk being desexed, a danger that was graphically realized in many press reports and political cartoons which depicted suffragettes as grotesque, mannish, and sexless harridans. For this reason, the militants often presented themselves as being forced to act against their own womanly instincts by the oppressiveness of their conditions. Simultaneously acknowledging and negotiating an existing Oedipalization of the revolutionary subject, militants portrayed their own actions as a strategic necessity rather than as the expression of a psychological imperative. Emmeline Pankurst, for example, frequently asserted that she was "by nature a law-abiding person . . . hating violence, hating disorder."[56] This discomfort—whether real or feigned is immaterial in this context—with certain aspects of the revolutionary tradition was particularly apparent in the care which suffragettes took over their appearance and dress. Various writers have commented on the distinctively elegant styles of self-presentation adopted by militant suffragettes even as en masse they smashed shop windows with hammers in Bond Street or resisted police arrest. Their feminine dress, large hats, and fashionable appearance deliberately avoided all suggestion of the masculine, seeking rather to conform to the middle-class stereotype of the womanly woman. Here the modern woman as feminist encountered the modern woman as consumer; as many photographs of the period showed, a suffragette could be both revolutionary *and* feminine.[57]

In drawing attention to their femininity in this way, however, suffragettes were confronted with the sedimented power of another cluster of representations which acknowledged a prior history of female radicalism only to pathologize it as dangerously irrational. French history in particular had spawned an image of the revolutionary woman as a deranged Fury driven by instinctual and bodily imperatives, graphically encapsulated in the figure of the *pétroleuse,* the mythic female incendiary of the Paris Commune. Contemporary press reports drew on this tradition in depicting the suffragettes as hysterical and frustrated women, a shrieking sisterhood with dangerously unbalanced psyches. Feminism, in this light, was nothing more than a species of sexual disorder, a condition of corporeal extremity.[58] The pervasive use of militaristic metaphors in feminist discourse sought to countermand such images of disorderly feminine bodies by creating a counter-image of a well-disciplined army marching inexorably toward success. As Martha Vicinus notes, "many middle-class women had watched their brothers go off and fight for the empire in South Africa and India. Fighting for a higher cause—with the weapons of moral superiority—seemed a natural way to describe the struggle for the vote. The language, iconography and ultimately the behavior of the WSPU portrayed an army at war with society."[59] This imagery of conflict, battle, and self-sacrifice became increasingly prominent with a radical section of the suffragette movement in the period leading up to the First World War. Eschewing any association of femininity with helplessness or weakness, figures such as Christabel Pankhurst expressed an unyielding rhetoric of revolutionary zeal that traded on motifs of martyrdom, devotion to the cause, and spiritual regeneration. Militant feminism defined itself as the voice of radical modernity campaigning against endemic forces of masculine reaction, stagnation, and conservatism.

Modernity and the Politics of the New

In his discussion of the philosophy and politics of the modern, Gianni Vattimo proposes the following base-line definition: "modernity is that era in which being modern becomes a value, or rather, it becomes *the* fundamental value to which all other values refer."[60] In other words, modernity is to be defined less in terms of its specific material forms, which may vary significantly across time and space, than as a condition epitomizing a distinctive logic of temporality which places ultimate value on innovation, even as it causes terms such as "old-fashioned" and "outmoded" to acquire automatically pejorative associations. To be modern is—tautologically—to define oneself as being such; that very gesture of self-naming, of assuming the necessary value of the new, enacts the very temporality that it seeks to describe.

If the valorization of the new can be seen as an inescapable feature of the modern condition, it nevertheless assumes different guises and may work to diverse ends. The designation of modernity as the "tradition of the new" acknowledges in its oxymoronic phrasing the central paradox of an era in which change itself becomes normalized and assumes a regulatory cultural function. The idea of progress symbolizes this institutionalization of the new, whereby change is assumed to be permanent and ongoing and is thereby homogenized as the necessary foundation of social processes. Western evolutionary narratives thus reveal an ossification of the dynamics of change into a rigid and prescriptive model of historical development. To be new in this context is merely to reenact the logic of the ever-same.[61]

This framing of the new within evolutionary, teleological time can be counterposed to the revolutionary vision of the new as a dramatic and violent rupture with the past. The idea of revolution can be seen in one sense as radically antihistorical in character, in that it affirms the schismatic nature of the transformative moment, as a qualitative leap toward an unimaginable future. In one sense, then, revolution subverts the ideology of progress through its rejection of developmental stages of continuity; it affirms that what will come will be radically other than what has gone before. Yet the metaphor of revolution can itself easily be assimilated back into a progressive teleology and a salvation history consisting of a sequence of revolutionary stages.

These two different yet interrelated perceptions of the new pervaded fin-de-siècle feminist discourse as women strove to represent their own status as historical beings. Shifting between figures of revolution and evolution, they sought to make sense of their status as modern women, as subjects of social processes rather than mere bystanders. In their writings, we can thus glimpse both the value and the inevitable limitations of modern imaginings of time. By placing women at the center of evolutionary narrative, for example, feminists challenged their own positioning outside history, endowing the old narrative of the new with fresh signification and a potentially resistive edge. The ideal of progress which they invoked was by no means identical to that which was enshrined in established paeans to Victorian and Edwardian culture. At the same time, however, they simultaneously relegated women and men of non-Western cultures to the zone of ahistoricity from which they had only just freed themselves. And although the rhetoric of evolution could be used to endow feminist struggles with the inexorable authority of natural law, this determinism could equally well undermine the very basis of political activism. Why, their contemporaries wondered, should suffragettes campaign so vehemently for an outcome that would emerge inevitably over time?

The appeal to revolution was one response to this dilemma which in turn opened up new ambiguities and problems. What did it mean for militant feminists to describe their struggle as a revolutionary one? By appropriating the uplifting power of a term which has marked some great political struggles of Western history, they sought to accelerate the speed of social transformation and to create a radical feminine subculture that would openly defy the authority of the patriarchal state. Yet this revolutionary ideology, rather than gathering sustained and widespread support, appears to have deepened existing schisms between the various factions of the suffragette movement. The growing conviction among the militants that their own ideals were radically incompatible with the values of the majority promoted a vanguardist consciousness, taking the form of what Janet Lyon describes as a "rhetoric of contempt which conceives and reifies as an oppressive cultural center a nonporous, undifferentiated 'public.'"[62] As a result, some militant feminists came to rely on an exaggerated sense of the political efficacy of their own acts of resistance, believing that a momentous transformation of society was directly imminent. Although it is difficult to assess the long-term effects of militant activities on public attitudes, at a purely strategic level the battle for the vote did not succeed. Female suffrage was not achieved until the end of the First World War, when it was first granted to a minority of women under a rather different set of political circumstances.

In our own time, the forms of historical consciousness that I have anatomized in this chapter have become far more problematic. For a variety of reasons, including the catastrophic legacy of two world wars, the history of Western imperialism, and the pseudo-innovation of consumerism and uncontrolled technological development, the grand narrative of modernity as evolution and progress is viewed as having been emptied of any meaningful content. Similarly, the failed experiments of twentieth-century Marxism have cast an irrevocable shadow on the category of revolution, which is now often cast in a sinister rather than a benevolent light. As a result of these crises in temporality, the postmodern is often seen as signaling the end of history and the death of the belief in the new. We live, it appears, in a world that is no longer historical.[63]

Yet in the very enunciation of these claims, one can often glimpse the continuing presence of the very historicity that is being disavowed. Is not

Lyotard's thesis of the end of grand narratives, as a number of commentators have suggested, itself a grand narrative of the first order? Vattimo is more cautious about the possibility of going "beyond" the aporias of the modern, recognizing that any such project of overcoming merely reenacts the fundamental imperative of modernity itself. Insisting that the postmodern needs to be seen as a critical moment within the modern, rather than a period that transcends it, he nevertheless uses language that reveals a continuing reliance on linearity and historicity in its references to advances, developments, and ends. The legacy of historical consciousness and temporality, it seems, is not as easily discarded as some of its critics might wish.

This is not to trivialize or to deny the force of the critique of Western historical-philosophical narratives, a critique which I have sought to incorporate at least partially into the writing of my own text. Yet to assume that we have simply transcended modern conceptualizations of history is to reinscribe precisely that confident superiority of the present to the misguided past that is ostensibly being called into question. Equally, such a claim denies the lived reality of our everyday interaction with the world, which continues to rely in a multiplicity of ways on notions of history as chronology and change. We may no longer subscribe to nineteenth-century grand visions of human development, but our very language betrays a continuing sense of historicity and of the irreversible flow of time. The difference lies, perhaps, in the fact that we have become more self-conscious about our own use of such narrative models and about their inevitable plurality, not in the fact that we have gone beyond them.

I have tried to show in my discussion that it is not only hegemonic but also subordinate groups that may benefit from such narratives; it is the latter, above all, who revitalize the dynamic of the new in offering a challenge to the status quo that is not simply a reproduction of the same. In this context, history emerges as a meaningful—nay vital—category for the disenfranchised, signaling not the legitimation of the real as the rational, but rather the articulation of passionate hopes for a different future. Thus when fin-de-siècle feminists spoke of evolution and revolution, they did not simply mimic an existing masculine discourse, but drew on and simultaneously reshaped the parameters of contemporary thought to offer alternative, female-centered visions of historical possibility. Political changes in gender relations were signaled through a reformulation of the project of history, an enunciation of new expectations of the future and of transformed understandings of the past. The challenge to male-centered narratives of modernity, rather than arising spontaneously out of the present historical moment, thus constitutes a recurring thread within the modern itself.

For Vattimo, our present postmodern condition is defined as one of *post-histoire*, where "what is new is not in the least 'revolutionary' or subversive; it is what allows things to stay the same."[64] In such accounts of the end of history, all newness, innovation, and historical change have been invalidated by their incorporation into an overarching systemic logic of domination which fetishizes the new even as it empties it of any meaning. Yet such a sweeping vision surely glosses over the fundamental distinction between various *kinds* of newness, between the revolutionary significance of a new political movement and that of a new brand of soap. If change has become omnipresent, then it becomes incumbent on us to struggle to distinguish between different forms of change in terms of their political and ethical significance and their wide-reaching structural implications. It is upon the making of such distinctions that politics must necessarily rest, even as "history," understood as both the construction of a past and the projection of a future, surely remains for many an unfinished rather than an already concluded project.

The Art of Perversion: Female Sadists and Male Cyborgs

> The theoretical interest of perversion extends even beyond the disruptive force it brings to bear upon gender. It strips sexuality of all functionality, whether biological or social; in an even more extreme fashion than "normal" sexuality, it puts the body and the world of objects to uses that have nothing whatever to do with any kind of "immanent" design or purpose ... Of course not all perversions are equally subversive, or even equally interesting.
>
> Kaja Silverman, *Male Subjectivity at the Margins*

In this chapter, I turn to the affiliations between the discourses of sexology and psychiatry and the texts of avant-garde art as they shape the formation of a distinctively modern vision of sexual desire. In this vision, which receives its earliest and most extensive articulation in France, the sexual deviant is identified with a transgressive extremity of experience beyond the boundaries of everyday social and sexual norms.[1] The heroization of the Marquis de Sade by the French intelligentsia is a particularly telling instance of this glamorization of perversion, which continues apace in our own time. Consider, for example, the ubiquity and interchangeability of "desire" and "transgression" as redemptive categories of contemporary cultural criticism as well as the increasing attention devoted to previously taboo sexual practices, such as S and M, in the mainstream media. The frisson of erotic transgression has, it seems, become a key moment in the formation of modern subjectivity. Through a reading of the works of Rachilde, a fin-de-siècle writer whose literary career was largely built on descriptions of "monstrous and deviant sexual behaviour,"[2] I consider some of the implications of the rapprochement of aesthetics and sexuality as markers of resistive identity. Moving away from the usual identification of perversion with a deviant/

defiant masculinity, I ask: What does it mean for a woman to be perverse?

My analytical focus should be distinguished from that of feminist scholars wishing to recuperate psychoanalysis as a model for theorizing female perversion. I am less interested in adjudicating between various explanations of the psychic etiology of sexual transgression than in exploring the specific cultural meanings adhering to the deployment of the perverse as an oppositional emblem by late-nineteenth-century artistic and intellectual elites. This does not imply a total negation of the psychoanalytic project; one of the arguments developed in this chapter is the historical significance of sexology and psychoanalysis as not just constraining but also enabling discursive phenomena, which make it possible to conceptualize and represent desire in new ways. I am, however, less persuaded of the utility of psychoanalysis for feminism as a technology of reading literary texts; in spite of their protestations to the contrary, such readings typically set in motion a reading machine which translates a heterogeneous range of texts into a single, self-contained master code organized around the privileged status of a few archetypal signifiers (the phallus, castration, the pre-Oedipal mother). My own concern, in any event, is less with the ultimate explanatory power of psychoanalysis than with an analysis of its historical relationship to other forms of discourse and the cultural self-definition of particular social groups.

Why, then, does sexuality emerge as such a powerful symbol in the contestatory culture of the avant-garde? What are the aesthetics and politics of perversion? Such a phenomenon seems unimaginable without the prior sexualization of the human body through the nineteenth-century development of biology, medicine, psychiatry, sexology, demography, and eugenics. It is through such processes of discursive mapping, as Michel Foucault and his followers have persuasively argued, that sexuality emerges as a fundamental marker of identity and a key to the truth of the self. The definitive contribution of Foucauldian theory has been to recast sexuality as a fundamental category of modern culture rather than as in some sense antithetical to it. Modernity in this account is equated with the initiation of sexual heterogeneity, the implantation of perversion through the multiplication of discursive categories. "Modern society is perverse" insists Foucault; it simultaneously creates, even as it pathologizes, a panoply of peripheral sexualities.[3]

While this historicization of the sexual usefully challenges the premises of a romantic erotic libertarianism, it may in turn encourage a functionalist perspective which reduces sexual identity to nothing more than an epiphenomenon of a self-reproducing discursive field. Yet the social construction of a category does not in itself explain its use; particular models of the sexed self are affirmed, contested, or reformulated by social agents within determinate contexts and to multifarious ends. As such phrasing suggests, moreover, it is misleading to interpret the history of sexuality as exemplifying a series of neat epistemological breaks, such that modernity signals the smooth replacement of a theological discourse of salvation by an alternative and radically incommensurate medical and psychiatric model of the self. Rather than an orderly sequential chain of epistemes, one needs to imagine a messy entanglement of discursive fields at any given moment; older conceptual frames do not simply disappear, but interact with newer paradigms in complicated processes of mutual contamination as well as active contestation.

This messy entanglement is well to the fore in the case of the richly ambiguous category of perversion. The term is best imagined as a nodal point, a zone of intersection for diverse and competing discourses of the self: moral/theological, scientific/deterministic, aesthetic/symbolic. Although a particular definition of the term may predominate in a particular enunciative statement, alternative meanings often retain a shadowy presence in the margins of the text. The origins of perversion lie in the doctrines of moral theology, where it describes any act of will against the law of God and nature. In this context, "perverse" refers to immoral or evil actions, understood as a form of rebellion or insurrection against the divine order.[4] It is only in the nineteenth century that perversion comes to acquire a distinctively psychopathological sense, marking the definitive instantiation of a medical model of sexuality. In *Psychopathia Sexualis* Krafft-Ebing attempts to enforce a clear separation of the medical from the moral; perversion, he insists, is a clinical term, a description of a biodegenerative condition over which the individual has no control, whereas perversity is a vice, describing a deliberate and hence immoral indulgence in abnormal sexual activities.[5] Yet in practice, the distinction between these two terms is not easily upheld, even as there are recurring movements in nineteenth-century texts between deterministic and voluntaristic accounts of the sexed subject. Instead of assuming a replacement of a religious and moral discourse of perversion by a medical one, it is more accurate to imagine a gradual overlaying of one conceptual grid by another to form a palimpsestic relationship. As Jonathan Dollimore notes, "structures developed within the concept of the sinfully perverse persist into modern theories of the sexually perverse."[6]

These multilayered associations of perversion are crucial to understanding its fascination for the early French avant-gardists. Profoundly influenced by contemporary medical and psychiatric discourses of sexuality, they simultaneously connected these discourses to their own conception of art as a symbolic refusal of the Law, a revolt against the constraints of both religious morality and bourgeois authority. This meshing of images of sexual deviance with an aesthetics of negativity and transgression has shaped much of our understanding of the relationship between sexuality and modernity. Yet until recently, there has been little discussion of the historical connections between literary and other discourses of sexuality in the late nineteenth century.[7] Instead, Foucauldian accounts of the development and circulation of medical and legal definitions of sexuality, couched largely in the vocabulary of history and social science, have developed in isolation from the literary-critical exploration of the transgressive desire operative in the avant-garde text. Yet there are significant parallels between the scientific depiction of sexual perversion and its appropriation by the intellectual and literary avant-garde as a privileged emblem of refusal. As Carolyn Dean argues, both share a conviction that the self is ontologically rooted in the libido, even as they draw quite different conclusions from this assumption.[8]

The association of art with deviant eroticism is not of course unique to the fin de siècle. In *The Romantic Agony* Mario Praz provides an extensive survey of the multifarious manifestations of dark and often violent erotic sensibility in nineteenth-century Romantic literature. In no other era, he notes, has sex played such a central part in the literary imagination.[9] It is in the late nineteenth century, however, that erotic desire is definitively medicalized and increasingly conceptualized in relation to various pre-Freudian theories of the unconscious. Within these new topographies of the self, sexuality becomes densely saturated with meaning as the ultimate, yet curiously enigmatic, marker of identity. It indicates both an intensified individualism, through the acknowledgment and simultaneous regulation of multiple and competing forms of idiosyncratic desire, and the potential dissolution of the self, through the mysterious subterranean workings of unconscious processes and instinctual impulses. The modern narrative of chronological and linear time is both affirmed and undermined in these proliferating discourses of sexuality. On the one hand, the ubiquity of perversion is seen to derive from the overrefined and oversophisticated nature of modern urban life, the exhausted endpoint of a protracted civilizing process. On the other hand, perversion is coded as a form of regression, signaling the resurgence of instinctual and uncontrolled libidinal forces. Thus the idea of the modern acquires particular temporal inflections in relation to contemporary discourses of sexuality; conjuring up a sense of exhaustion and decadence, the rhetoric of desire simultaneously signifies a vision of atavistic return and the enigmatic ahistoricity of the unconscious.

In creating an elaborate taxonomy of the irrational, the emergent disciplines of sexology and psychiatry provided rich material for avant-garde artists whose cultural identity hinged on a bohemian disdain for the bour-

geois credo of reason. A Romantic tradition of the *poète maudit* was reformulated in terms of a rhetoric of pathology; appropriating discourses of
degeneration which depicted artistic creativity as perverse, writers in turn
transvalued sexual deviance by depicting it as a privileged epistemological
standpoint from which to question social values and fixed truths. The alliance of the literary with the erotically aberrant manifested itself not simply
in the content of particular texts but in the broader subcultural formations
which helped to define the contemporary parameters for their reception.
Within the more bohemian circles of fin-de-siècle Paris, it became a form of
radical chic to present oneself as a sexual rebel and an acolyte of the perverse,
although the relation of this public self-stylization to an individual's actual
erotic preferences and practices was not necessarily a transparent or straightforward one.

While literary decadence encouraged a sexualization of art that was to
characterize many of the later texts of high modernism, it also promoted an
aestheticization of sexuality. In the discourse of sexology, the category of
perversion effectively embraced every sexual practice that did not serve the
ends of reproduction; as a synonym for any form of erotic pleasure without
function, it pointed to a disturbing loosening of desire from the moorings of
the procreative impulse. Decadent writers adopted and affirmed this separation of sexuality from reproduction; the libidinal was stylized, aestheticized, transformed into a self-contained and self-legitimating spectacle.
Present-day juxtapositions of sexuality and textuality have their historical
roots in this aestheticization of desire and the perceived affinities between
free-floating eroticism and a self-reflexive poetics. As evidenced in the epigraph to this chapter, perversion is thereby conceptualized as a quasi-Kantian
aesthetic zone of pleasure without purpose, resisting the tyrannical yoke of
instrumentality and function. Yet, inevitably, the refusal of purpose itself
acquires a purpose, assuming specific meanings and functions in the force
field of social relations. In the realm of perversion, as in aesthetics, there is
no disruption that is not also in some sense a reinscription of power differentials.

Rachilde is an ideal figure through whom to approach this complicated
question of the politics of perversion and the mutual entanglement of literary
and medical discourses of sexuality. Her work comprises an extensive and
exhaustive register of erotic deviations that surpassed the efforts of even her
more outré colleagues, containing descriptions of necrophilia, bestiality, male
masochism, female sadism, autoeroticism, homosexuality, transvestism,
fetishism, voyeurism, exhibitionism, and so on. Her biographer, Claude
Dauphiné, notes in this context that much of her work reads like a literary

illustration of the popular French manuals of psychopathology that were widely read during the period.[10] Just as Rachilde drew upon contemporary medical and sexological sources in the delineation of her characters, her work was in turn to become an object of clinical and scientific scrutiny. In later editions of Krafft-Ebing's *Psychopathia Sexualis,* for example, Rachilde's novel *La marquise de Sade* is referenced alongside Heinrich von Kleist's *Penthesilea* as an exemplary illustration of the rare malady of female sadism.[11]

Born in 1860 as Marguerite Eymery, Rachilde became an instant literary celebrity with the *succès de scandale* of her fourth novel, *Monsieur Venús* (1884). This story of a female artist who wears men's clothes and transforms a working-class man into her adoring and submissive "mistress" was condemned as pornographic and banned on its first publication in Belgium; it created an aura of provocation and scandal around Rachilde that shaped much of her later literary career. Known as the "queen of the decadents" and as "Mademoiselle Baudelaire," she went on become a prominent figure of the Parisian avant-garde and a prolific writer of novels about the pathological and morbid dimensions of sexuality. She was also an esteemed critic and reviewer and an early editor of one of the most prestigious of French literary journals, *Mercure de France.* A staunch supporter of writers such as Verlaine, Rachilde was a guiding force of the Parisian literary scene over many years, attracting both established and aspiring critics and writers to her famous Tuesday salons.

Rachilde has not, however, fared well in the annals of literary history; relegated to a footnote or a passing sentence in most standard surveys of the period, she has been classified as a minor and overly sensationalist writer of the decadent movement. The appearance of a recent critical biography by Claude Dauphiné as well as proliferating references to her work suggests that a rediscovery of Rachilde may be under way. As Dauphiné notes, *Monsieur Vénus* must surely emerge as a major novel in any feminist rewriting of literary history. Yet Rachilde's status in relation to feminism remains a fraught and uneasy one. Her work has been read by some critics as espousing a conservative, male-identified ideology that panders to conventional fantasies of the femme fatale. More recently, the renewed interest in psychoanalysis as well as the turn toward performance and cross-dressing in feminist theory has engendered a more affirmative response to her work as a subversive and even proto-feminist destabilization of gender roles.[12] I differ from the former critics in my emphasis on the distinctive features of Rachilde's imaginative reworkings of decadent mythology; rather than simply repeating established themes, I argue that her work requires us to rethink male-centered definitions of sadism, fetishism, and other perversions. At the same time, one cannot ignore Rachilde's own relationship to questions of gender politics as spelled out in the title of her pamphlet *Pourquoi je ne suis pas féministe (Why I Am Not a Feminist)*. We need to take her at her word. While I hope to show that Rachilde's texts open up suggestive and important directions for feminist criticism, her espousal of the perverse cannot simply be aligned with a political commitment to improving the condition of women.

In a sense, the issue at stake here is how to read the texts of an exceptional woman without either pathologizing or deifying her. Unlike my previous subjects, Marie Corelli and the early suffragettes, Rachilde cannot be legitimated as an object of study by dint of her own claim to represent a broader constituency such as that of "women" or the "people." On the contrary, she was avowedly elitist, contemptuous of other female writers, and a snob; her literary career appears to have been built upon a self-defined identity as a unique and exceptional figure. At the same time, her texts offer evocative scenarios of female power and perversion that remain unsurpassed in their bold formulation of desires traditionally forbidden to women. The task at hand thus becomes one of offering a politically aware reading of Rachilde's writing without forcing it into a feminist straitjacket that the author herself consistently repudiated. Such a reading may in turn open the way for a feminist rethinking of perversion that can move beyond the gender stereotypes which continue to shape much psychoanalytical thought.

The Modernization of Desire

The formal scientific study of sexual pathology emerged in Europe in the late 1870s and early 1880s, its most well-known practitioners including such figures as Krafft-Ebing, Havelock Ellis, Iwan Bloch, Albert Moll, and Charles Feré. These pioneering sexologists had two major aims: to identify and classify the various forms of perversion and to solve the riddle of their etiology. Krafft-Ebing's exhaustive and influential study, for example, included discussions of sadism, masochism, necrophilia, exhibitionism, male and female inversion, nymphomania, coprophilia, fetishism, and numerous other sexual variations, many of which he was instrumental in identifying and naming. *Psychopathia Sexualis* and similar texts undoubtedly helped create a public consciousness of the ubiquity and variety of perversions in the modern era, even though their scientific and Latinate vocabulary simultaneously encouraged a sense of the pathological and exotic nature of such erotic variations. Portrayed as an aberrant and marginal figure, the pervert also came to epitomize the unstable and problematic nature of modern sexual identity in general. Sexual science inaugurated a new genre of writing, the psychopathography, as individual case histories documenting the various categories and subcategories of sexual obsession were collected and arrayed in sequence like rare specimens in a museum.[13]

While there was a certain consensus as to what constituted a perversion, there was much less agreement as to its causes. Frank Sulloway has charted the rapid shifts in theories of sexuality between the 1880s and the 1900s, as disputes occurred between those sexologists who attributed perversion to hereditary and instinctual forces and those who placed greater weight on environmental factors and the influence of upbringing and chance.[14] In general, however, there was a growing recognition of the determining centrality of sexual feeling to social life, as a powerful yet inchoate force over which the individual exercised relatively little control. Furthermore, an emphasis on the physiological determination of erotic desire was not incompatible with recognizing its historical variability. The popular degeneration theories of the late nineteenth century frequently combined biological and social explanations, arguing that the proliferation of sexual pathologies arose from a distinctively modern condition of nervous enfeeblement caused by the stressful and unnatural conditions of fin-de-siècle urban life.[15]

Lawrence Birken has made an extended case for the centrality of sexology to the intellectual history of modernity, as part of a more general paradigm shift from a productivist and dimorphous model of the self to a consumerist and genderless one. Distancing himself from dystopian accounts of the emergence of sexual science as a repressive form of discursive regimentation, he argues for the real if ambiguous freedoms arising out of this new ideology of desire. The sexological revolution beginning with Darwin and ending with Freud, according to Birken, brought with it changing models of sexuality and the self that paralleled the increased emphasis on consumption within economic thought as expressed in the rise of marginal utility theory. The acknowledgment of an undifferentiated and polymorphous libidinality as the basis of human relations brought about the potential for a democratization of desire, allowing for a recognition of perversion as a variation on a sexual continuum rather than an expression of absolute deviance. Sexology thus made possible, even if in its early stages it did not fully enact, an individualization of the desiring subject.

Most provocative, from a feminist perspective, is Birken's claim that the discourse of sexology was ultimately enabling for women in acknowledging their status as desiring subjects and hence conferring upon them a form of symbolic citizenship. The sexualization of culture brought with it a gradual process of democratization. Owing to the influence of evolutionary theory, the perception of a natural and ahistorical difference between the sexes was replaced by a model of differentiation from a common sameness; such a conception of an originary bisexuality helped to erode the perception of absolute gender opposition. Within such a model, it became possible to recognize women's status as sexed subjects within a general economy of desire, even while the growing recognition of perversions as simple variations bore witness to an increasing emphasis on the idiosyncratic nature of sexual taste. It was in this sense, he concludes, that the sexological tradition culminating in Freud both made and unmade gender distinctions; its new conception of a "sexonomy" of desiring and consuming individuals helped to undermine previously fixed conceptions of natural sexual difference, even though in practice it often reinscribed many of those same differences.[16]

This question of the relationship between modern discourses of sexuality and the emancipation of women has of course an extended and passionately debated history within feminism itself. Against those positions which deem our existing conceptions of sexuality to be inherently and irredeemably masculine, I would side with Birken's account of the paradigm of desire as constitutive of our modern sense of subjectivity as such. Hence the importance of psychoanalysis for feminism, as has often been noted, lies in its framing of both sexual and sexed identity as a conditional and labile positioning within a general libidinal economy rather than as a natural or fixed essence. As Teresa de Lauretis writes, "the seductiveness of psychoanalysis for women owes to its acknowledging woman . . . as subject of desire and to the power it grants women in the transferential contract—the power of seducing and being seduced as *sexed* and *desiring* subjects."[17] In this sense, while feminists have been critical of specific manifestations of male sexuality, they too have drawn on the extended legacy of Freudian thought in affirming women's status as erotic agents and subjects of desire. At the same time, they have developed detailed critiques of the misogynistic underpinnings of the intellectual and institutional histories of sexology, psychiatry, and psychoanalysis. Birken's paucity of references to such scholarship is symptomatic of his tendency to skim over issues of gender politics as they affected the formation of sexual science.

The absence of any mention of hysteria is particularly striking in this regard, given the centrality of that category to fin-de-siècle discussions of female sexuality. Thus hysteria was to become the exemplary instance of the medical pathologization of the female body, a catchall term that was increasingly used to label any form of behavior not consonant with established social norms of femininity. Its indeterminate and protean symptoms resisted neat classification, presenting a chaotic clinical picture that engendered considerable bewilderment among doctors.[18] As Elaine Showalter points out, the volatility of hysteria was linked to the essence of the feminine in numerous ways. "Its vast, unstable repertoire of emotional and physical symptoms—fits, fainting, vomiting, choking, sobbing, laughing, paralysis—and the rapid passage from one to another suggested the lability and capriciousness traditionally associated with the feminine nature."[19] Rather than contributing to a democratization of desire, the prevalence of the hysteria diagnosis reaffirmed a vision of the distinctively irrational and unstable nature of femininity.

Hysteria was of course not a modern category, but one with origins in the time of the ancient Greeks. Yet its popularity as a diagnosis was to accelerate dramatically throughout the nineteenth century, peaking during the fin de siècle. This increase has been interpreted by some feminists as evidence of ever greater social constraints placed upon women's lives, but it may also have been directly related to changing classificatory practices on the part of doctors. At La Salpetrière, for example, where Jean Martin Charcot carried out his famous experiments on female patients, the incidence of diagnosis was dramatically higher than at neighboring hospitals. The professionalization of psychiatry expressed itself in a form of expansionism which sought to place ever larger sections of society under its jurisdiction. The popularization of hysteria became one means of persuading women to view their emotional distress as a medical condition to be treated by a physician rather than a moral or spiritual crisis requiring the guidance of a priest.[20]

This expansionism in turn manifested itself in a gradual loosening of hysteria from its moorings in the female body. Through its reclassification as a nervous disorder rather than a malfunctioning of the womb, the existence of male hysteria became a medical possibility; thus Charcot's research into the etiology and characteristics of the disorder uncovered a significant percentage of male hysterics among his patients.[21] Nevertheless, hysteria remained symbolically a feminine malady that was conventionally described in terms of the labile and capricious features of the feminine psyche and exemplified through scientific measurements and displays of the disorderly female body. Male hysterics by contrast were typically differentiated from their female counterparts in terms of the distinctive tenacity and permanence of their symptoms.[22] The move away from a purely anatomical model of hysteria did not dramatically alter its powerfully gendered connotations.

While hysteria remained a feminine erotic disorder, perversion remained a primarily masculine pathology, despite the acknowledgment of its occasional appearance in women. Although the reconceptualization of perversion as a medical problem and a degenerative disorder appeared to render it gender neutral, it nevertheless remained identified with an insurrectionary intensity of desire that was strongly aligned with a cultural norm of male subjectivity. In the studies of most turn of the century sexologists, women constitute a small minority of cases, their perverse desires usually limited to the specific phenomena of cross-dressing and female inversion. Krafft-Ebing cites women's lack of sensuality and aggression as an explanation for this almost total absence, noting that "intrinsic and extraneous factors—modesty and custom—naturally constitute in women insurmountable obstacles to the expression of perverse sexual instinct."[23] Similarly, the French psychiatrist Gatian de Gaeton de Clérambault, in his investigation of instances of fetishism among both male and female patients, was convinced that women lacked the transgressive erotic imagination characteristic of the true pervert.[24]

On the one hand, then, sexology and psychiatry encouraged a perception that everyone was potentially deviant; on the other, they inaugurated a differentiation between the pathologies of men and women, as new medical vocabularies intersected with common-sense conceptions of male and female identity, traditional moral and religious frameworks, and an Oedipal model of sexual transgression. This differentiation would become explicit in Freud's well-known definition of "feminine" neurosis as the negative of "masculine" perversion. "Quite frequently a brother is a sexual pervert," Freud writes, "while his sister, who, being a woman, possesses a weaker sexual instinct, is a neurotic whose symptoms express the same inclinations as the perversions of her sexually more active brother. And correspondingly, in many families the men are healthy, but from a social point of view immoral to an undesirable degree, while the women are high-minded and over-refined, but severely neurotic."[25] Hysteria was of course the exemplary manifestation of this female inclination toward neurosis, which was classified by Freud as a form of repudiated perversion.[26] Given prevailing psychic and social constraints on femininity, women, it seemed, could express their rebellious wishes and desires only unconsciously, in somatic form.

It is against this systematic if not univocal gendering of nineteenth-century forms of pathology that I wish to situate Rachilde's depictions of female sexuality. The importance of her writing, I will contend, lies in an appropriation of modern sexological and psychoanalytical notions of the decentered, desiring subject which simultaneously refuses their typical representations of femininity. Guided by her own self-description as a "hysteric of letters," some feminist critics have sought to make sense of Rachilde's texts through the conventional psychoanalytical equation of deviant femininity with hysteria.[27] I will argue, however, that a closer reading reveals Rachilde's heroines to be not hysterical but perverse. That is, they do not express desires and psychic conflicts unconsciously through the involuntary symptoms of the body, but consciously enact a willed refusal of social and moral norms. Rather than embodying a nonverbal and incoherent somatization of repressed wishes, they engage in a linguistically and aesthetically self-conscious performance of deviant sexuality. In creating a vision of the knowing, desiring, and perverse female subject, Rachilde's writings thus explore themes of obvious interest to contemporary feminist theory.

Why, then, should Rachilde have described herself as a hysteric? At first sight, such a self-designation seems puzzling, given the powerfully negative connotations of hysteria in the late nineteenth century and Rachilde's own highly ambivalent relationship to femininity. Hysteria had, however, become a fashionable term in the latter half of the century among such writers as Flaubert, Mallarmé, and Verlaine;[28] appropriated as a metaphor of transgression by the artistic elite, it became yet another instance of the imaginary male identification with the feminine. In such a context, Rachilde's self-naming becomes understandable, given her passionate affiliation with the values of the French artistic and intellectual avant-garde. In defining herself as a hysteric, Rachilde was not so much acknowledging a repressed femininity as masquerading as an avant-garde man masquerading as a woman. Only under such conditions could a woman's adoption of the role of hysteric signify transgression and revolt rather than involuntary pathology at a time when the transvaluation of hysteria by second-wave feminism had yet to take place.

The Cruel Woman

What are the semiotics and erotics of female sadism? How do women's fantasies of destruction and revenge express themselves in textual form? Merely to pose such a question is immediately to reveal the striking absence of writing on this topic. While feminist interest in male masochism has grown, there has been a conspicuous silence on the question of female sadism, on women's potential investment and pleasure in representations of violence. Such a question undoubtedly strikes at the heart of our most deeply held beliefs about the distinctive emotional susceptibilities and moral qualities of the female sex. Yet unless one subscribes to a belief in the innate and inevitable absence of aggressive impulses in women, it seems necessary to explore this question and to begin to consider the distinctive textual features of female fantasies of power, violence, and destruction.

Of course, cultural prohibitions against the expression of female aggression have often meant that such fantasies could be expressed only in covert and hidden form. It is here that the work of Rachilde is significant; her positioning within French decadent culture provided her with an intellectual and aesthetic alibi for creating explicit images of female deviance, which both draw upon and significantly transform the conventional fin-de-siècle iconography of the cruel woman. Thus *La marquise de Sade* (1887) remains a startling text even today; the heroine's frank declaration of war on the male sex and her nonchalant delight in the mutilation and destruction of the male body have not lost their power to shock. This novel is perhaps Rachilde's most elaborate and detailed representation of female cruelty in a literary oeuvre filled with depictions of autocratic heroines sending feeble and effeminate men to their madness and death. Such couplings of female pleasure and power with the deliberate infliction of suffering render Rachilde's work disturbing and provocative, if only because of the rare experience of encountering literary depictions of eroticized violence narrated from the woman's point of view.

La marquise de Sade combines the genre of the psychopathography with an elaborate reworking of decadent symbolism in its delineation of the origins of a sadistic personality. We first encounter the novel's heroine, Mary Barbe, as a young girl accompanying her aunt on an errand, she is told, to get fresh milk for her sickly mother. They arrive at an abattoir, where Mary, having wandered into the back room, encounters the horrifying sight of a bull slowly dying in convulsions of agony, blood pouring from its opened neck into a pail. The liquid her mother will imbibe, Mary realizes, is not milk but fresh blood, a common tonic for anemia during the period; the friendly and fatherly butcher is suddenly revealed as an agent of death. This nightmarish vision of secret slaughter brings the young girl to the point of collapse and engenders an intense, recurring identification with the figures of executioner and victim in later life. Childhood innocence is irrevocably shattered by this early formative trauma, embodied in the discovery of a father figure who loves and kills and a mother whose nourishment is not milk but blood.[29]

This graphic opening sequence sets the scene for the subsequent narration of Mary's lonely and anomic childhood. Her father, a harsh and authoritarian army officer, resents her for not having been born a boy; her mother is an emotionally distant invalid who dies after giving birth to a long-awaited son. Jealous of the attention lavished on her brother, Mary comes to realize that her own inferiority derives from the fact of her sex. Growing ever more isolated and distrustful of emotional attachments, she becomes preoccupied with fantasies of destroying her brother, whom she perceives as her mother's executioner. Silently watching as he is accidentally suffocated by a sleeping nurse, Mary deliberately decides not to intervene—one of her first declarations of warfare against the male sex.

After the death of her father, Mary is placed in the care of her elderly uncle, a renowned scientist and doctor. For several years she is ignored by him, forced to recognize her own redundancy in an intellectual milieu based on the exclusion of femininity. With puberty, however, comes the possibility of access to power and revenge. By seducing her uncle, Mary gradually shifts the balance of power between them; succumbing to the unfamiliar lure of erotic infatuation, the magisterial thinker becomes a besotted dotard eager to grant his precocious niece her every wish. At the same time, she decides to marry an aging libertine as a means of attaining adult freedoms and the protection afforded by social rank. On her wedding night, Mary informs her astonished husband that she will be his mistress, not his wife, threatening to poison him if he attempts to impregnate her. Expressing her revulsion at a reproductive imperative that offers women only the prospect of subjugation, suffering, and frequently death, she affirms her own contempt for the horrors of maternity and her refusal to endorse the mindless self-replication of a monstrous humanity.

Mary's next victim is a penurious young student, Paul, who is ultimately revealed as her husband's illegitimate son. A passive and self-effacing figure, he suffers from copious nosebleeds, which excite Mary and arouse her to a state of delirious erotic frenzy. She takes delight in biting and scratching his vulnerable flesh to accelerate the flow of mysterious red liquid pouring from his veins; both cannibal and vampire, Rachilde's heroine draws her power and strength from her lover's copious loss of blood. Thus her youthful dreams of revenge on the male sex are finally fulfilled in this incestuous scenario of calculating erotic domination over men of three generations. Her uncle finally kills himself, humiliated by his own impotence and abjection, and her husband collapses and dies, poisoned by the aphrodisiacs that she has been secretly feeding him. Discovering that Mary is his father's murderer, Paul flees from her in horror, tearing himself away from her devouring teeth.

In the last chapter, Mary has been transformed into a figure of myth. An exotic vampirelike figure surrounded by a bevy of retainers, she roams the streets of Paris at night in a restless search for vicarious and perverse pleasures, hoping to catch a glimpse of acts of obscenity and murder in the brothels and cheap hotels of the underworld. A late-night encounter with a group of transvestites at a ball engenders a murderous fantasy of the ultimate limit experience.

Her nostrils dilated behind the velvet of her mask. She would take an ideal pleasure in the death agony of one of these men, incapable of defending himself against a woman. One spring night, she would toss her handkerchief into this heap of animals for sale, bring him home, cover him with her jewels, wind him around with her laces, intoxicate him with her best wines, and then, asking nothing in exchange but his repulsive life, tie him with satin ribbons to her antique bed and kill him with pins glowing red from the fire.[30]

This sadistic dream is followed by a return to the scene of her original trauma. Feigning a lung complaint, she travels to a bar near the Parisian abattoirs where she can buy wine mixed with blood, savoring its taste while surrounded by the coarse talk of the butchers' apprentices. The smell of slaughtered animals intoxicates her with a mystic voluptuousness as she again surrenders to dreams of erotic destruction. The imagined moment of sacrificial slaughter promises the ultimate limit experience, the descent into the abyss and the ecstatic redemption of the self. "And she dreamed of the forthcoming pleasure of murder, carried out before everyone, if the desire took her too strongly, the murder of one of those fallen males which she would carry out with a serene heart, dagger up in the air!"[31]

Rachilde's text bears an obvious debt to the Sadean cult of the fin de siècle, a cult that was evidenced not just in literature but also in a growing array of scholarly works which sought to turn the eighteenth-century libertine into an exemplary nineteenth-century pervert. Like de Sade, Rachilde affirms the inexorable interconnection of eroticism and power, passion and domination, rejecting any sentimental myth of natural love or equality between the sexes. Mary Barbe is supremely indifferent to moral values, delighting in the suffering and destruction of others without revealing any trace of compassion or remorse. One might write of her what Angela Carter writes of de Sade's heroines: "their liberation from the limitations of femininity is a personal one, for themselves only. They gratify themselves fully, but it is a liberation without enlightenment and so becomes an instrument for the oppression of others, both women and men."[32] Rachilde's vision of female desire refuses the values of intimacy, affect, and other-relatedness and replaces them with an alternative ethos of individualism, amorality, and cruelty, systematically negating the myth of natural female virtue.

Yet there are also important differences between the erotic scripts and fantasy scenarios of de Sade and Rachilde. It is not enough to distinguish between the textual worlds of sadism and masochism, as Deleuze argues in his reading of Sacher-Masoch. Rather, one must also consider the specifically gendered dimensions of fantasy, the ways in which eroticized hierarchies are inflected by male or female subject positioning. Thus Rachilde's texts do not simply repeat the ideas and formal motifs of de Sade, nor can they be read as merely the mirror image of the text of male masochism. Rather, they reveal a specific aesthetic logic structured around the viewpoint and sexual and social positioning of the female subject. This logic in turn endows her work with an implicit social dimension through its self-conscious depiction of the hierarchical relationship of men and women; although its imaginary solution is defiantly individualistic and perverse, it nevertheless confronts the specifically gendered, rather than simply human or metaphysical, dimensions of inequality. It is in this sense that Rachilde's texts offer a distinctive refashioning of the script of sadistic desire.

The organizing principle of the Sadean text, as a number of writers have noted, is that of negation. It depicts the compulsive and mechanical repetition of acts of erotic violence by the solitary ego as a means of negating the reality of the other and affirming the absolute sovereignty of the self. Gilles Deleuze develops the notion of the institution to describe the distinctive quality of de Sade's representations of aggression: power is exercised in a relentless and absolute manner by an authority that sets itself above the law. The scenario of the Sadean fantasy is that of unconditional mastery, of "a torturer seizing upon a victim and enjoying her all the more because she is unconsenting and unpersuaded."[33] Sexual pleasure relies on and requires the obliteration of the other's agency and identity by means of an impersonal and curiously detached violence. For Deleuze, as for Adorno and Horkheimer, de Sade serves as the ultimate manifestation of the instrumental logic of Enlightenment reason.

Such a scenario constitutes an almost unimaginable basis for female-authored erotic fantasy, particularly in a nineteenth-century context. The radical solipsism of the Sadean hero remains unattainable, even for a literary heroine as alienated and solitary as Rachilde's Mary Barbe; the woman cannot escape recognition of the male other insofar as she is constantly forced to confront the reality of his authority and power. Similarly, the idea of institutionalized possession is not easily translatable across the gender divide, epitomizing a taken-for-granted sovereignty over others that is profoundly at odds with the psychic and social formation of the female subject. My intent here is not to argue that there is any simple or unicausal relationship between social gender and the scripting of erotic fantasy—clearly the opposite is true—but merely to suggest that prevailing cultural forms of masculinity and femininity may place certain limits upon what can be imagined and found pleasurable by the fantasizing subject.

Thus the systematic and impersonal enactment of violence against others is not a feature of Rachilde's novel. The female sadist finds herself in a peculiarly contradictory and conflictual position: her ultimate desire is to inflict pain as a means of achieving pleasure; yet she has no self-evident means of enforcing her own desire through the simple mastery and negation of the other. The logic of sadism as portrayed in Rachilde's text thus cannot be grasped through the Deleuzian alternatives of institutionalized possession (de Sade) or contractual alliance (Sacher-Masoch), but is, I would suggest, best understood through the structuring principle of *seduction*. Mary Barbe can overcome her own powerlessness only through indirect means; it is by seducing men—her uncle, her husband, his son—that she in turn acquires the power to subjugate and destroy them. Women's strategic deployment of their own desirability emerges as a necessary precondition for their acquisition of the ability to inflict violence upon others.

This structural logic in turn explains the less abstract and depersonalized quality of Rachilde's text. Seduction, after all, requires an acknowledgment of and engagement with the subjectivity of the other, even if only at the level of strategy. Thus the instrumental rationality of the Sadean text, with its compulsive, mathematically choreographed enactment of violence, is replaced by a seductive cruelty that is both more ironic and more discreet. Mary must simulate desirability, must rely on the power of artifice, lure, and maneuver in order to achieve her own ultimate desire. Sadism, rather than exemplifying a brutal corporeal imposition of the will, is thus redefined as a fundamentally semiotic and aesthetic phenomenon; female cruelty and violence is enacted in an oblique and mediated fashion via duplicitous tactics of performance and masquerade.

"Seduction," Jean Baudrillard writes, "never belongs to the order of nature, but that of artifice—never to the order of energy, but that of signs and rituals."[34] Baudrillard's own idealization of seduction as feminine, however, explicitly denies its imbrication in gender power relations; rather, it becomes the privileged space of indeterminacy and masquerade, epitomizing a ludic strategy and play of veils that resists the prevailing phallic economies of power and sex. The texts of Rachilde, by contrast, suggest a very different vision of seduction that is intimately linked to, rather than severed from, hierarchical dynamics of power and the articulation of sadistic desire. Furthermore, Baudrillard's distinction between the "supple ceremonial" of seduction and the uncompromising rigidity of perversion loses much of its force in the context of Rachilde's fiction, where, as I hope to show, deviance is always already aestheticized. In other words, addressing perversion in its gender specificity requires us to rethink its established definitional history, even as it may bring to light forms of the perverse, such as female sadism, not previously recognizable as such.

Moreover, if the structuring principle of the female sadistic fantasy is seduction, its motivating force is *revenge*. In this sense, its logic is a reactive one, a violent response to a prior condition of powerlessness and impotent rage. Mary Barbe's hostility to the male sex springs from a childhood which consistently reminds her of the invisibility and inferiority of femininity. Female sadism thus arises not out of a disavowal of sexual difference, as in the case of de Sade, but rather out of a profound recognition of its inescapable reality and power. Insofar as it is not just a recognition of but a protest against this condition, however, it also shows the woman attempting to wrest herself free from the debilitating constraints of femininity. Mary Barbe's horror of motherhood emerges in this context as an inevitable consequence of her desire to avoid all association with female powerlessness and abjection. Here Rachilde's heroine echoes the dandy's fear of the reproductive body, even though the context of this fear is a significantly different one. Maternity is depicted as a sacrifice of female autonomy for the reproductive imperative of the patriarchal family, exemplified most graphically in Mary's own mother's death in childbirth. Her conflictual relationship to the feminine is further evidenced—and this is true of many of Rachilde's heroines—in her intense erotic attraction to passive and effeminate young men. By seducing and dominating such men, she is able to subjugate and crush a signifier of femininity as well as to take revenge on the male sex. The disturbing final scenario of the murder of a transvestite takes this logic to its chilling conclusion. In fantasizing such an action, Mary Barbe symbolically annihilates the image of her own femininity, even as she simultaneously kills a man made vulnerable by his transvestism. The sadistic fantasy allows her to simultaneously ally herself with the power of the masculine, to enact violence upon men, and to negate her femininity as reflected back to her in the mimicry of the transvestite.

Here it is significant that the symbolism of blood, with all its multivalent and abject resonances, pervades this text of female cruelty. A long-standing equation of blood lust with sexual voracity and aggression is invoked in Rachilde's depiction of the female vampire who takes unalloyed pleasure in biting and penetrating her lover's flesh and causing it to bleed. This active oral sadism on the part of the phallic woman is in turn paralleled by the displacement of feminine abjection onto the body of the male. Paul's recurring nosebleeds identify him with the culturally taboo figure of the menstruating woman; constantly tormented by unexpected flows of blood which he struggles to conceal for fear of social disapprobation, he becomes a graphic symbol of shameful and polluted corporeality. It is as if the representation of failed and fallen males, of men associated with conventional signifiers of abject or devalued femininity, were a necessary precondition for literary imaginings of female power. Thus the blood which pours from Paul's body is endowed with a sacramental quality as a token within a cannibalistic rite of purification and regeneration. Like the animals in the slaughterhouse glimpsed by Mary Barbe as a young child, the male victim must be sacrificed in order to nourish and strengthen the woman; it is his blood which enables her to survive and triumph.

Like many of Rachilde's other novels, *La marquise de Sade* creates a fantasy scenario of a woman whose pursuit of deviant and violent desires is celebrated rather than punished. The prevalence of powerful and often overtly masculine women in Rachilde's fiction in turn raises questions about the status of lesbianism in her cataloging of fin-de-siècle perversions. How does Rachilde's questioning of prevalent norms of femininity relate to contemporary imaginings of female same-sex desire? In her classic study, *Sex Variant Women in Literature*, Jeannette Foster points to evidence of repressed homosexual inclinations in Rachilde's work, primarily on the basis of her recurring fascination with the figure of the woman in drag. This association of the mannish woman with the lesbian was a commonplace during a period which typically defined sexual preference through gender identification; yet it is striking how vehemently Rachilde seeks to keep these two categories apart.[35] Her female characters, like the author herself, frequently announce their disdain for the fashionable vice of lesbianism. For Mary Barbe, sapphism is nothing more than the neurotic fad of schoolgirls, while Raoule de Vénérande, the transvestite heroine of *Monsieur Vénus*, is equally blunt in her condemnation of such vulgar forms of love: "to be Sapphic would be like everyone! My upbringing forbids me the crime of the boarding school girl or the prostitute's foibles."[36] This repeated and phobic act of self-distancing can perhaps by explained by the passionate affiliation with a masculine principle evident in many of Rachilde's novels; to experience same-sex desire is to risk being reidentified with a contaminating, because powerless, femininity at the level of object choice. This does not necessarily refute Foster's argument if one assumes that disavowal may also bespeak desire, but it suggests that the work of Rachilde, unlike that of later writers such as Renée Vivien and Nathalie Barney, cannot be unproblematically assimilated into a lesbian canon. Its perversity undoubtedly remains selective.

Given the vehemence of this identification with a principle of masculine power, it may be asked if there is anything liberating in the fantasy image of the cruel woman. The claim that Rachilde's texts exemplify an image of female freedom seems implausible in this respect, given their insistence on the pervasiveness of sexual hierarchy and the inescapability of the master/ slave dialectic. Neither can they be seen as a subversive expression of previously silenced female desires; on the contrary, they hook into an existing and widely disseminated repertoire of images of female cruelty within the French decadent tradition. Yet there are also important differences in Rachilde's refashioning of this tradition. As Mary Ann Doane has recently noted, "the femme fatale overrepresents the body . . . she is attributed with a body which is itself given agency independently of consciousness."[37] The figure of the deadly woman exemplifies the power of demonic nature as embodied in the power of a newly discovered unconscious; her power is instinctual, irrational, and destructive.

By contrast, Mary Barbe, like many of Rachilde's other heroines, is a highly conscious and self-conscious agent. Rather than simply representing the body, these characters partake of a knowing and reflective subjectivity. Their perversity is deliberate rather than instinctual, expressing an individual revolt against a condition of female subordination; they are privileged agents, as I will shortly demonstrate, of the realm of art and culture rather than of nature. The significance of Rachilde's writing thus lies in its expansion of the symbolic field to acknowledge women's potential status as insurrectionary subjects through a usurpation of a traditionally masculine realm of intense and violent eroticism. As such, they challenge one of our most persistent cultural taboos by exploring women's anger, violence, and desire for revenge. Rachilde's fantasies of female cruelty—and it is important to stress in this context that unlike de Sade's, they are *only* fantasies[38]—refuse prevailing wisdoms about the gendering of transgression and deviance. Instead, they postulate a dissident, nonconformist, yet triumphant femininity that is perverse in all senses of the word: erotic, moral, and aesthetic.

Performing the Perverse

While *La Marquise de Sade* retains many of the features of realist representation in its biographical portrayal of the origins of a sadistic personality, many of Rachilde's other works are more stylized and aesthetically self-conscious in form. Their representation of female perversion challenges the diagnostic gaze of the clinician; there is behind the mask no fixed personality whose inner compulsions can be charted and deciphered. Instead, sexuality is presented as performance rather than essence; desire is inseparable from its cultural mediation and irrevocably severed from any notion of organic interiority.

La jongleuse (*The Juggler*, 1900) explicitly centers on this thematics of aestheticized sexuality and masquerade. The text stages a series of encounters between the glamorous and enigmatic Eliante Dolanger, a thirty-five-year-old widow, and Léon Reille, a young medical student whom she meets at a ball and invites to her home. Bewitched by her seductive persona and excited by her bold initiation of their encounters, Léon confidently assumes that she will soon become his mistress. Eliante, however, constantly frustrates and baffles his expectations of sexual union; appearing before him at different times in a variety of roles and costumes, from the highly erotic to the primly bourgeois, she juggles with his desires as adeptly as she juggles with knives. Outwitting him at every turn, she orchestrates their encounters in the manner of a chess game (the text is plotted throughout in a stylized symbolism of black and white). Her final triumph, a dazzling and morbid denouement, is the deft substitution of one female body for another in an elaborately choreographed climax of simultaneous love and death.

In this evocative exploration of female exhibitionism, Rachilde addresses the status of modern woman as image and spectacle. Adopting a diversity of costumes—bourgeois widow, exotic dancer, solicitous aunt, juggling acrobat, black-sheathed vamp—Eliante reveals femininity itself to be a disguise. Displaying without revealing, she exposes a body whose identity remains enigmatic and undecipherable to a male spectator depicted as powerless rather than powerful in his simultaneous desire and failure to penetrate to its essence. The linked imperatives of scopophilia and epistemophilia, the desire to look as exemplifying the desire to know, are blocked by the blankness of a body that is nothing but surface, an empty screen that simultaneously attracts and repels the hermeneutic gaze. Femininity thus becomes wholly theatrical and impersonal, a tribal mask of idealized display; the formality and iconicity of this self-presentation refuses the viewer any psychological access, whether real or imagined.[39]

The pleasures of exhibitionism are not of course uncontaminated; rather, they arise from the characteristic positioning of women in the scopic field of modernity, their condition of to-be-looked-at-ness. Eliante's performance of the feminine thus invokes the split consciousness of the woman who, in John Berger's well-known phrase, is constantly watching herself being watched.[40] In Berger's argument, this condition of self-surveillance is portrayed as a symptom of women's profound alienation, as exemplified in their lack of access to a unitary identity. Rachilde's text, however, offers a reevaluation of the status of femininity and a striking rearticulation of the gender symbolism of modernity. If the modern subject is split, decentered, deeply aware of its own formation through exteriority and structures of cultural mediation, then it is woman who has become the exemplary modern individual. Rather than symbolizing undifferentiated nature and unconscious desire, women's positioning in relation to the gaze of the other endows them with a degree of self-consciousness that men can never attain. In a powerful reversal of the representations of modernity examined in earlier chapters, it is now the male subject who clings nostalgically to an illusory sense of unitary and noncontradictory identity, whereas woman epitomizes the double, divided, and contradictory self fully conscious of her own exterior determination. Feminity is revealed as the privileged figure of an authentic modernity.

Rachilde, however, does not limit the narrative agency of her heroines to a parodic performance of their status as objects of desire; if women are exhibitionists, they can also be voyeurs. Long before the emergence of feminist debates about the possibility of women's appropriation of the gaze, Rachilde's novel *Monsieur Vénus* depicted the male body as an object of female desire. Reversing the conventional narrative of an aristocratic hero who seduces a woman from a lower class, Rachilde's novel portrays the sexual liaison between the wealthy and well-born Raoule de Vénérande and Jacques Silvert, a working-class flower-maker and an aspiring but untalented artist. On first encountering him, Raoule is immediately infatuated by the young man's striking and unusual beauty. Feigning an interest in his mediocre paintings, she installs him in a sumptous apartment, seduces him, and gradually turns him into a submissive and docile lover.

Throughout the novel, the reader is offered numerous descriptions of Jacques's body as seen through Raoule's eyes, descriptions which trace its curves, contours, and shadows in suggestive erotic detail. At their first meeting, for example, we are given a precise delineation of Jacques's various body parts that fragments the unity and autonomy conventionally ascribed to masculinity; his flesh is sized up and evaluated with the detached and practiced eye of a butcher or a pimp. The narratorial gaze moves from a measured assessment of his jutting hips and slim ankles to an inspection of his adorable dimpled chin and the creases in his neck. Rather than being represented as active, dynamic, and powerful, the male body is infantilized and feminized, transformed into a helpless, charming, and seductive object. Yet Jacques's physique is simultaneously presented as that of a working-class man; he is depicted as stocky and robust rather than ethereally feminine. As Raoule confides to one of her friends, "he isn't even a hermaphrodite, not even impotent; he is a handsome male of twenty-one years, whose soul, with its feminine instincts, is in the wrong container."[41] It is this ambiguous positioning of Jacques, as simultaneously of both genders and hence of neither, which provides the titillating erotic contrasts that Raoule's jaded palate requires.

As she confidently assumes the traditional rights of the male lover in their relationship, so Jacques in turn comes to enjoy his own role as a cosseted yet controlled sex object. Raoule is the active partner, the one who initiates and choreographs their sexual encounters; a jealous and demanding lover, she seeks constantly to dominate her partner, to control his actions and to bend him relentlessly to her own desires. The organizing centrality of the female gaze plays a central role in this insistent transformation of the male into "une chose." Jacques is often described at moments when he is asleep or unaware that he is being watched, his body presented as erotic, enticing yet highly vulnerable. In a key scene that recasts the conventional topos of the man spying upon the naked woman, Raoule surreptitiously watches him bathing. He is increasingly discomfited and embarrassed by her gaze, yet helpless to free himself from her visual control.

> Prone on the floor, behind the curtain, Mademoiselle de Vénérande could see him without troubling herself in the least. The taper's softly gleaming light grazed his blond skin that was downy all over like the skin of a peach . . .
>
> The small of the back, where the spine's curve is drawn into a voluptuous smoothness that then rises in two adorably firm, plump contours akin to the marble of Paros with its amber transparencies, was worthy of a Venus Callipyge. The thighs, though somewhat less robust than those of a woman, had yet a solid rotundity that belied their sex. The calves were set high, seeming to give the torso a jutting impertinence that was all the more piquant in a body that seemed unaware of itself. The well-turned heel was so rounded that its tapering line was scarcely perceptible.[42]

If fetishism is conventionally defined as entailing a disavowal of phallic absence, such passages by contrast enact a disavowal of phallic presence through their softening and feminizing of masculinity. Jacques's body is interpreted, framed, and rendered meaningful in relation to the ideal referent of the represented female form. In striking contrast to his depiction in their first encounter, he has become aestheticized through the idealizing force of Raoule's desire; no longer portrayed as a coarse, physically robust representative of working-class masculinity, his body has become transformed into a source of erotic awe and delight, its planes and surfaces rendered with the careful precision of a still-life painting. In Rachilde's text, it is masculinity that becomes the object of mechanisms of textual transfiguration, that is fetishized, idealized, and transmuted from the realm of nature into art.

Monsieur Vénus thus disrupts the traditional invisibility of the male body. Rather than constituting the taken-for-granted and hence absent norm, it is made into an object of detailed scrutiny and thus rendered simultaneously material and semiotic, at once fleshly envelope and complexly meaningful sign. Raoule, herself an artist, constantly textualizes her lover's body, depicting it as an exquisite *objet d'art* awaiting the gaze of the knowing female connoisseur. Janet Beizer notes that "Jacques's body traverses a semiotic spectrum in this novel, alternately becoming a poem, a text, a painting, a sculpture: in short a semiotic object to be read, deciphered, interpreted, viewed, written, painted, and molded."[43] Raoule does not just interpret Jacques's body but ultimately helps to create it, training, schooling, and transforming an uncouth working-class youth into a much admired figure of feminine elegance. Through her pedagogic formation of another subject, this female Pygmalion even threatens to usurp the ultimate prerogative. Visiting Jacques one night, Raoule finds him asleep; posed charmingly among his feminine bedclothes, he is no longer recognizable as a man. She watches him for a moment, "wondering with a kind of superstitious terror whether she had not, in the manner of God, created a being in her own image."[44] Disdaining the usual path allotted women of creation through reproduction, Rachilde's heroine defiantly reenacts the story of Genesis in the feminine. Through the power of her own act of narcissistically inspired creative will, the new Adam has been remade as a woman.

This aestheticization of masculinity is taken to its logical conclusion in the final pages of *Monsieur Vénus*. Freed from any sense of organic identity or integral personality, Jacques no longer exists as a human subject but is merely a collection of body parts that can be plundered and reassembled at will. After his eventual death in a duel instigated by Raoule, she arranges for his body to be simultaneously preserved and reformed in the shape of a wax mannequin, a kind of male automaton. This mannequin is enshrined in a concealed room of her house, where she visits it secretly at night, dressed sometimes as a man, sometimes as a woman. Half-natural, half-artificial, the mannequin is the perfect simulacrum, a male body preserved in docile and immutable form.

> On the shell-shaped couch guarded by a marble Eros, there lies a wax mannequin covered in a skin of transparent rubber. His red hair, his blond lashes, the golden down upon his chest are natural; the teeth that adorn his mouth, the nails of his hands and feet have been torn from a corpse. His enamel eyes have an adorable look in them . . .
>
> A spring set inside the lower body is connected to the mouth and makes it move.
>
> This mannequin, an anatomical masterpiece, was manufactured by a German.[45]

This final image of a male cyborg, as Naomi Schor observes, is a telling countermodel to the female automaton of Villiers de L'Isle Adam's *L'Eve future*.[46] Preserved in the beauty of his youth, transcending the terrors of time and bodily putrefaction, Jacques has become the perfect *objet d'art* for the female collector, a grotesque blend of religious icon and sex puppet. Raoule genuflects before him as if to worship before the displayed effigy of a martyr or a saint; yet she can also probe between his open thighs, causing his mouth to open obediently at her touch. The abject nature of this cyborg figure lies in its uncanny blurring of conventional systems of binary classification; both organism and machine, animate yet inanimate, living yet dead, it resists the aesthetic coherence that can be ascribed to the neighboring marble cupid even as it bears bodily witness to its own material and organic origins.

Recent feminist discussions of this figure seem unsure whether to interpret it as an instance of female fetishism; yet it clearly incorporates the simultaneous morcellization and idealization of the body that fetishism typically signifies. If, as Anne McClintock has argued, we put to one side a hermeneutic which persistently reduces the question of the fetish to an exclusively phallic economy, it becomes possible to consider the complex and culturally shifting meanings of various fetishistic investments and practices and the potential status of women as erotic agents and subjects of perverse desire. "Since fetishes involve the displacement onto impassioned objects of a host of social contradictions, they defy reduction to a single originary trauma or the psychopathology of the individual subject."[47] Death is of course a major occasion for fetishistic activity, when photographs, locks of hair, and items of clothing come to stand in for the body of the lost beloved and hence to be invested with a hyperbolic intensity of meaning. In Rachilde's novel, however, the relic is not merely a part that metonymically invokes the whole; rather it reproduces the whole in the form of an uncanny replica that approaches the realm of the hyperreal.

In this sense, the male cyborg functions less as partial compensation for an absent masculinity than as its ideal substitute; it is the logical endpoint of the series of docile and feminized males to be found in Rachilde's texts. The artificial man neither punishes nor prohibits female desire, but rather bears eloquent testimony to its creative and imaginative powers. In a discussion of the significance of wax models and preserved corpses in the history of Western representations of femininity, Elisabeth Bronfen suggests that such figures encapsulate a desire to control and distance the threat of both female sexuality and death by transforming their disruptive and indeterminate powers into a frozen, immobile, and atemporal form.[48] Here, however, it is a male body that has been solidified into anatomically correct art and that emerges as an object of erotic yet reverent contemplation. The ultimate exemplar of an obedient and sexually receptive masculinity, the mannequin simultaneously functions as a *memento mori* for the existentially self-conscious female subject, as eros and death are conjoined in Raoule's necrophilic embrace.

If masculinity can be turned into an artifact, it can also be replaced by one; thus *The Juggler* invokes the scenario of a feminine autoeroticism that is divorced from the demands and constraints of male sexual desire. Eliante warns her suitor, Léon, of her own distaste for conventional forms of sexual union, which, she claims, serve only to humiliate and subjugate women. She refuses the predictable script of heterosexual courtship, in which a man pursues a woman only to abandon her after her surrender. Her own sense of erotic pleasure, she insists, is polymorphous and diffuse and does not require the presence of a male sexual organ. While he watches in shocked disbelief, she turns toward an elegant amphora of human proportions and androgynous shape whose immutable and ancient beauty she has just extravagantly soliloquized.

> Eliante, now poised over the neck of the white amphora, stretched up from nape to heels. She was not offering herself to the man, she was giving herself to the alabaster vase, the insentient person in the room. Without a single indecent gesture, her arms chastely crossed over the slender form, neither girl nor youth, she clenched her fingers a little, in complete silence, and then the man saw her closed eyes part, her lips half open, and starlight pour from the white of her eyes and the bright enamel of her teeth; a slight tremor ran through her body—a ripple creasing the mysterious waves of her silk dress—and she gave a little imperceptible groan of pleasure, the authentic breath of the orgasmic spasm.[49]

Freed from any necessary connection to heterosexuality or even human contact, feminine eroticism is presented as a polymorphous yet celebral perversity that can be unleashed by a multiplicity of objects. The erotic and aesthetic sensitivity of Rachilde's heroines allows them to experience libidinal gratification from a variety of sources, to achieve erotic self-sufficiency through a sexualization of the inanimate and inorganic. Perverse both in their object choice and in their form of gratification, these heroines embody a fantasy of feminine pleasure outside traditional heterosexual norms. It is genital intercourse between women and men that becomes the almost unimaginable taboo in Rachilde's fiction.

Within this fiction, then, it is women who personify the aestheticized self-consciousness of modernity, whereas men remain for the most part naive and overliteral interpreters of their environment. In an ironic—perverse—rewriting of themes examined previously, the male subject can be transmuted into a work of art, yet lacks the capacity for attaining a heightened self-reflexivity. This discrepancy is illustrated most clearly in relation to the overarching motif of transvestism in *Monsieur Vénus*, a governing metaphor for the formulaic, iterable, and hence transferable nature of gender identity. Raoule revels in her mimicry and impersonation of the conventions of masculinity, revealing a chameleonlike ability to simulate perfectly the role of the rakish aristocratic gentleman. Similarly, Jacques gradually adopts stereotypically feminine traits, becoming flirtatious, petulant, and submissive as he grows accustomed to his new role as kept mistress. Maleness and femaleness are presented as products of linguistic, sartorial, and behavioral codes, modes of performative self-presentation that are governed by contingent hierarchies of social relations rather than by innate instincts and desires.

The crucial difference between the two characters, however, is that Raoule retains a mobility of gender identity that Jacques lacks, delighting in her shifting persona as she switches freely from male to female attire. Jacques, by contrast, soon becomes fatally immured in his new identity as a conventionally feminine heterosexual woman and is unable to transcend it. When he catches sight of Rachilde's breasts during their love-making, he is deeply agitated: the illusion of her masculinity that is necessary for his own nascent sense of femininity has been shattered. After a visit to a brothel reveals that he is no longer able to experience any desire for women, his sexual preferences shift accordingly. "Confusing men with Raoule and Raoule with men," unable to distinguish between the facsimile and the real, Jacques-as-a-woman begins to desire men and as a result himself becomes the object of homosexual desire. Rarely have the complex entanglements of gender identity and sexual object choice been plotted so adeptly as in Rachilde's novel, which resembles a hall of mirrors in its dazzling choreographing of the proliferations and mutations of modern erotic relations.

Contradicting Deleuze's claim that sadism is inherently hostile to the aesthetic attitude, *La jongleuse* and *Monsieur Vénus* thus combine a thematics of female domination narrated from the viewpoint of the heroine with a highly stylized and self-reflexive form. The rationalist, quasi-mathematical grammar of the Sadean text with its relentless repetitions and combinations of sexual partners is replaced by the structural pre-eminence of detail, surface, and ornament. The deliberate obscenity of de Sade's lists of organs and orgasms gives way to an eroticism that is cerebral rather than genital, that is less interested in the goal of climactic release than the devious and deviant pleasures to be found en route. If perversion is defined as pleasure without function, then Rachilde's oeuvre can be seen as the ultimate exemplar of the perverse in terms of both content and form. Just as her female characters resist the goal of reproduction and genital sexuality, so her texts refuse any straightforward mimetic reading by flaunting their status as texts and by overtly displaying their own fictionality through parodistic citation of numerous fin-de-siècle novelistic clichés.[50]

This ludic aesthetic, however, also reveals its own mechanisms of disavowal, embodied in an aristocratic disdain not simply for the values of productivity and function, but for their somatic materialization in the working—and working-class—body. Inevitably, economic privilege serves as a fundamental prerequisite for a self-conscious espousal of deviance in the fin de siècle; it is only because of their position within the class structure that Rachilde's heroines can defy prevailing conceptions of gender identity and sexual practice without incurring the dangers of either surveillance or incarceration. The cultivation of a self-consciously aestheticized personality in turn presumes a certain distance from the realm of immediate need; not everyone, after all, can live life as a work of art. Here the perverse woman meets the figure of the dandy in their shared distaste for the vulgarity of the lower classes, who epitomize an unmediated closeness to the material body that is defined as the antithesis of the stylized rituals of perverse performance.

Interpreted within such a class rubric, Rachilde's texts appear in an obviously more problematic light. The subversive destabilization of gender in *Monsieur Vénus* is simultaneously an erasure of the working-class body whose labor forms the necessary precondition for Raoule's own freedom to disdain any imperatives of function and need. This erasure is evidenced in the form of Jacques's dramatic transformation, which effaces his class position as well as his gender; his metamorphosis magically erases all corporeal signs of his economic origins and his previous history of work and productivity. Working-class masculinity is thus both acknowledged and negated through Jacques's subsumption into Raoule's elegant social sphere, as if such an *Aufhebung* were to denote the possibility of miraculously transcending the unpalatable bodily reminders of a class-stratified social structure. A similar anxiety is apparent in the text's treatment of Jacques's sister, Marie Silvert, a working-class prostitute who conspicuously lacks the sumptuous glamor of the high-class courtesan. Her province is not the elegant boudoir but rather the gutter, the brothel, and the street. A grotesque and foul-mouthed harridan, she is depicted as a vocal enemy of Raoule who is compulsively driven by a sordid greed for money. If erotic desire acquires a transgressive aura in Rachilde's writing, the yearning for hard cash that is felt by the poor is not endowed with the same exalted and idealized status. Rather, the working-class woman epitomizes a vulgar urgency of need that the ambiguously gendered aesthete has transcended. She is a body that must be expunged from the text, because she remains trapped within her own nature and materiality, a telling symbol of corporeal abjection. Her occluded labor and desire thus mark the necessary limits of the aesthetics and erotics of fin-de-siècle experimentation.

Historicizing Perversion

My detailed discussion of Rachilde's texts has, I hope, been justified both by their relative unfamiliarity and by their pertinence to theorizing questions of sexual politics and the female avant-garde. These texts echo a general fascination with sexual deviance as a privileged metaphor for an avant-garde aesthetics of indeterminacy; the pervert does not embody an inborn truth of sexuality so much as the fact that there is no such truth, testifying to the mysterious and labile workings of erotic desire. But it is woman who has become the exemplary bearer of this vision and whose subtle and perverse passions both draw on and challenge the received wisdoms about female sexuality that pervade medical, sexological, and psychoanalytical discourse. Refusing dominant views of female passionlessness, passivity, and conservatism, Rachilde presents woman as a modern, self-conscious, and triumphantly erotic subject.

Rachilde herself explicitly distinguished such a modernist erotics and aesthetics from the political modernity of public life. For her, as for many other writers and artists in fin-de-siècle Paris, public politics was a domain irredeemably compromised by the philistinism, vulgarity, and mediocrity of bourgeois society. She seems to have felt little sympathy for the French feminists of the turn of the century, regarding them merely as dupes of the system in their single-minded pursuit of the chimera of political equality. This disdain for modern politics is exemplified in the portrait in *The Juggler* of Missy, an earnest young bluestocking whose knowledgeable and forthright manner merely serves to underscore her utter blindness to the understated and erotic nuances of interaction between women and men. Whereas seduction and masquerade constitute strategies of feminine power, the figure of the new woman is risible and ultimately pathetic in her struggle to enter the public world on an equal footing with men.

Rachilde touches on these issues in more detail in *Pourquoi je ne suis pas féministe,* published toward the end of her literary career. Commenting on her lack of faith in women and her own desire to have been a man, she also denies this wish has any broader political ramifications. "This propensity towards masculine behavior did not inspire in me any desire to seize rights which were not mine. I have always acted as an *individual,* without thinking of founding a society or overthrowing the existing one."[51] Similarly, she downplays her own history of cross-dressing—during the 1880s Rachilde was one of only three women in France given police authorization to wear men's clothes—as a decision made on purely economic and practical grounds. Rachilde then launches into a disparagement of women's attempts to enter French political and cultural life by insisting upon their innate weaknesses and the fundamental inferiority of her own sex. In this response, one can glimpse Rachilde's discomfort with the popularization of her own subversive stance; by the 1920s women en masse were beginning to demand access to sexual freedoms and forms of behavior previously seen as exclusively masculine. Such a democratization could only appear to be a vulgarization to Rachilde, whose own aristocratic and individualistic perspective defined itself in explicit opposition to mainstream attitudes.

She was hardly alone in holding this view in fin-de-siècle France. The antithesis between artistic and political visions of liberation seemed absolute; very few individuals, it appeared, could imagine a fusion of social engagement and a broad-based politics with an individual vision of libidinal and aesthetic freedom. In recent times, by contrast, such a connection is repeatedly affirmed in critical appeals to an aesthetics of everyday life and a micropolitics of desire. The heritage of 1968, with its impassioned commitment to an ideal of sexual liberation, lives on in a recognition of the intermeshing of erotics and politics and the insistence on erotics *as* politics. Second-wave feminism has played a central role in reconfiguring the relations between social, aesthetic, and libidinal domains, even though feminists reveal differing and often conflicting responses to existing representations of sexual deviance. Does perversion bespeak instinctual compulsion or conscious rebellion? Is it a sign of real or illusory erotic freedom?

In a book entitled *Female Perversions,* the feminist therapist Louise Kaplan explicitly condemns the contemporary idealization of the pervert. Rather than being a modish symbol of erotic freedom, she insists, "the pervert has no choice. His sexual performance is obligatory, compulsive, fixated, and rigid."[52] While expanding established definitions of sexual deviance to incorporate relatively common forms of female behavior, Kaplan insists that perversion, whether female or male, is a form of pathology. Perverts are not free but imprisoned, trapped by their own compulsive fixations, forced to enact a script not of their own making. By contrast, Mandy Merck's recent *Perversions* reinstates and reaffirms the equation between perverse sexuality and a rebellious defection from doctrine and stifling orthodoxy. Merck reads perversion not as an expression of psychic unfreedom, but rather as epitomizing an aestheticized realm of irony, parody, and performance. The term registers a deliberate choice of existence on the margins, an attempt to live askew, that gains specific resonances in the context of Merck's professed alliance with queer theory. Perversion thus becomes symptomatic of a more general commitment to challenging fixed truths and valuing partiality and ambiguity.[53]

The dissonances between these two texts are striking, arising less from a disagreement over the meaning of a phenomenon than from the incommensurate positioning of that phenomenon within the differing registers of therapeutic and aesthetic discourse. These contrasting conceptions of perversion are explicitly juxtaposed within the space of a few lines in an article by Parveen Adams on lesbian sadomasochism. While conceding that from the standpoint of psychoanalysis lesbian sadomasochism must necessarily qualify as a perversion, Adams seeks nevertheless to distinguish between the compulsory pathology of the traditional pervert and the liberatory perversion of the lesbian.

> For the clinical pervert things have to be just so. The fetishist is immobilized by his fetish, the masochist plays and replays the scene that is essential to him. The rigidity and repetition constitute the compulsion and the enigma of the masochist's sexuality. For the lesbian sadomasochist, on the other hand, there is an erotic plasticity and movement; she constructs fetishes and substitutes them; she multiplies fantasies and tries them on like costumes. All this is done quite explicitly as an incitement of the senses, a proliferation of bodily pleasures, a transgressive excitement; a play with identity and a play with genitality. It is a perverse intensification of pleasure.[54]

The perversion of the heterosexual is rigid, compulsive, and pathological, whereas that of the lesbian sadomasochist is aesthetic, free-floating, and mobile. The conflicting interpretations of perversion that I have traced in late-nineteenth-century psychiatry and aesthetics reappear in Adam's distinction between perversion as involuntary pathology and as transgressive play.

Although I am not convinced that lesbian sexual practices can transcend psychic and social determination in quite the way Adams suggests, such celebrations of the perverse are clearly connected both to the development of lesbian and gay rights movements and to the more recent emergence of queer politics and theory. Given the long-standing interpretation of same-sex desire as one of the primary forms of sexual deviance, it is unsurprising that perversion has emerged as a defining term within recent sexuality debates. Significantly, however, such a reclamation of the perverse requires a recuperation of both its aesthetic and its (im)moral, as well as its erotic, dimensions; only when interpreted as an act of symbolic refusal rather than as merely a product of biological or psychic determination can perversion be redeemed as a category of cultural resistance. In this sense, the multilayered meanings of perversion live on in the ways it is currently deployed.

This aestheticization of the perverse links into a widespread interest in the politics of the performative which is also currently in evidence in postmodern theory, cultural studies, and feminism. The prominence of such texts as Judith Butler's *Gender Trouble* and Marjorie Garber's *Vested Interests* epitomizes the current trend toward viewing gender and sexuality as labile, shifting, and performative acts. Yet critical deployments of metaphors of performance, masquerade, and transvestism do not always sustain their own political claims at the level of either social theory or historical particularity. The aestheticization of politics may result in a simple conflation of aesthetics with politics and an unproblematic affirmation of "deviant" sexual expression as a utopian site of transgressive excess. Here Danae Clark's recent analysis of "commodity lesbianism" provides a useful corrective in its subtle analysis of the complex intermeshings and affiliations between contemporary sexual subcultures and the marketing strategies of a consumer society increasingly oriented toward style, performance, and the exploitation of sexual ambiguity. This is not to demonize commodification as signaling the inevitable corruption of an authentic prior identity, but merely to note that any assessment of the present-day politics of perversion cannot avoid the question of its extensive entanglement with consumer culture and the paradoxical mainstreaming of the deviant.[55]

In Rachilde's time, of course, the conditions determining the production and reception of a perverse aesthetic were of a very different order. Rather than suffering from either popularization or commodification, her texts were largely defined by the author's own positioning in and identification with a relatively small and self-consciously marginal coterie of decadent intellectuals. A broader female or feminist constituency for Rachilde's writing did not exist, not that the author herself would have had time for such a notion. Instead, her writings circulated within an almost exclusively male artistic circle; since she was the token woman in this subculture, it seems unlikely that her work had any substantive impact on existing gender attitudes. Although I have highlighted some of the more provocative aspects of her writing as seen from a present-day perspective, her male colleagues remained oblivious to these same features. Published commentaries on her work, such as Maurice Barrès's preface to *Monsieur Vénus*, typically frame her work as the titillating outpourings of a precocious yet naive nymphet, invoking precisely the stereotype of instinctual femininity that I have argued Rachilde's work is at great pains to problematize.[56]

Yet although Rachilde herself refused the label of feminist, her work nevertheless contains powerful representations of the multifarious and perverse trajectories of female sexuality which continue to speak beyond the particularities of their own time. Turning her back on contemporary views of woman as either angel in the house or earnest suffragette, she created a distinctively modern vision of female erotic and aesthetic agency. In this sense, she exemplified, in her own words, a "revolutionary spirit" in sexual matters that was rare for a woman of her era. In the present, as women begin to claim their own right to be perverse, her work is again coming into its own. We do not need to claim Rachilde as an exemplary feminist forerunner in order to appreciate the startling and innovative power of her representations of female sexuality, even while we also acknowledge their limits.

Afterword:
Rewriting the Modern

Rachilde is perhaps a fitting subject with which to bring my discussion to a close. The current growth of feminist interest in her work underlines the protean and unstable constitution of the cultural traditions of modernity, their continuing interpretation and redefinition from the desires and perspectives of the present. It is unlikely that an analysis of Rachilde would have appeared in a critical text of this kind ten years ago; its inclusion thus serves as a useful illustration and reminder of the shifting state of feminist discourse itself and its concomitant redefinitions of the history of women and gender relations. As new paradigms and ideological concerns come into view, the past and our relationship to it is subject to an ongoing process of contestation and revision. In this sense, as Nietzsche was one of the first to emphasize, history does not give us a neutral record of an already established reality, but assumes diverse rhetorical forms and works to various psychological and social ends.

Nietzsche's essay on the use and abuse of history has often been interpreted as an ironic debunking of the pretensions of historical knowledge and its claims to truth. Yet this is surely to oversimplify a complex argument which simultaneously insists upon the necessity and inescapability of history. While Nietzsche is scathing in his dismissal of the sway of Hegelian historicism and the disabling effects of a craven antiquarianism, he is equally insistent that we cannot escape the burden of historical consciousness. The issue is not one of going "beyond" history, but rather one of acknowledging that the act of constructing a relationship to one's past is always already invested with interests and prejudice (prejudgment) rather than embodying the creation of value-free science. For Nietzsche, then, historical knowledge is intimately connected to questions of human needs, rather than being an absolute and self-evident value in itself.[1]

Nietzsche's untimely meditations have themselves become timely in an era that is marked by the questioning of History but also by a proliferation of histories. History may no longer stand as an absolute guarantor of meta-physical truths (did it ever really do so?), but magisterial proclamations of its imminent demise coexist, often on the same bookshelf, with a tumultous array of references to history, tradition, and the past across a variety of cultural forms and genres. In this disjuncture, one can glimpse yet another instance of the nonsynchronicity often noted in discussions of the post-modern, the dissonance between the discourses of those intellectuals mourning or celebrating the death of their own guiding meta-narratives and the very different perspectives of other disenfranchised groups who are begin-ning to gain access to the public construction of their own genealogies and histories. Drawing on yet simultaneously questioning many of the established genres of historiography and historical fiction, such groups are beginning to create new understandings and formulations of temporality and the past.

Part of that project of historical reconstruction remains the reading and writing of the ambivalent legacy of modernity. One of the reasons for the renewed interest in the idea of the modern in contemporary theory is the dethroning of the white bourgeois male as privileged subject of history, which re-opens and leaves unresolved the question of what modernity might mean for women and other subaltern groups. If recent feminist criticism is said to involve a return to history, what might history signify in the aftermath of challenges to epochal unity and unilinear narrative? How can we rethink the temporality of texts in such a way as to do justice to issues of gender politics? My own analysis has sought to provide a partial response to this question by unraveling some of the irreducible complexities of the history of the modern as they might be seen in relation to contemporary feminist concerns. I have contended that to write about modernity is always to be implicated, whether unwittingly or self-consciously, in hierarchies of sexual difference, but also that the history of the modern itself contains an extended tradition of questioning and contesting dominant gender norms.

In one sense, of course, this argument for complexity is not in itself particularly new. In Carl Schorske's classic text on fin-de-siècle Vienna, one can find the following lines: "what the historian must now abjure, and nowhere more so than in confronting the problem of modernity, is the positing in advance of an abstract categorical common denominator—what Hegel called the *Zeitgeist* and Mill 'the characteristic of the age.' Where such an intuitive discernment of unities once served, we must now be willing to undertake the empirical pursuit of pluralities as a precondition to finding unitary patterns in culture."[2] Of course, as Schorske's text, and my own, clearly demonstrate, there are obvious limits affecting any individual's capacity to achieve such a pursuit of plurality and to remain receptive to the differentiated particularities of a historical era. I have sought nevertheless to destabilize a periodizing category that has often been simplistically defined in the context of feminist theory in order to explore some of the varying ways in which woman have been seen, and have seen themselves, as modern subjects. In this project, I have been guided by the view that different genres of discourse can tell different stories about the same culture at the same moment, as Carol Clover notes in a different context, and that a particular kind of writing may illuminate certain facets of women's modernity that another text serves to obscure.[3] There are, nevertheless, many facets of the gender/modernity relationship which I have been unable to pursue. Some of these absences can, and undoubtedly will, be read symptomatically as deriving from the blind spots of my own social history and disciplinary training. At the same time, they are also a reminder of the necessary limits of any one work of theory, which can no longer claim, if it ever could, to encapsulate the entire meaning of the modern era.

There are, furthermore, obvious limits to the doctrine of plurality and heterogeneity; not all stories which a particular epoch tells about itself will appear equally persuasive or equally plausible. Indeed, the very process of textual selection and interpretation, the identification of certain works as more worthy of discussion than others, presupposes certain assumptions about the constitution of reality or particular aspects of it, just as these schemata may themselves be modified through the act of reading in an endless hermeneutic spiral. Any form of politically inflected and hence critical reading, moreover, is necessarily committed to investigating, however tentatively, the interactive flows of influence, determination, and causality linking particular texts to broader structures of power. In the present context, I have focused on key issues which seem particularly significant in theorizing cultural representations of women and modernity; these include commodification and consumerism, the private/public distinction, female sexuality, the politics of avant-garde aesthetics and mass culture, the organizational power of historical narrative, and the differentiation yet simultaneous contamination of political, religious, and scientific vocabularies. By discussing a number of these motifs in more than one chapter, I have also sought to establish meaningful connections and parallels across individual analyses of particular texts. My argument thus assumes a messy and multidimensional entanglement of socio-discursive relations that are marked by family resemblances, points of connection, and shared causal relationships as well as by moments of disjuncture and contradiction.

One of my primary concerns has been to identify and to disentangle, even if only partially, the murky and often confusing elision of the descriptive and the normative that distinguishes many discussions of modernity. To define someone or something as modern is, almost inevitably, to communicate a value judgment about that person's or object's worth. In my introductory chapters I noted that representations of the modern have repeatedly positioned women in a zone of ahistorical otherness and have thereby sought to minimize their agency, contemporaneity, and humanity. In a sense, the rest of the book is a critical response to this view and an argument for the significance of women and the feminine in the history of modernity. I have attempted to render visible women's contributions to the more entrenched institutions of the modern as well as to reconceptualize certain aspects of culture often not seen in such a light. This is not to argue that women have been autonomous creators of their own history, but rather to elucidate the complex interactions of determination and agency shaping women's (and men's) responses to the world into which they are born. Such a project has involved, inevitably, not simply a reconceptualization of women as modern subjects, but also a significant revision and rearticulation of the defining categories of the modern itself.

One of the most striking—and for me unexpected—results of this rereading of the modern through the figure of woman has been the new prominence and visibility of cultural expressions of yearning, dissatisfaction, and restlessness in nineteenth-century culture. Rather than reiterating a confident belief in the superiority of modern Western society, most of the texts that I have examined rely on mechanisms of temporal or spatial displacement to locate meaning elsewhere, whether in an edenic past, a projected future, or a zone of cultural otherness. Such articulations of longing are of course not necessarily oppositional—on the contrary, I have tried to show how they are tied up in complicated ways with the logics of consumerism and the politics of colonialism as well as with struggles for social change. Nevertheless, they serve to underscore the fundamental ambivalences entangled with the idea of the modern. Rather than being limited to the contestatory culture of the twentieth-century avant-garde, textual expressions of contradiction and ambiguity can be found in many nineteenth-century texts that reveal a profound awareness of the conflicts and crises engendered by processes of modernization. The figure of woman and the idea of the feminine have emerged as a key zone for the expression of such ambivalences by both men and women.

My argument for women's modernity should not, however, be confused with a wholesale defense and affirmation of all aspects of that modernity. On the contrary, my aim has been to question sweeping evaluations of the modern as either a liberating or a repressive phenomenon by addressing its multidimensional and contradictory manifestations. As Peter Stallybrass has argued, "it is impossible to define 'the modern' as if it had a single referent. Rather, one needs to look at the particular classifications, practices and institutions which the term is used to initiate and support."[4] These different practices and institutions will clearly possess varying meanings and values when viewed from the standpoint of feminist theory and politics. Indeed, my own text has repeatedly resorted to norms and value judgments—some overt, some covert—in reading the history of femininity and modernity. Here I find myself in agreement with Steven Connor's recent argument for the inescapability of normativity and hierarchies of value, which remain evident—implicitly if not explicitly—in the practice of contemporary theory.[5] The point is, however, that these judgments are tied to assessments of the contingent gender politics of particular dimensions of the modern; they do not arise out of a global historical vision which freezes women in an unchanging relationship to an inexorable temporal logic.

In the final stages of this project, as I have become more familiar with debates in postcolonial theory, I have been struck by the manifest correspondences and points of connection between much of this theoretical work and my own concerns. A major area of commonality derives from the perceived intellectual and political bankruptcy of the tradition/modernity opposition as elaborated in dichotomies of authenticity and alienation, nature and culture, timelessness and history, and so on. Such polarizations have marked much of the critique of the oppressive trajectories of Western imperialism, and they continue to determine many feminist responses to modernity. In the writings of such theorists as Homi Bhabha, Trinh Minh-ha, and Gayatri Spivak, however, this idealization of the authentic native other as existing outside modernity and the legacy of colonialism has been replaced by an insistence upon hybridity, contamination, and intermixture as fundamentally constitutive of cultural identity.[6] In particular, much of this writing has sought to radically destabilize the concept of tradition, as exemplified in Western nativist nostalgia for timeless, noncontradictory ethnic identities, and to insist on the complex temporalities and disjunctive cultural logics operative in non-Western societies.

The ramifications of this critique for our understanding of the history and racial dynamics of the modern itself has, however, been less systematically explored. In this context, Paul Gilroy's recently published *The Black Atlantic: Modernity and Double Consciousness* provides a major contribution to and revision of existing theories of modernity. Gilroy is critical of what he describes as a volkish trend within cultural criticism which seeks to construct an autonomous tradition of black history and identity grounded in an ideal of racial authenticity. Such antimodernist positions are themselves, he notes, deeply if often unconsciously indebted to nineteenth-century theories of nationalism shaped by the heritage of German Romanticism. Instead, Gilroy develops an alternative, transcultural, and transnational notion of the black Atlantic as a web of hybrid diasporic identities, a complex intermixture of African and European philosophical and cultural systems and ideas. Without denying the terrible legacy of modernity exemplified in its heritage of slavery and racism, he seeks to investigate the ways in which black individuals have themselves drawn selectively on the tradition of the modern through practices of both affirmation and critique. Black culture is for Gilroy thus a "counter-culture of modernity," even though the recognition of the centrality of race to the modern brings with it a need to reconceptualize many of the periodizing and theoretical categories through which the modern has been understood. Thus, Gilroy writes, the diaspora of the black Atlantic is constituted as "a non-traditional tradition, an irreducibly modern, ex-centric, unstable and asymmetrical cultural ensemble that cannot be apprehended through the manichean logic of binary coding."[7]

I would not wish to overstate the similarities between Gilroy's argument and my own; this would be to elide their distinct and diverging political agendas. Nor do I seek to appropriate his text in order to legitimate my own work, which must inevitably stand or fall on its own merits. Gilroy's subtle and complex argument, however, further intensifies my own conviction that the history of the modern needs to be rethought in terms of the various subaltern identities that have contributed to its formation. In expanding our understanding of the inescapable plurality of modern subjects, such a project involves a major fracturing and reshaping of established temporal schemata and periodizing structures. Received wisdoms about the aesthetics and politics of the modern will thereby be subjected to processes of contestation and revision, as the heterogeneous, often nonsynchronous, yet intersecting modernities of different social groups come into view. The history of the modern is thus not yet over; in a very real sense, it has yet to be written.

Notes

Introduction

1. Louis A. Montrose, "Professing the Renaissance: The Poetics and Politics of Culture," in *The New Historicism*, ed. H. Aram Veeser (New York: Routledge, 1989), p. 23. For discussions of the textual dimensions of historical representation, see, among others, Hayden White, *Metahistory: The Historical Imagination in Nineteenth-Century Europe* (Baltimore: The Johns Hopkins University Press, 1973), and *Tropics of Discourse: Essays in Cultural Criticism* (Baltimore: The Johns Hopkins University Press, 1978); Dominick LaCapra, *History and Criticism* (Ithaca: Cornell University Press, 1985); and Lionel Gossman, *Between History and Literature* (Cambridge: Harvard University Press, 1990).

2. Marshall Berman, *All That Is Solid Melts into Air: The Experience of Modernity* (London: Verso, 1983), pp. 53–54.

3. Ibid., p. 57.

4. See, e.g., Jessica Benjamin, *The Bonds of Love: Psychoanalysis, Feminism, and the Problem of Domination* (New York: Pantheon, 1988).

5. Gail Finney, *Women in Modern Drama: Freud, Feminism, and European Theater at the Turn of the Century* (Ithaca: Cornell University Press, 1989), p. 13. See also Elaine Showalter, *The Female Malady: Women, Madness, and English Culture, 1830–1980* (London: Virago, 1987).

6. See also Harry Redner, *In the Beginning Was the Deed: Reflections on the Passage of Faust* (Berkeley: University of California Press, 1982).

7. Douglas Kellner, *Critical Theory, Marxism, and Modernity* (Baltimore: The Johns Hopkins University Press, 1989), p. 91.

8. Theodor Adorno and Max Horkheimer, *Dialectic of Enlightenment* (London: Verso, 1979), p. xvi.

9. Andrew Hewitt, "A Feminine Dialectic of Enlightenment? Horkheimer and Adorno Revisited," *New German Critique*, 56 (1992): 147.

10. Patricia Jagentowicz Mills, *Woman, Nature, and Psyche* (New Haven: Yale University Press, 1987), p. 89.

11. Ibid., pp. 192–195.

12. Horst Ruthrof, "The Hidden Telos: Hermeneutics in Critical Rewriting," *Semiotica*, 100, 1 (1994): 90–91.

1. Modernity and Feminism

Epigraph: Meaghan Morris, "Things to Do with Shopping Centres," in *Grafts: Feminist Cultural Criticism*, ed. Susan Sheridan (London: Verso, 1988), p. 202.

1. Bryan S. Turner, "The Rationalization of the Body: Reflections on Modernity and Discipline," in *Max Weber: Rationality and Modernity*, ed. Sam Whimster and Scott Lash (London: Allen and Unwin, 1987), p. 223.

2. David Frisby, *Fragments of Modernity* (Cambridge: MIT Press, 1986), p. 4.

3. Matei Calinescu, *Five Faces of Modernity: Modernism, Avant-Garde, Decadence, Kitsch, Postmodernism* (Durham: Duke University Press, 1987), p. 91.

4. Susan J. Hekman, *Gender and Knowledge: Elements of a Postmodern Feminism* (Cambridge: Polity Press, 1990), p. 188.

5. *Modernism, 1890–1930*, ed. Malcolm Bradbury and James McFarlane (Harmondsworth: Penguin, 1976), p. 41.

6. Marshall Berman, *All That Is Solid Melts into Air: The Experience of Modernity* (London: Verso, 1983), p. 14.

7. See Jürgen Habermas, *The Philosophical Discourse of Modernity* (Cambridge: Polity Press, 1987), and *Habermas and Modernity*, ed. Richard J. Bernstein (Cambridge: Polity Press, 1985).

8. Vincent Descombes, "Le Beau Moderne," *Modern Language Notes*, 104, 4 (1989): 787–803.

9. Lawrence E. Cahoone, *The Dilemma of Modernity: Philosophy, Culture, and Anti-Culture* (Albany: State University of New York Press, 1988), p. 1.

10. My discussion here draws on Mike Featherstone's helpful gloss, "In Pursuit of the Postmodern," *Theory, Culture, and Society*, 5, 2/3 (1988): 195–215.

11. See Frisby, *Fragments of Modernity*, and Mike Featherstone, "Postmodernism and the Aestheticization of Everyday Life," in *Modernity and Identity*, ed. Scott Lash and Jonathan Friedman (Oxford: Basil Blackwell, 1992).

12. See, e.g., Charles Taylor, *Sources of the Self: The Making of the Modern Identity* (Cambridge: Harvard University Press, 1989).

13. Calinescu, *Five Faces of Modernity*, pp. 23–35.

14. On the complicity of Western notions of history and modernity with the legacy of imperialism, see, e.g., Robert Young, *White Mythologies: Writing History and the West* (London: Routledge, 1990).

15. Joan B. Landes, *Women and the Public Sphere in the Age of the French Revolution* (Ithaca: Cornell University Press, 1988), p. 204.

16. Gianni Vattimo, *The End of Modernity: Nihilism and Hermeneutics in a Post-Modern Culture* (Baltimore: The Johns Hopkins University Press, 1988), p. 4.

17. See, e.g., Carole Pateman, *The Disorder of Women: Democracy, Feminism, and Political Theory* (Stanford: Stanford University Press, 1989); *Feminist Interpretation and Political Theory*, ed. Mary Lyndon Stanley and Carole Pateman (Cambridge: Polity Press, 1991); R. A. Sydie, *Natural Women, Cultured Men: A Feminist Perspective on Sociological Theory* (Milton Keynes: Open University Press, 1987); T. R. Kandal, *The Woman Question in Classical Sociological Theory* (Miami: Florida International University Press, 1988).

18. Susan Buck-Morss, "The Flâneur, the Sandwichman, and the Whore: The Politics

of Loitering," *New German Critique*, 39 (1986): 119. The flâneur has emerged as a key figure in recent feminist accounts of modernity, though opinions vary as to the possibility of a female flâneur. See Janet Wolff, "The Invisible Flâneuse: Women and the Literature of Modernity," *Theory, Culture, and Society*, 2, 3 (1985): 37–46; Griselda Pollock, "Modernity and the Spaces of Femininity," in her *Vision and Difference: Femininity, Feminism and the Histories of Art* (New York: Routledge, 1988); Deborah Epstein Nord, "The Urban Peripatetic: Spectator, Streetwalker, Woman Writer," *Nineteenth-Century Literature*, 46, 3 (1991): 351–375; and Elizabeth Wilson, "The Invisible Flâneur," *New Left Review*, 191 (1992): 90–110.

19. Juliet Flower MacCannell, *The Regime of the Brother: After the Patriarchy* (London: Routledge, 1991). On fraternity, see also Carole Pateman, *The Sexual Contract* (Stanford: Stanford University Press, 1988).

20. Landes, *Women and the Public Sphere*, and Pollock, "Modernity and the Spaces of Femininity."

21. See Iris Marion Young, "The Ideal of Community and the Politics of Difference," in *Feminism/Postmodernism*, ed. Linda Nicholson (New York: Routledge, 1990).

22. Elaine Showalter, *Sexual Anarchy: Gender and Culture at the Fin de Siècle* (New York: Viking Penguin, 1990); Sandra M. Gilbert and Susan Gubar, *No Man's Land: The Place of the Woman Writer in the Twentieth Century*, vol. 1: *The War of the Words* (New Haven: Yale University Press, 1988), and *No Man's Land*, vol. 2: *Sexchanges* (New Haven: Yale University Press, 1989); Elizabeth Wilson, *Adorned in Dreams: Fashion and Modernity* (Berkeley: University of California Press, 1987), and *The Sphinx in the City: Urban Life, the Control of Disorder, and Women* (London: Virago, 1991); Christine Buci-Glucksmann, *La raison baroque: de Baudelaire à Benjamin* (Paris: Editions Galilée, 1984); Rachel Bowlby, *Just Looking: Consumer Culture in Dreiser, Gissing, and Zola* (Methuen: New York, 1985); Nancy Armstrong, *Desire and Domestic Fiction: A Political History of the Novel* (Oxford: Oxford University Press, 1987); Andreas Huyssen, "Mass Culture as Woman: Modernism's Other" and "The Vamp and the Machine: Fritz Lang's *Metropolis*," in his *After the Great Divide: Modernism, Mass Culture, and Postmodernism* (Bloomington: Indiana University Press, 1986); Patrice Petro, *Joyless Streets: Women and Melodramatic Representation in Weimar Germany* (Princeton: Princeton University Press, 1989).

23. Mary Poovey, *Uneven Developments: The Ideological Work of Gender in Mid-Victorian England* (Chicago: University of Chicago Press, 1988), p. 8.

24. Christine Buci-Glucksmann, "Catastrophic Utopia: The Feminine as Allegory of the Modern," *Representations*, 14 (1986): 222.

25. Recent discussions of the prostitute as a symbol of modernity influenced by the work of Walter Benjamin include Buck-Morss, "The Flâneur, the Sandwichman, and the Whore," and Angelika Rauch, "The *Trauerspiel* of the Prostituted Body or Woman as Allegory of Modernity," *Cultural Critique*, 10 (1989): 77–88. See also T. J. Clark, *The Painting of Modern Life* (Princeton: Princeton University Press, 1984), ch. 2; Charles Bernheimer, *Figures of Ill-Repute: Representing Prostitution in Nineteenth-Century France* (Cambridge: Harvard University Press, 1989); Alain Corbin, *Women for Hire: Prostitution and Sexuality in France after 1850* (Cambridge: Harvard University Press, 1990); Lynda Nead, *Myths of Sexuality: Representations of Women in Victorian Britain* (Oxford: Basil Blackwell, 1988); and Judith Walkowitz, *Prostitution and Victorian Society: Women, Class,*

and the State (Cambridge: Cambridge University Press, 1980), and *City of Dreadful Delight: Narratives of Sexual Danger in Late-Victorian London* (Chicago: University of Chicago Press, 1992).

26. Charles Baudelaire, *The Painter of Modern Life and Other Essays* (London: Phaidon Press, 1984), p. 36.

27. Philippe Auguste Villiers de L'Isle Adam, *Tomorrow's Eve,* trans. Robert Martin Adams (Urbana: University of Illinois Press, 1982). See also, e.g., Mary Ann Doane, "Technophilia: Technology, Representation, and the Feminine," in *Body/Politics: Women and the Discourse of Science,* ed. Mary Jacobus, Evelyn Fox Keller, and Sally Shuttleworth (New York: Routledge, 1990); Annette Michelson, "On the Eve of the Future: The Reasonable Facsimile and the Philosophical Toy," in *October: The First Decade, 1976–1986,* ed. Annette Michelson et al. (Cambridge: MIT Press, 1987); Rodolphe Gasché, "The Stelliferous Fold: On Villiers de L'Isle-Adam's *L'Eve future,*" *Studies in Romanticism,* 22 (1983): 293–327; Peter Gendolla, *Die lebenden Maschinen: Zur Geschichte der Maschinen-menschen bei Jean Paul, E. T. A. Hoffmann, und Villiers de L'Isle Adam* (Marburg: Guttandin und Hoppe, 1980).

28. My discussion of the mechanical woman is indebted to Huyssen's "The Vamp and the Machine." For the cyborg, see Donna Haraway, "A Manifesto for Cyborgs: Science, Technology, and Socialist Feminism in the 1980s," in her *Simians, Cyborgs, and Women* (New York: Routledge, 1991).

29. Thais E. Morgan, "Male Lesbian Bodies: The Construction of Alternative Mascu-linities in Courbet, Baudelaire, and Swinburne," *Genders,* 15 (1992): 41. See also Walter Benjamin, *Charles Baudelaire: A Lyric Poet in the Era of High Capitalism* (London: New Left Books, 1973), pp. 89–93, and Lillian Faderman, *Surpassing the Love of Men: Romantic Friendships and Love between Women from the Renaissance to the Present* (London: Junc-tion Books, 1981), pp. 254–276.

30. Teresa de Lauretis, *Technologies of Gender* (Bloomington: Indiana University Press, 1987).

31. Eugene Lunn, *Marxism and Modernism* (London: Verso, 1985), pp. 33–37.

32. Malcolm Bradbury and James McFarlane, "The Name and Nature of Modernism," in Bradbury and McFarlane, *Modernism,* p. 27.

33. Marianne DeKoven, *Rich and Strange: Gender, History, Modernism* (Princeton: Princeton University Press, 1991), p. 12.

34. Suzette Henke, *James Joyce and the Politics of Desire* (London: Routledge, 1990).

35. See, e.g., Shari Benstock, *Women of the Left Bank: Paris, 1900–1940* (Austin: Uni-versity of Texas Press, 1986); Gillian Hanscombe and Virginia L. Smyers, *Writing for Their Lives: The Modernist Women, 1910–1940* (London: Women's Press, 1987); and *The Gender of Modernism: A Critical Anthology,* ed. Bonnie Kime Scott (Bloomington: Indiana Uni-versity Press, 1990).

36. Celeste Schenk, "Charlotte Mew," in *The Gender of Modernism,* p. 320, note 1.

37. Laura Marcus, "Feminist Aesthetics and the New Realism," in *New Feminist Dis-courses,* ed. Isobel Armstrong (London: Routledge, 1992), p. 14. For a detailed discussion of the mimetic claims implicit in much modernist aesthetic theory, see Astradur Eysteinsson, *The Concept of Modernism* (Ithaca: Cornell University Press, 1990).

38. DeKoven, *Rich and Strange,* p. 8.

39. Alain Corbin, "Backstage," in *A History of Private Life*, vol. 4: *From the Fires of Revolution to the Great War*, ed. Michelle Perrot (Cambridge: Harvard University Press, 1990), p. 503.

40. Calinescu, *Five Faces of Modernity*, p. 43.

41. Martin Pumphrey, "The Flapper, the Housewife, and the Making of Modernity," *Cultural Studies*, 1, 2 (1987): 181.

42. Here I am thinking of the above-mentioned texts by Petro, Huyssen, and Wilson, but also of such landmark works in feminist cultural studies as Tania Modleski, *Loving with a Vengeance: Mass-Produced Fantasies for Women* (New York: Methuen, 1984); Ien Ang, *Watching Dallas* (New York: Methuen, 1985); and Janice Radway, *Reading the Romance: Women, Patriarchy, and Popular Literature* (Chapel Hill: University of North Carolina Press, 1984).

43. Ludmilla Jordanova, *Sexual Visions: Images of Gender in Science and Medicine between the Eighteenth and Twentieth Centuries* (New York: Harvester Wheatsheaf, 1989), p. 2.

44. Nancy Fraser, *Unruly Practices: Power, Discourse, and Gender in Contemporary Social Theory* (Minneapolis: University of Minnesota Press, 1989).

2. On Nostalgia

Epigraph: Susan Stewart, *On Longing: Narratives of the Miniature, the Gigantic, the Souvenir, the Collection* (Baltimore: The Johns Hopkins University Press, 1984), p. 23.

1. Bryan S. Green, *Literary Methods and Sociological Theory: Case Studies of Simmel and Weber* (Chicago: University of Chicago Press, 1988), p. 6.

2. Wolf Lepenies, *Between Literature and Science: The Rise of Sociology* (Cambridge: Cambridge University Press, 1988), p. 1.

3. Charles Lemert, "Sociology: Prometheus among the Sciences of Man," *Boundary 2*, 2, 2/3 (1985): 84.

4. "Georg Simmel," in Lewis A. Coser, *Masters of Sociological Thought*, 2nd ed. (New York: Harcourt Brace Jovanovich, 1977), pp. 194–196.

5. David Frisby, *Sociological Impressionism: A Reassessment of Georg Simmel's Social Theory* (London: Heinemann, 1981). See also David Frisby, *Simmel and Since: Essays on Georg Simmel's Social Theory* (London: Routledge, 1992).

6. For a comparison of Simmel and Jacques Derrida, see Green, *Literary Methods and Sociological Theory*. For a discussion of Simmel as postmodernist, see Deena Weinstein and Michael A. Weinstein, *Postmodern(ized) Simmel* (London: Routledge, 1993).

7. Lieteke van Vucht Tijssen, "Women and Objective Culture: Georg Simmel and Marianne Weber," *Theory, Culture, and Society*, 8, 3 (1991): 204. See also Suzanne Vromen, "Georg Simmel and the Cultural Dilemma of Women," *History of European Ideas*, 8, 4/5 (1987): 563–579; Klaus Lichtblau, "Eros and Culture: Gender Theory in Simmel, Tönnies, and Weber," *Telos*, 82 (1989): 89–110; Heinz-Jürgen Dahme, "Frauen- und Geschlechterfrage bei Herbert Spencer und Georg Simmel," *Kölner Zeitschrift für Soziologie und Sozialpsychologie*, 38 (1986): 490–509; and Silvia Bovenschen, *Die imaginierte Weiblichkeit: Exemplarische Untersuchungen zu kulturgeschichtlichen und literarischen Präsentationsformen des Weiblichen* (Frankfurt am Main: Suhrkamp, 1979),

pp. 19–43. For an important early feminist critique of Simmel, see Marianne Weber's "Die Frau und die objektive Kultur," in her *Frauenfragen und Frauengedanken: Gesammelte Aufsätze* (Tübingen: T. C. B. Mohr, 1919).

8. *Georg Simmel: On Women, Sexuality, and Love,* trans. and ed. Guy Oakes (New Haven: Yale University Press, 1984), p. 54.

9. Margaret Homans, *Women Writers and Poetic Identity: Dorothy Wordsworth, Emily Brontë, and Emily Dickinson* (Princeton: Princeton University Press, 1980), p. 13. On Rousseau, see, e.g., Sarah Kofman, "Rousseau's Phallocratic Ends," in *Revaluing French Feminism: Critical Essays on Difference, Agency, and Culture,* ed. Nancy Fraser and Sandra Lee Bartky (Bloomington: Indiana University Press, 1992).

10. See, e.g., Lawrence Stone, *The Family, Sex, and Marriage in England, 1500–1800* (London: Weidenfeld and Nicholson, 1977). The notion of "women's time" is taken from Julia Kristeva's article of the same name, republished in *The Kristeva Reader,* ed. Toril Moi (Oxford: Basil Blackwell, 1986).

11. Cynthia Eagle Russett, *Sexual Science: The Victorian Construction of Womanhood* (Cambridge: Harvard University Press, 1989), pp. 50–54.

12. See, e.g., Peter J. Bowler, *The Invention of Progress: The Victorians and the Past* (Oxford: Basil Blackwell, 1989).

13. Fred Davis, *Yearning for Yesterday: A Sociology of Nostalgia* (New York: The Free Press, 1979), pp. 1–2.

14. Michael S. Roth, "The Time of Nostalgia: Medicine, History, and Normality in Nineteenth-Century France," *Time and Society,* 1, 2 (1992): 282. See also Michael S. Roth, "Returning to Nostalgia," in *Home and Its Dislocations in Nineteenth-Century France,* ed. Suzanne Nash (Albany: State University of New York Press, 1993).

15. Roth, "The Time of Nostalgia," pp. 273–277.

16. Davis, *Yearning for Yesterday,* pp. 54–56.

17. Simmel, "The Problem of the Sexes," in *On Women, Sexuality, and Love,* p. 116. The Freudian reference here is to the discussion of the mother's body as the "former *Heim* of all human beings . . . the place where each of us lived once upon a time and in the beginning. There is a joking saying that 'Love is home-sickness'; and whenever a man dreams of a place or a country and says to himself, while he is still dreaming: 'this place is familiar to me, I've been here before,' we may interpret the place as being his mother's genitals or her body." See Sigmund Freud, "The 'Uncanny,'" in *The Standard Edition of the Complete Psychological Works of Sigmund Freud,* vol. 17 (London: The Hogarth Press, 1955), p. 245.

18. Coser, "Georg Simmel," p. 191.

19. Georg Simmel, "The Metropolis and Mental Life," in *Georg Simmel: On Individuality and Social Forms,* ed. and intro. Donald N. Levine (Chicago: University of Chicago Press, 1971). For a discussion of the simultaneously liberating and alienating dimensions of modernity as presented in Simmel's social theory, see Daniel Miller, *Material Culture and Mass Consumption* (Oxford: Basil Blackwell, 1987), ch. 5.

20. Simmel, "Female Culture," in *On Women, Sexuality, and Love,* p. 67.

21. Simmel, "The Relative and the Absolute in the Problem of the Sexes," in *On Women, Sexuality, and Love,* p. 103.

22. Ibid., p. 104.

23. Ibid., p. 103.

24. Ibid., p. 113.

25. Susan J. Hekman, *Gender and Knowledge: Elements of a Postmodern Feminism* (Cambridge: Polity Press, 1990), p. 100.

26. Elizabeth Boa, *The Sexual Circus: Wedekind's Theatre of Subversion* (Oxford: Basil Blackwell, 1987), p. 181. See also the discussion of Hegel and gender in Patricia Jagentowicz Mills, *Woman, Nature, and Psyche* (New Haven: Yale University Press, 1987), and in Seyla Benhabib, "On Hegel, Women, and Irony," in *Situating the Self: Gender, Community, and Postmodernism in Contemporary Ethics* (Cambridge: Polity Press, 1992).

27. Simmel, "The Problem of the Sexes," in *On Women, Sexuality, and Love*, p. 122.

28. Ibid., p. 132.

29. Ibid., p. 107.

30. Otto Weininger, *Sex and Character* (London: Heinemann, 1906).

31. Lichtblau, "Eros and Culture," p. 93.

32. Simmel, "Female Culture," p. 86.

33. Marshall Berman, *All That Is Solid Melts into Air: The Experience of Modernity* (London: Verso, 1983), p. 15, and David Harvey, *The Condition of Postmodernity* (Oxford: Basil Blackwell, 1989), p. 104. Both these writers are of course drawing on Marx's view of capitalist development as unleashing a process of unending renewal and transformation.

34. Simmel, "The Problem of the Sexes," p. 129.

35. Lichtblau, "Eros and Culture," p. 96.

36. Simmel, "Female Culture," p. 94.

37. In other words, to view domestic work as a craftlike activity enabling authentic female self-expression is to ignore the commodified nature of the modern household. This commodification, Simmel argues elsewhere, has caused housework to take on the quality of ceremonial fetishism. See Simmel, *The Philosophy of Money* (London: Routledge, 1981), p. 460.

38. Georg Simmel, "Fashion," in *Georg Simmel: On Individuality and Social Forms*.

39. See Ursula Vogel, "Rationalism and Romanticism: Two Strategies for Women's Liberation," in *Feminism and Political Theory*, ed. Judith Evans et al. (London: Sage, 1986).

40. See the useful discussion by Nike Wagner, *Geist und Geschlecht: Karl Kraus und die Erotik der Wiener Moderne* (Frankfurt am Main: Suhrkamp, 1982).

41. Elizabeth Fee, "The Sexual Politics of Victorian Social Anthropology," in *Clio's Consciousness Raised: New Perspectives on the History of Women*, ed. Mary Hartman and Lois W. Banner (New York: Harper and Row, 1974), p. 90. See also Gilles Deleuze, *Coldness and Cruelty*, in *Masochism* (New York: Zone, 1989), pp. 52–53.

42. J. J. Bachofen, *Myth, Religion, and Mother Right* (Princeton: Princeton University Press, 1967).

43. Sigmund Freud, *Civilization and Its Discontents* (London: The Hogarth Press, 1975), p. 41.

44. Judith Van Herik, *Freud on Femininity and Faith* (Berkeley: University of California Press, 1982), p. 21. See also John Brenkman, *Straight Male Modern: A Cultural Critique of Psychoanalysis* (New York: Routledge, 1993).

45. See Biddy Martin, *Woman and Modernity: The (Life)styles of Lou Andreas-Salomé* (Ithaca: Cornell University Press, 1991), ch. 7.

46. "Der Mensch als Weib," in Lou Andreas-Salomé, *Die Erotik: Vier Aufsätze* (Munich: Ullstein, 1986), pp. 9–10. I quote here from Biddy Martin's translation in *Woman and Modernity*, p. 151.

47. Simmel, "The Problem of the Sexes," p. 128.

48. Anne McClintock, "The Return of Female Fetishism and the Fiction of the Phallus," *New Formations*, 19 (1993): 7–10.

49. Donald. N. Levine, *The Flight from Ambiguity: Essays in Social and Cultural Theory* (Chicago: University of Chicago Press, 1985), p. 180, and Frank J. Sulloway, *Freud, Biologist of the Mind: Beyond the Psychoanalytical Legend* (London: Burnett, 1979), ch. 10.

50. Georg Stauth and Bryan S. Turner, *Nietzsche's Dance: Resentment, Reciprocity, and Resistance in Social Life* (Oxford: Basil Blackwell, 1988), p. 32. See also Bryan S. Turner, "A Note on Nostalgia," *Theory, Culture, and Society*, 4, 1 (1987): 147–156, and Fritz Ringer, *The Decline of the German Mandarins: The German Academic Community, 1890–1933* (Cambridge: Harvard University Press, 1969).

51. Janet Wolff, "The Invisible Flâneuse: Women and the Literature of Modernity," *Theory, Culture, and Society*, 2, 3 (1985): 37–46.

52. Ferdinand Tönnies, *Community and Society* (New Brunswick: Transaction Books, 1986). For a feminist critique of Durkheim, Marx, and Weber, see R. A. Sydie, *Natural Women, Cultured Men: A Feminist Perspective on Sociological Theory* (Milton Keynes: Open University Press, 1987).

53. Robert A. Nisbet, *Social Change and History: Aspects of the Western Theory of Development* (New York: Oxford University Press, 1969), pp. 202–203. See also Levine, *The Flight from Ambiguity*, and Johannes Fabian, *Time and the Other: How Anthropology Makes Its Object* (New York: Columbia University Press, 1983).

54. Nancy Armstrong, *Desire and Domestic Fiction: A Political History of the Novel* (Oxford: Oxford University Press, 1987); Jacques Donzelot, *The Policing of Families* (London: Hutchinson, 1980); Friedrich A. Kittler, *Discourse Networks, 1800/1900* (Stanford: Stanford University Press, 1990).

55. See Bruce Mazlish, *A New Science: The Breakdown of Connections and the Birth of Sociology* (New York: Oxford University Press, 1989).

56. Karen Horney, "The Flight from Womanhood: The Masculinity Complex in Women As Viewed by Men and by Women," in *Psychoanalysis and Women*, ed. Jean Baker Miller (Harmondsworth: Penguin, 1973), pp. 5–20.

57. Ute Frevert, *Women in German History: From Bourgeois Emancipation to Sexual Liberation* (New York: Berg, 1989), p. 127. See also the brief discussion in Lieteke Van Vucht Tijssen, "Women between Modernity and Postmodernity," *Theories of Modernity and Postmodernity*, ed. Bryan S. Turner (London: Sage, 1990), and Harriet Anderson, *Utopian Feminism: Women's Movements in Fin-de-Siècle Vienna* (New Haven: Yale University Press, 1992).

58. On critical nostalgia, see James Clifford, "On Ethnographic Allegory," in *Writing Culture: The Poetics and Politics of Ethnography*, ed. James Clifford and George E. Marcus (Berkeley: University of California Press, 1986), p. 114. Clifford is paraphrasing Raymond Williams's discussion of pastoral in *The Country and the City* (London: The Hogarth Press, 1985).

59. Malcolm Chase and Christopher Shaw, "The Dimensions of Nostalgia," in *The Imagined Past: History and Nostalgia,* ed. Malcolm Chase and Christopher Shaw (Manchester: Manchester University Press, 1989), p. 9.

60. Keith Tester, "Nostalgia," in his *The Life and Times of Post-Modernity* (London: Routledge, 1993), p. 66.

3. Imagined Pleasures

Epigraph: Colin Campbell, *The Romantic Ethic and the Spirit of Modern Consumerism* (Oxford: Basil Blackwell, 1987), p. 227.

1. The phrase "dream worlds" is taken from Rosalind Williams, *Dream Worlds: Mass Consumption in Late Nineteenth-Century France* (Berkeley: University of California Press, 1982). The "dream world" is of course also central to Walter Benjamin's understanding of modernity as exemplifying a re-enchantment rather than demythification of the social. See Susan Buck-Morss, "Dream World of Mass Culture," *The Dialectics of Seeing: Walter Benjamin and the Arcades Project* (Cambridge: MIT Press, 1989). Other recent attempts to rethink the history of modernity through the category of consumption include Grant McCracken, *Culture and Consumption: New Approaches to the Symbolic Character of Consumer Goods and Activities* (Bloomington: Indiana University Press, 1990); Neil McKendrick, John Brewer, and J. H. Plumb, *The Birth of a Consumer Society: The Commercialization of Eighteenth-Century England* (Bloomington: Indiana University Press, 1982); and Chandra Mukerji, *From Graven Images: Patterns of Modern Materialism* (New York: Columbia University Press, 1983).

2. Williams, *Dream Worlds,* p. 308.

3. See, among others, Mica Nava, "Consumerism and Its Contradictions" and "Consumerism Reconsidered: Buying and Power," in Nava, *Changing Cultures: Feminism, Youth, and Consumerism* (London: Sage, 1992).

4. See, for example, Patricia Williams, *The Alchemy of Race and Rights* (Cambridge: Harvard University Press, 1991), ch. 3.

5. Mary Ann Doane, *The Desire to Desire: The Woman's Film of the 1940s* (Bloomington: Indiana University Press, 1987), p. 22.

6. Paul Morand, quoted in Williams, *Dream Worlds,* p. 60. For discussions of the great exhibition in England and France, see Thomas Richards, *The Commodity Culture of Victorian England: Advertising and Spectacle, 1851–1914* (Stanford: Stanford University Press, 1990), and Deborah Silverman, *Art Nouveau in Fin-de-Siècle France: Politics, Psychology, and Style* (Berkeley: University of California Press, 1989).

7. Gail Reekie, *Temptations: Sex, Selling, and the Department Store* (Sydney: Allen and Unwin, 1993), p. 16.

8. Elaine S. Abelson, *When Ladies Go A-Thieving: Middle-Class Shoplifters in the Victorian Department Store* (Oxford: Oxford University Press, 1989), p. 61.

9. Citations are taken from the following translations: Gustave Flaubert, *Madame Bovary,* ed. and trans. Paul de Man (New York: Norton, 1965); Emile Zola, *Nana,* trans. George Holden (Harmondsworth: Penguin, 1972); and Emile Zola, *The Ladies' Paradise* (Berkeley: University of California Press, 1992).

10. Williams, *Dream Worlds,* pp. 11–12.

11. Reekie, *Temptations*, p. xii.

12. Besides Reekie and Abelson, see Elizabeth Wilson, *Adorned in Dreams: Fashion and Modernity* (Berkeley: University of California Press, 1985); Rachel Bowlby, *Just Looking: Consumer Culture in Dreiser, Gissing, and Zola* (New York: Methuen, 1985); Rémy G. Saisselin, *Bricabracomania: The Bourgeois and the Bibelot* (London: Thames and Hudson, 1985); and William R. Leach, "Transformations in a Culture of Consumption: Women and Department Stores, 1890–1925," *The Journal of American History*, 71, 2 (1984): 319–342.

13. See the notes to the Livre de Poche edition of *Au bonheur des dames* (Paris: Fasquelle, 1984), p. 491.

14. Wilson, *Adorned in Dreams*, p. 150.

15. Paul Dubuisson, quoted in Michael Miller, *The Bon Marché: Bourgeois Culture and the Department Store, 1869–1920* (Princeton: Princeton University Press, 1981), p. 229.

16. On shoplifting, see Abelson, *When Ladies Go A-Thieving*; Miller, *The Bon Marché*, pp. 197–205; Leslie Camhi, "Stealing Femininity: Department Store Kleptomania as Sexual Disorder," *Differences*, 5, 1 (1993): 26–50; and Ann-Louise Shapiro, "Disorderly Bodies / Disorderly Acts: Medical Discourse and the Female Criminal in Nineteenth-Century Paris," *Genders*, 4 (1989): 68–86.

17. Zola, *The Ladies' Paradise*, p. 98.

18. Griselda Pollock, *Vision and Difference: Feminism, Femininity, and the Histories of Art* (London: Routledge, 1988), p. 67.

19. Bowlby, *Just Looking*, pp. 29–32.

20. Zola, *The Ladies' Paradise*, pp. 69–70.

21. As noted in Zola's preliminary sketch for the text, quoted in the commentary on *Au bonheur des dames*, p. 490.

22. See Tania Modleski, *Loving with a Vengeance: Mass-Produced Fantasies for Women* (New York: Methuen, 1985), ch. 2, and Jan Cohn, *Romance and the Erotics of Property* (Durham: Duke University Press, 1988).

23. See Miller, *The Bon Marché*, pp. 194–198.

24. See, e.g., Klaus Theweleit, *Male Fantasies, 1: Women, Floods, Bodies, History* (Minneapolis: University of Minnesota Press, 1987); for the French context, see Susanna Barrows, *Distorting Mirrors: Visions of the Crowd in Late Nineteenth-Century France* (New Haven: Yale University Press, 1981); on Zola specifically, see Naomi Schor, *Zola's Crowds* (Baltimore: The Johns Hopkins University Press, 1978).

25. Zola, *The Ladies' Paradise*, p. 214.

26. Ibid., p. 236.

27. Abelson, for example, refers to the endless journalistic discussions of women who ran up huge store bills and whose husbands refused to pay for their purchases. See *When Ladies Go A-Thieving*, p. 56.

28. Peter Brooks, "Storied Bodies, or Nana at Last Unveil'd," *Critical Inquiry*, 16, 1 (1989): 8.

29. Zola, *Nana*, p. 439.

30. See Patrice Petro, *Joyless Streets: Women and Melodramatic Representation in Weimar Germany* (Princeton: Princeton University Press, 1989).

31. For the English etymology of consumption, see Raymond Williams, *Keywords: A*

Vocabulary of Culture and Society (London: Fontana, 1983), and for the French, Rosalind Williams, *Dream Worlds*, pp. 5–7.

32. Zola, *Nana*, pp. 409–410.

33. See Charles Bernheimer, *Figures of Ill-Repute: Representing Prostitution in Nineteenth-Century France* (Cambridge: Harvard University Press, 1989), p. 201.

34. Zola, *Nana*, p. 434.

35. Bram Dijkstra, *Idols of Perversity: Fantasies of Feminine Evil in Fin-de-Siècle Culture* (New York: Oxford University Press, 1986), p. 366.

36. See, e.g., G. J. Barker-Benfield, "The Spermatic Economy: A Nineteenth Century View of Sexuality," in *The American Family in Social-Historical Perspective*, ed. Michael Gordon (New York: St Martin's Press, 1978), and Lawrence Birken, *Consuming Desire: Sexual Science and the Emergence of a Culture of Abundance, 1871–1914* (Ithaca: Cornell University Press, 1988), ch. 2.

37. Zola, *Nana*, p. 298.

38. Colin Campbell, *The Romantic Ethic and the Spirit of Modern Consumerism* (Oxford: Basil Blackwell, 1987), pp. 85–90. Campbell's book is a highly suggestive resource for feminist approaches to consumption, though the author does not begin to address the obvious gender implications of his own analysis until its closing pages.

39. Zola, *Nana*, p. 336.

40. Naomi Schor, "Idealism and the Novel: Recanonizing Sand," *Yale French Studies*, 75 (1988): 56–73.

41. On this point, see Dominick LaCapra, *Madame Bovary on Trial* (Ithaca: Cornell University Press, 1982).

42. Huyssen, "Mass Culture As Woman," p. 45.

43. Fredric Jameson, "Reification and Utopia in Mass Culture," *Social Text*, 1 (1979): 130–148. For discussion of the deleterious effects of novel reading, see Peter de Bolla, *The Discourse of the Sublime: Readings in History, Aesthetics, and the Subject* (Oxford: Basil Blackwell, 1989), pp. 252–278, and Campbell, *The Romantic Ethic*, pp. 26–27.

44. See Huyssen, "Mass Culture As Woman"; Kirsten Drotner, "Intensities of Feeling: Modernity, Melodrama, and Adolescence," *Theory, Culture, and Society*, 8, 1 (1991): 57–87; Terry Lovell, *Consuming Fiction* (London: Verso, 1987); Christine Gledhill, "The Melodramatic Field: An Investigation," in *Home Is Where the Heart Is: Studies in Melodrama and the Woman's Film*, ed. Christine Gledhill (London: British Film Institute, 1987), p. 34.

45. Larry Riggs, "Bovarysme Reconsidered: Self-Promotion, Commercialized Print, and the Birth of a Consumer Culture," in *East Meets West: Homage to Edgar C. Knowlton, Jr.*, ed. Roger L. Hadlich and J. D. Ellsworth (Honolulu: University of Hawaii, Department of European Languages and Literature, 1988), p. 235.

46. Leo Bersani, *A Future for Astyanax: Character and Desire in Literature* (Boston: Little, Brown and Co., 1976), p. 92.

47. Janice Radway, "Reading Is Not Eating: Mass-Produced Literature and the Theoretical, Methodological, and Political Consequences of a Metaphor," *Book Research Quarterly*, 2, 3 (1986): 10–11. See also James Strachey, "Some Unconscious Factors in Reading," *International Journal of Psychoanalysis*, 11 (1930): 322–331.

48. Flaubert, *Madame Bovary*, p. 26.

49. Ibid., p. 24.

50. Bersani, *A Future for Astyanax*, p. 93; Eric Gans, *Madame Bovary: The End of Romance* (Boston: G. K. Hall, 1989), p. 44. For a negative assessment of Emma's reading, see Sarah Webster Goodwin, "Libraries, Kitsch, and Gender in *Madame Bovary*," *L'Esprit Créateur*, 28, 1 (1988): 56–66.

51. Jameson, "Reification and Utopia in Mass Culture."

52. Rosemary Lloyd, *Madame Bovary* (London: Unwin Hyman, 1990), p. 93.

53. Carla L. Peterson, "*Madame Bovary*: Dionysian Rituals," in *Emma Bovary*, ed. Harold Bloom (New York: Chelsea House, 1994), pp. 124–127.

54. Flaubert, *Madame Bovary*, p. 41.

55. Ibid., p. 28.

56. Ibid., p. 26.

57. Nathaniel Wing, "Emma's Stories: Narrative, Repetition, and Desire in *Madame Bovary*," in Bloom, *Emma Bovary*, p. 140.

58. Flaubert, *Madame Bovary*, p. 163.

59. On Emma's narcissism, see Michal Peled Ginsburg, *Flaubert Writing: A Study in Narrative Strategies* (Stanford: Stanford University Press, 1986), ch. 3; on the motif of fusion, see Leo Bersani, "Flaubert and Madame Bovary: The Hazards of Literary Fusion," in *Gustave Flaubert's Madame Bovary*, ed. Harold Bloom (New York: Chelsea House, 1988).

60. *Pages from the Goncourt Journal*, ed. Robert Baldick (Harmondsworth: Penguin, 1984), p. 136.

61. Clearly, this view is far from superseded in our own time. In relation to Woody Allen's 1985 film *The Purple Rose of Cairo*, for example, Mary Ann Doane writes: "There is a certain naiveté assigned to women in relation to systems of signification—a tendency to deny the processes of representation, to collapse the opposition between the sign (the image) and the real . . . Proximity rather than distance, passivity, overinvolvement and overidentification . . . these are the tropes which enable the women's assumption of the position of 'subject' of the gaze" (Doane, *The Desire to Desire*, pp. 1–2). In the case of the female reader, in other words, aesthetics is reduced to erotics, to an emotionally and sexually charged reponse to the text; she remains incapable of appreciating the formal and self-conscious qualities of the art work in their own terms.

My own favorite recent fictional example of this theme is Stephen King's horror novel *Misery*. See my "Kitsch, Romance Fiction, and Male Paranoia: Stephen King Meets the Frankfurt School," in *Feminist Cultural Studies*, ed. Terry Lovell (London: Edward Elgar, in press).

62. LaCapra, *Madame Bovary on Trial*, p. 59.

63. Bruce Robbins, "Modernism and Literary Realism: Response," in *Realism and Representation*, ed. George Levine (Madison: University of Wisconsin Press, 1993), pp. 227–228. Jonathan Culler also notes that formalist readings of *Madame Bovary* have often been tied to misogynistic assumptions about the triviality of its content. See *Flaubert: The Uses of Uncertainty* (Ithaca: Cornell University Press, 1985), pp. 236–237.

64. Jann Matlock, *Scenes of Seduction: Prostitution, Hysteria, and Reading Difference in Nineteenth-Century France* (New York: Columbia University Press, 1994), p. 252. Matlock is quoting the Catholic journalist Alfred Nettement.

65. Flaubert, *Madame Bovary*, p. 42.

66. Wilson, *Adorned in Dreams*, p. 245.

67. This is also true of more recent analyses, such as Walter Benn Michael's *The Gold Standard and the Logic of Naturalism: American Literature at the Turn of the Century* (Berkeley: University of California Press, 1987).

68. See Birken, *Consuming Desire*, ch. 6.

69. See, e.g., Williams, *Dream Worlds*, pp. 307–308, and Reekie, *Temptations*, ch. 7.

70. Leach, "Transformations in a Culture of Consumption," p. 342. See also Martin Pumphrey, "The Flapper, the Housewife, and the Making of Modernity," *Cultural Studies*, 1, 2 (1987): 179–194.

71. I do not mean that categories of race and gender do not have economic effects; I simply mean that their rationale and significance cannot be understood purely in such terms.

4. Masking Masculinity

Epigraph: Tania Modleski, *Feminism without Women: Culture and Criticism in a "Postfeminist" Age* (New York: Routledge, 1991), p. 101.

1. See, e.g., Jacques Le Rider, *Modernité viennoise et crises de l'identité* (Paris: Presses Universitaires de France, 1990), and Christine Buci-Glucksmann, *La raison baroque: de Baudelaire à Benjamin* (Paris: Editions Galilée, 1984).

2. See Elaine Showalter, *Sexual Anarchy: Gender and Culture at the Fin de Siècle* (New York: Viking Penguin, 1990), in particular chs. 1 and 9.

3. Texts are cited from the following editions: J. K. Huysmans, *Against the Grain* (New York: Dover, 1969); Leopold von Sacher-Masoch, *Venus in Furs*, in *Masochism* (New York: Zone Books, 1989); Oscar Wilde, *The Picture of Dorian Gray* (Harmondsworth: Penguin, 1985).

4. Thus, as Carl Schorske notes, "the Austrian aesthetes were neither as alienated from their society as their French soul-mates nor as engaged in it as their English ones." See Carl E. Schorske, *Fin-de-Siècle Vienna: Politics and Culture* (Cambridge: Cambridge University Press, 1981), p. 304.

5. Such appropriations are numerous. See, e.g., Gaylyn Studlar, *In the Realm of Pleasure: Von Sternberg, Dietrich, and the Masochistic Aesthetic* (Urbana: University of Illinois Press, 1988), and Kaja Silverman, "Masochism and Male Subjectivity," in her *Male Subjectivity at the Margins* (New York: Routledge, 1992). For a critique, see Tania Modleski, *Feminism without Women: Culture and Criticism in a "Postfeminist" Age* (New York: Routledge, 1991).

6. For the origin of the term "counterdiscourse," see Richard Terdiman, *Discourse/Counter-Discourse: The Theory and Practice of Symbolic Resistance in Nineteenth-Century France* (Ithaca: Cornell University Press, 1985).

7. As Christine Battersby notes, "the great artist is a *feminine male*." See her *Gender and Genius: Towards a Feminist Aesthetic* (London: Women's Press, 1989) for a discussion of interconnections between vocabularies of aesthetic praise and those of sexual difference. See also Alan Richardson, "Romanticism and the Colonization of the Feminine," in *Romanticism and Feminism*, ed. Anne K. Mellor (Bloomington: Indiana University Press, 1988).

8. Charles Baudelaire, *The Painter of Modern Life and Other Essays*, trans. Jonathan Mayne (London: Phaidon Press, 1964), pp. 29–34.

9. Max Nordau, *Degeneration* (London: Heinemann, 1913).

10. Regenia Gagnier, *Idylls of the Marketplace: Oscar Wilde and the Victorian Public* (Stanford: Stanford University Press, 1986), p. 59.

11. George L. Mosse, *Nationalism and Sexuality: Middle-Class Morality and Sexual Norms in Modern Europe* (Madison: University of Wisconsin Press, 1985), p. 44.

12. Sacher-Masoch, *Venus in Furs*, p. 152.

13. See Rémy G. Saisselin, *Bricabracomania: The Bourgeois and the Bibelot* (London: Thames and Hudson, 1985).

14. Ellen Moers, *The Dandy: Brummell to Beerbohm* (New York: Viking, 1960), p. 13. See also Marie-Christine Natta, *La grandeur sans convictions: essai sur le dandysme* (Paris: Editions du Félin, 1991), and Jessica R. Feldman, *Gender on the Divide: The Dandy in Modernist Literature* (Ithaca: Cornell University Press, 1993).

15. Wilde, *Dorian Gray*, p. 160.

16. Ibid., p. 160.

17. Sacher-Masoch, *Venus in Furs*, p. 175.

18. Rachel Bowlby, "Promoting Dorian Gray," *Oxford Literary Review*, 9, 1/2 (1987): 152.

19. Wilde, *Dorian Gray*, p. 48.

20. Ed Cohen, "Writing Gone Wilde: Homoerotic Desire in the Closet of Representation," *PMLA*, 102, 5 (1987): 808.

21. Wilde, *Dorian Gray*, p. 174.

22. Walter Benjamin, *Charles Baudelaire: A Lyric Poet in the Era of High Capitalism* (London: Verso, 1983), p. 167. See also Susan Stewart, *On Longing: Narratives of the Miniature, the Gigantic, the Souvenir, the Collection* (Baltimore: The Johns Hopkins University Press, 1984), pp. 151–169.

23. Rosalind Williams, *Dream Worlds: Mass Consumption in Late Nineteenth-Century France* (Berkeley: University of California Press, 1982), p. 119.

24. Wilde, *Dorian Gray*, p. 26.

25. Gilles Deleuze, *Coldness and Cruelty*, in *Masochism* (New York: Zone Books, 1989), p. 33.

26. Gertrud Lenzer, "On Masochism: A Contribution to the History of a Phantasy and Its Theory," *Signs*, 1, 2 (1975): 295.

27. Bowlby, "Promoting Dorian Gray."

28. Quoted in Bram Dijkstra, *Idols of Perversity: Fantasies of Feminine Evil in Fin-de-Siècle Culture* (New York: Oxford University Press, 1986), p. 101.

29. Huysmans, *Against the Grain*, p. 98.

30. Richard Dellamora, *Masculine Desire: The Sexual Politics of Victorian Aestheticism* (Chapel Hill: University of North Carolina Press, 1990), p. 167.

31. Susan Sontag, "Notes on 'Camp,'" in her *Against Interpretation and Other Essays* (New York: Octagon, 1978), pp. 275–292. See also Andrew Ross, "Uses of Camp," in his *No Respect: Intellectuals and Popular Culture* (New York: Routledge, 1989).

32. Ed Cohen, *Talk on the Wilde Side: Towards a Genealogy of a Discourse on Male Homosexuality* (New York: Routledge, 1993), pp. 1–2.

33. Cohen, "Writing Gone Wilde," p. 811. See also Eve Kosofsky Sedgwick, *Epistemology of the Closet* (Berkeley: University of California Press, 1990), ch. 3. For an earlier reading of Wilde's novel, see Jeffrey Meyers, "Wilde: *The Picture of Dorian Gray*," in his *Homosexuality and Literature, 1880–1930* (London: Athlone Press, 1977), pp. 20–31.

34. Jonathan Dollimore, "Differential Desires: Subjectivity and Transgression in Wilde and Gide," *Textual Practice*, 1, 1 (1987): 48–67. An extended version of this argument is developed in *Sexual Dissidence: Augustine to Wilde, Freud to Foucault* (Oxford: Oxford University Press, 1991).

35. Neil Bartlett, *Who Was That Man? A Present for Mr. Oscar Wilde* (London: Serpent's Tail, 1988), pp. 163–164.

36. Mosse, *Nationalism and Sexuality*, pp. 45–65.

37. Dollimore, *Sexual Dissidence*, ch. 3.

38. This is one of the problems of Jack Babuscio's otherwise illuminating discussion "Camp and the Gay Sensibility," in *Gays and Film*, ed. Richard Dyer (London: British Film Institute, 1977), pp. 40–57. For a critique of the notion of a "gay sensibility," see Dollimore, *Sexual Dissidence*, pp. 308–313.

39. Sontag, "Notes on Camp," p. 289. See also Bartlett, "Possessions," in *Who Was That Man?*

40. See Cohen, *Talk on the Wilde Side*.

41. Wilde, *Dorian Gray*, p. 60 and p. 231.

42. Sacher-Masoch, *Venus in Furs*, p. 174.

43. Huysmans, *Against the Grain*, p. 20.

44. For an interesting discussion of changing historical representations of the lower-class body, see Peter Stallybrass and Allon White, *The Politics and Poetics of Transgression* (Ithaca: Cornell University Press, 1986).

45. Andreas Huyssen, "Mass Culture As Woman: Modernism's Other," in his *After the Great Divide: Modernism, Mass Culture, and Postmodernism* (Bloomington: Indiana University Press, 1986).

46. Bowlby, "Promoting Dorian Gray."

47. Huysmans, *Against the Grain*, p. 137.

48. Ibid.

49. A. E. Carter, *The Idea of Decadence in French Literature: 1830–1900* (Toronto: University of Toronto Press, 1958).

50. Huysmans, *Against the Grain*, p. 162.

51. Wilde, *Dorian Gray*, p. 76.

52. Ibid., p. 120.

53. Sacher-Masoch, *Venus in Furs*, p. 192.

54. Ibid., p. 174.

55. Wilde, *Dorian Gray*, p. 138.

56. Ibid, pp. 82–83.

57. Quoted in Marshall Berman, *All That Is Solid Melts into Air: The Experience of Modernity* (London: Verso, 1983), p. 156.

58. Natta, *La grandeur sans convictions*, p. 152.

59. Rodolphe Gasché, "The Falls of History: Huysmans's *A Rebours*," *Yale French Studies*, 74 (1988): 195.

60. This motif is of course already apparent in Baudelaire's celebration of the artificial as exemplifying a pursuit of the ideal through the transcendence of nature. See *The Painter of Modern Life,* in particular pp. 31–34.

61. Wilde, *Dorian Gray,* p. 72.

62. Matei Calinescu, *Five Faces of Modernity: Modernism, Avant-Garde, Decadence, Kitsch, Postmodernism* (Durham: Duke University Press, 1987), p. 172.

63. Charles Bernheimer, "Huysmans: Writing against (Female) Nature," in *The Female Body in Western Culture,* ed. Susan Suleiman (Cambridge: Harvard University Press, 1987), pp. 373–386.

64. Benjamin, *Charles Baudelaire,* p. 166.

65. Sacher-Masoch, *Venus in Furs,* p. 143.

66. Christine Buci-Glucksmann, "Catastrophic Utopia: The Feminine as Allegory of the Modern," *Representations,* 14 (1986): 224.

67. Sacher-Masoch, *Venus in Furs,* p. 192.

68. Wilde, *Dorian Gray,* p. 133.

69. Ibid., p. 131.

70. Huysmans, *Against the Grain,* p. 99.

71. Sacher-Masoch, *Venus in Furs,* p. 163.

72. Deleuze, *Coldness and Cruelty,* p. 22. For a useful discussion of Sacher-Masoch's life and work, see Albrecht Koschorke, *Leopold von Sacher-Masoch: die Inszenierung einer Perversion* (Munich: Piper, 1988).

73. Quoted in Natta, *La grandeur sans convictions,* p. 153.

74. For a related discussion of this dialectic of modernism and modernization, see Huyssen, "Mass Culture As Woman," pp. 55–58.

75. Charles Bernheimer, *Figures of Ill-Repute: Representing Prostitution in Nineteenth-Century France* (Cambridge: Harvard University Press, 1989), p. 266.

76. Ibid., p. 273.

77. Rosi Braidotti, "The Becoming-Woman of Philosophy," in her *Patterns of Dissonance: A Study of Women in Contemporary Philosophy* (Cambridge: Polity Press, 1991)

78. Charles Bernheimer, "The Politics of Aversion in Theory," in *Men Writing the Feminine,* ed. Thais Morgan (Albany: State University of New York Press, 1994); Modleski, *Feminism without Women,* pp. 99–103. For the misogynistic frankness of his appropriation of the feminine, the example of Jean Baudrillard is hard to beat. See, for example, *Cool Memories* (London: Verso, 1990), p. 7, where he writes, "it is not the Revolution which will turn me into a woman. That will come about by my espousing here and now—passionately—the position of femininity itself. Now for feminists this is unpardonable. For this position is more feminine, with all the supreme femininity it implies, than that of women will ever be."

5. Love, God, and the Orient

Epigraph: Suzanne Clark, *Sentimental Modernism: Women Writers and the Revolution of the Word* (Bloomington: Indiana University Press, 1991), p. 2.

1. Brian Masters, *Now Barabbas Was a Rotter: The Extraordinary Life of Marie Corelli* (London: Hamish Hamilton, 1978), p. 6. Masters is Corelli's most recent, and most

blatantly misogynistic, biographer; his passing reference to the "spluttering irrationality that she evoked from normally sane men" (p. 8) is nowhere more evident than in his own text. Nevertheless, a number of suggestive insights can be found in his biography if one is prepared to stomach its patronizing sexism. Also useful are Eileen Bigland, *Marie Corelli: The Woman and the Legend* (London: Jarrolds, 1953); George Bullock, *Marie Corelli: The Life and Death of a Best-Seller* (London: Constable, 1940); and William Stuart Scott, *Marie Corelli: The Story of a Friendship* (London: Hutchinson, 1955). By contrast, T. F. G. Coates and R. S. Warren Bell's *Marie Corelli: The Writer and the Woman* (Philadelphia: G. W. Jacobs, 1903) and Bertha Vyver's *Memoirs of Marie Corelli* (London: A. Rivers, 1930) are hagiographies of the first order.

2. Quoted in Masters, *Now Barabbas Was a Rotter*, p. 142 and p. 222.

3. Quoted in Scott, *Marie Corelli*, p. 30. On a similar note, the *Daily Express* concluded: "she was a squat, tubby, little woman who pretended to a non-existent ancestry, gave herself out to be ten years younger than she was, wrote a series of novels which for pretentiousness and bosh have never been approached and which, though they were torn to pieces by the critics, took in nine-tenths of the reading public of this country." Also quoted in Scott, *Marie Corelli*, p. 25.

4. Masters, *Now Barabbas Was a Rotter*, p. 74.

5. For a discussion of the interconnection between realism and idealism in Victorian fiction, see John R. Reed, *Victorian Conventions* (Athens: Ohio University Press, 1975), ch. 1.

6. Christine Gledhill, "The Melodramatic Field: An Investigation," in *Home Is Where the Heart Is: Studies in Melodrama and the Woman's Film*, ed. Christine Gledhill (London: British Film Institute, 1987), p. 34.

7. Q. D. Leavis, *Fiction and the Reading Public* (London: Chatto and Windus, 1965), pp. 64–65.

8. Thomas Richards, *The Commodity Culture of Victorian England: Advertising and Spectacle, 1851–1914* (Stanford: Stanford University Press, 1990), p. 88.

9. For a more detailed discussion of the relationship between femininity and kitsch, see Rita Felski, "Kitsch, Romance, and Male Paranoia: Stephen King Meets the Frankfurt School," in *Feminist Cultural Studies*, ed. Terry Lovell (London: Edward Elgar, in press). See also Robert C. Solomon, "On Kitsch and Sentimentality," *The Journal of Aesthetics and Art Criticism*, 49, 1 (1991): 1–14.

10. Hermann Broch, "Notes on the Problem of Kitsch," in *Kitsch: The World of Bad Taste*, ed. Gillo Dorfles (New York: Universe Books, 1969), p. 73.

11. See Pierre Bourdieu, *Distinction: A Social Critique of the Judgement of Taste* (Cambridge: Harvard University Press, 1984).

12. See, in particular, Jean-François Lyotard, "The Sublime and the Avant-Garde," in his *The Inhuman* (Stanford: Stanford University Press, 1991).

13. Patricia Yaeger, "Toward a Female Sublime," in *Gender and Theory: Dialogues on Feminist Criticism*, ed. Linda Kauffman (Oxford: Basil Blackwell, 1989). Samuel Monk's history of the sublime, for example, discusses a number of eighteenth-century women writers, devaluing their "crude emotionalism" in comparison with the later philosophical maturity of figures such as Wordsworth. See *The Sublime* (Ann Arbor: University of Michigan Press, 1960).

14. Ann Cvetkovich, *Mixed Feelings: Feminism, Mass Culture, and Victorian Sensationalism* (New Brunswick: Rutgers University Press, 1992), p. 35. Some time after formulating this notion of the popular sublime, I came across James Donald's *Sentimental Education: Schooling, Popular Culture, and the Regulation of Liberty* (London: Verso, 1992). Donald's discussion of "the vulgar sublime" in chapter 5 puts forward a similar case for the centrality of the sublime in contemporary popular culture, though with much greater emphasis on its abject and uncanny dimensions.

15. Celeste Olalquiaga, *Megalopolis: Contemporary Cultural Sensibilities* (Minneapolis: University of Minnesota Press, 1992), ch. 3.

16. Monk, *The Sublime*, p. 232.

17. Naomi Schor, "Idealism in the Novel: Recanonizing Sand," *Yale French Studies*, 75 (1988): 73.

18. Peter Brooks, *The Melodramatic Imagination: Balzac, Henry James, and the Mode of Excess* (New York: Columbia University Press, 1984), pp. 11–12.

19. Marie Corelli, *The Sorrows of Satan* (Philadephia: J. P. Lippincott, 1896), p. 198.

20. Brooks, *The Melodramatic Imagination*, p. 41.

21. See, e.g., Bullock, *Marie Corelli*, pp. 54–59.

22. Masters, *Now Barabbas Was a Rotter*, p. 110.

23. Carolyn Steedman, *Landscape for a Good Woman: A Story of Two Lives* (London: Virago, 1986), p. 123.

24. Brooks, *The Melodramatic Imagination*, p. 15.

25. Ibid., p. 4.

26. Quoted in Masters, *Now Barabbas Was a Rotter*, p. 102.

27. Quoted in Scott, *Marie Corelli*, p. 33.

28. Masters, *Now Barabbas Was a Rotter*, pp. 12–13.

29. See Brooks, *The Melodramatic Imagination*, pp. 41, 42.

30. For critical surveys of this tradition, see Gledhill, "The Melodramatic Field: An Investigation," and E. Ann Kaplan, *Motherhood and Representation: The Mother in Popular Culture and Melodrama* (London: Routledge, 1992), ch. 4.

31. Suzanne Clarke, *Sentimental Modernism: Women Writers and the Revolution of the Word* (Bloomington: Indiana University Press, 1991), p. 8.

32. Marie Corelli, *Temporal Power* (New York: Dodd, Mead and Co., 1902), p. 461.

33. Ibid., p. 554.

34. Marie Corelli, *Ziska: The Problem of a Wicked Soul* (London:. Methuen, 1960), pp. 172–173.

35. See Janice Radway, "Reading Is Not Eating: Mass-Produced Literature and the Theoretical, Political, and Methodological Consequences of a Metaphor," *Book Research Quarterly*, 2, 3 (1986): 17.

36. Corelli, *Sorrows of Satan*, p. 311.

37. Marie Corelli, *Free Opinions Freely Expressed* (London: Archibald Constable, 1905), p. 182.

38. Ibid, p. 156.

39. Thus one of Corelli's friends and biographers wrote, "She is about the only forceful woman writer whom no one has dared to endow with a 'masculine mind.'" See Scott, *Marie Corelli*, p. 151.

40. Corelli, *Temporal Power*, p. 17.

41. Cvetkovich, *Mixed Feelings*, p. 111.

42. Masters, *Now Barabbas Was a Rotter*, pp. 277–278.

43. Bridget Fowler, *The Alienated Reader: Women and Popular Romantic Literature in the Twentieth Century* (Brighton: Harvester, 1991), p. 1.

44. See, e.g., Janet Oppenheim, *The Other World: Spiritualism and Psychic Research in England, 1850–1914* (Cambridge: Cambridge University Press, 1985), and Robert Laurence Moore, *In Search of White Crows: Spiritualism, Parapsychology, and American Culture* (New York: Oxford University Press, 1987).

45. Brooks, *The Melodramatic Imagination*, p. 16.

46. Much the same could be said about our own time, where "postmodern" experiences of fragmentation and indeterminacy coexist with the rise of religious fundamentalisms and New Age philosophies. For some sociological speculations on the role of religion in the postmodern, see Stjepan. G. Mestrovic, *The Coming Fin de Siècle* (London: Routledge, 1991), pp. 136–162.

47. For example, Dr. Anne Kingsford, Annie Besant, and Madame Blavatsky. See Oppenheim, *The Other World*, ch. 5.

48. Ibid., p. 59.

49. For a thorough discussion of the connections between feminism and spiritualism, see Alex Owen, *The Darkened Room: Women, Power, and Spiritualism in Late Victorian England* (Philadelphia: University of Pennsylvania Press, 1990).

50. Marie Corelli, *A Romance of Two Worlds* (New York: Thomas Y. Crowell and Co., n.d.), p. 205.

51. Ibid., p. 168.

52. See the discussion of the interrelations between spiritualism, Eastern religions, and feminism in Sandra M. Gilbert and Susan Gubar, *No Man's Land: The Place of the Woman Writer in the Twentieth Century*, vol. 2: *Sexchanges* (New Haven: Yale University Press, 1989), pp. 26–32.

53. See Patrick Brantlinger, *Rule of Darkness: British Literature and Imperialism, 1830–1914* (Ithaca: Cornell University Press, 1988), ch. 8.

54. Sara Mills, *Discourses of Difference: An Analysis of Women's Travel Writing and Colonialism* (London: Routledge, 1991).

55. Chris Bongie, *Exotic Memories: Literature, Colonialism, and the Fin de Siècle* (Stanford: Stanford University Press, 1991), p. 40. See also Lisa Lowe, *Critical Terrains: British and French Orientalisms* (Ithaca: Cornell University Press, 1992).

56. Brantlinger, *Rule of Darkness*, p. 246.

57. Quoted in Masters, *Now Barabbas Was a Rotter*, p. 16.

58. Corelli, *Ziska*, p. 7.

59. Ibid., p. 11.

60. Ibid., p. 34.

61. Ibid., p. 45.

62. Ibid., pp. 181–182.

63. Ibid, p. 53.

64. For interesting discussions of *The Sheik* as novel and film, see Billie Melman, "1919–28: 'The Sheik of Araby'—Freedom in Captivity in the Desert Romance," in her

Women and the Popular Imagination in the Twenties: Flappers and Nymphs (London: Macmillan, 1988), and Miriam Hansen, "The Return of Babylon: Rudolph Valentino and the Female Spectator," in her *Babel and Babylon: Spectatorship in American Silent Film* (Cambridge: Harvard University Press, 1991).

65. Virginia M. Allen, *The Femme Fatale* (Troy, N.Y.: Whitston Publishing Co., 1983), ch. 8.

66. Meg Armstrong develops the notion of the exotic sublime in "'A Jumble of Foreignness': The Sublime Musayms of Nineteenth-Century Fairs and Expositions," *Cultural Critique,* 23 (1992–93): 199–250. See also Rosalind Williams's discussion of department-store exoticism in *Dream Worlds: Mass Consumption in Late Nineteenth-Century France* (Berkeley: University of California Press, 1982), pp. 66–78, and Thomas Richards's discussion of imperial kitsch in *The Commodity Culture of Victorian England: Advertising and Spectacle, 1851–1914* (Stanford: Stanford University Press, 1990), ch. 3.

67. Hugh Ridley, *Images of Imperial Rule* (London: Croom Helm, 1983), p. 17.

68. Nina Baym, *Woman's Fiction: A Guide to Novels by and about Women in America, 1820–1870* (Ithaca: Cornell University Press, 1978), and Jane Tompkins, *Sensational Designs: The Cultural Work of American Fiction, 1790–1860* (Oxford: Oxford University Press, 1985).

69. Cvetkovich, *Mixed Feelings,* p. 38.

70. Ibid., p. 7.

71. Patricia Stubbs, *Women and Fiction: Feminism and the Novel, 1880–1920* (London: Methuen, 1981), p. 45.

72. Charles Augustin Sainte-Beuve, "*Madame Bovary* by Gustave Flaubert," in *Madame Bovary,* ed. and trans. Paul de Man (New York: Norton, 1965), p. 331.

6. Visions of the New

Epigraph: Lisa Tickner, *The Spectacle of Women: Imagery of the Suffrage Campaign, 1907–1914* (London: Chatto and Windus, 1987), pp. 182–192.

1. I borrow the term "time-text" from Anthony Kemp, who uses it to designate "the communal narrative of which individual histories are expressions. This metahistorical time-text, far from being bound or limited by an objective, independent, past-in-itself, is capable ... of extreme variation, of violent and irreconcilable change." See Anthony Kemp, *The Estrangement of the Past: A Study in the Origins of Historical Consciousness* (Oxford: Oxford University Press, 1991), p. vii. My critical reassessment of the gender politics of historical thought derives from a skepticism regarding the purported distinction between a masculine, linear time and a feminine temporality based on rhythm, cyclicality, and repetition. Such an opposition, I will argue, is insufficiently nuanced to engage with the varying conceptions and experiences of time among women and men as shaped by the particularities of sociohistorical context. See in this regard Julia Kristeva, "Women's Time," in *The Kristeva Reader,* ed. Toril Moi (Oxford: Basil Blackwell, 1986).

2. See Malcolm Bradbury and James McFarlane, "The Name and Nature of Modernism," in *Modernism: 1890–1930,* ed. Malcolm Bradbury and James McFarlane (Harmondsworth: Penguin, 1976), pp. 37–38; Holbrook Jackson, *The Eighteen Nineties* (New York: Capricorn Books, 1966), pp. 21–22; *1915, the Cultural Moment: The New Politics,*

the New Woman, the New Psychology, the New Art, and the New Theatre in America, ed. Adele Heller and Lois Rudnick (New Brunswick: Rutgers University Press, 1991).

3. See Penny Boumelha, "Women and the New Fiction 1880–1900," in her *Thomas Hardy and Women: Sexual Ideology and Narrative Form* (Brighton: Harvester, 1982); Ann Ardis, *New Women, New Novels: Feminism and Early Modernism* (New Brunswick: Rutgers University Press, 1990); Susan M. Gilbert and Susan Gubar, "Home Rule: The Colonies of the New Women," in their *No Man's Land: The Place of the Woman Writer in the Twentieth Century*, vol. 2: *Sexchanges* (New Haven: Yale University Press, 1989); Elaine Showalter, "New Women," in her *Sexual Anarchy: Gender and Culture at the Fin de Siècle* (New York: Viking Penguin, 1990); Carroll Smith-Rosenberg, "Discourses of Sexuality and Subjectivity: The New Woman, 1870–1936," in *Hidden from History: Reclaiming the Gay and Lesbian Past*, ed. Martin Duberman, Martha Vicinus, and George Chauncey, Jr. (Harmondsworth: Penguin, 1991); Lucy Bland, "The Married Woman, the 'New Woman,' and the Feminist: Sexual Politics of the 1890s," in *Equal or Different? Women's Politics, 1800–1914*, ed. Jane Rendall (London: Basil Blackwell, 1987); Gail Cunningham, *The New Woman and the Victorian Novel* (New York: Macmillan, 1978). For a discussion of the influence of feminism on male novelists in England, see Patricia Stubbs, *Women and Fiction: Feminism and the Novel, 1880–1920* (London: Methuen, 1981).

4. Katherine Stern, "The War of the Sexes in British Fantasy Literature of the Suffragette Era," *Critical Matrix*, 3, 3 (1987): 78–109.

5. See, e.g., Donald M. Lowe, "Temporality," in his *History of Bourgeois Perception* (Chicago: University of Chicago Press, 1982), and Matei Calinescu, *Five Faces of Modernity: Modernism, Avant-Garde, Decadence, Kitsch, Postmodernism* (Durham: Duke University Press, 1987), p. 13.

6. See the discussion of the two terms in Raymond Williams, *Keywords: A Vocabulary of Culture and Society* (London: Fontana, 1983).

7. For a critique of the concept of the "revolutionary personality," see Marie Marmo Mullaney, "Women and the Theory of the 'Revolutionary Personality': Comments, Criticisms, and Suggestions for Further Study," *The Social Science Journal*, 21, 2 (1984): 49–70. Recent feminist accounts of the French Revolution include Joan Landes, *Women and the Public Sphere in the Age of the French Revolution* (Ithaca: Cornell University Press, 1988), and Dorinda Outram, "*Le langage mâle de la vertu*: Women and the Discourse of the French Revolution," in *The Social History of Language*, ed. Peter Burke and Roy Porter (Cambridge: Cambridge University Press, 1987). For a useful reassessment of feminist critiques of the French Revolution and liberal political theory, see the more nuanced account recently offered by Lynn Hunt in *The Family Romance of the French Revolution* (Berkeley: University of California Press, 1992).

8. Lorna Duffin, "Prisoners of Progress: Women and Evolution," in *The Nineteenth-Century Woman: Her Cultural and Physical World*, ed. Sara Delamont and Lorna Duffin (London: Croom Helm, 1978), and Christine Crosby, *The Ends of History: Victorians and the Woman Question* (London: Routledge, 1991). See also Jill Conway, "Stereotypes of Femininity in a Theory of Sexual Evolution," in *Suffer and Be Still: Women in the Victorian Age*, ed. Martha Vicinus (Bloomington: Indiana University Press, 1972).

9. Peter Osborne, "Modernity Is a Qualitative, Not a Chronological Category," *New Left Review*, 192 (1992): 67.

10. Susan Kingsley Kent, *Sex and Suffrage in Britain, 1860–1914* (London: Routledge, 1990), p. 3. See also Martha Vicinus, "Male Space and Women's Bodies: The Suffragette Movement," in her *Independent Women: Work and Community for Single Women, 1850–1920* (Chicago: University of Chicago Press, 1985), and Jane Marcus, "Introduction: Re-reading the Pankhursts and Women's Suffrage," in *Suffrage and the Pankhursts*, ed. Jane Marcus (London: Routledge, 1987).

11. I borrow the term "symbolic politics" from Joan Landes, whose discussion of the eighteenth-century public sphere provides an illuminating account of the interconnections between systems of political and cultural representation.

12. Lynn Hunt, *Politics, Culture, and Class in the French Revolution* (Berkeley: University of California Press, 1982), pp. 14, 24. See also *The New Cultural History*, ed. Lynn Hunt (Berkeley: University of California Press, 1989).

13. Lisa Tickner, *The Spectacle of Women: Imagery of the Suffrage Campaign, 1907–1914* (London: Chatto and Windus, 1987). The term "semiotics and somatics of woman's suffrage" comes from Jane Marcus, "The Asylums of Antaeus: Women, War, and Madness—Is There a Feminist Fetishism?" in *The New Historicism*, ed. H. Aram Veeser (New York: Routledge, 1989), p. 142.

14. Janet Lyon, "Militant Discourse, Strange Bedfellows: Suffragettes and Vorticists before the War," *Differences*, 4, 2 (1992): 100–133, and "Transforming Manifestoes: A Second-Wave Problematic," *The Yale Journal of Criticism*, 5, 1 (1991): 101–127.

15. Vicinus, "Male Space and Women's Bodies," p. 254.

16. Ibid., p. 264. See also the discussion of feminist autobiographies of the period in Tricia Davis et al., "'The Public Face of Feminism': Early Twentieth-Century Writings on Women's Suffrage," in *Making Histories: Studies in History-Writing and Politics*, ed. Richard Johnson et al. (London: Hutchinson, 1982).

17. Tickner, *The Spectacle of Women*, p. 151.

18. See Tickner, *The Spectacle of Women*, p. 108, and also Gillian Beer, *Darwin's Plots: Evolutionary Narrative in Darwin, George Eliot, and Nineteenth-Century Fiction* (London: Routledge, 1985).

19. Quoted in Conway, "Stereotypes of Femininity," p. 141.

20. Tickner, *The Spectacle of Women*, p. 186.

21. For a discussion of eugenics and its relationship to feminism, see Jeffrey Weeks, *Sex, Politics, and Society: The Regulation of Sexuality since 1800* (London: Longman, 1981), and Penny Boumelha, "Sexual Ideology and the 'Nature' of Woman, 1880–1900," in *Thomas Hardy and Women*.

22. Quoted in Ruth First and Ann Scott, *Olive Schreiner: A Biography* (New Brunswick: Rutgers University Press, 1990), p. 285. See also Ruth Brandon's *The New Women and the Old Men: Love, Sex, and the Woman Question* (London: Flamingo, 1991) for a discussion of personal networks and relationships among Schreiner, Ellis, Pearson, and other members of the Men and Women's Club.

23. Olive Schreiner, *Woman and Labour* (London: Virago, 1978), p. 12. The quotation from Geddes and Thomson's *The Evolution of Sex* is taken from Conway's "Stereotypes of Femininity," p. 146.

24. Schreiner, *Woman and Labour*, p. 82.

25. Ibid., p. 259.

26. For a careful delineation of Schreiner's relationship to the dominant evolutionary theories of her day, see Joyce Avrech Berkman, *The Healing Imagination of Olive Schreiner: Beyond South African Colonialism* (Oxford: Plantin, 1990), ch. 3.

27. Schreiner, *Woman and Labour*, p. 283.

28. Elaine Showalter, *A Literature of Their Own: English Women Novelists from Brontë to Lessing* (London: Virago, 1978), p. 203.

29. Schreiner, *Woman and Labour*, p. 282.

30. See "Press Notices on the First Edition," in Frances Swiney, *The Awakening of Women, or Woman's Part in Evolution*, 3rd ed. (London: William Reeves, 1908).

31. Ibid., p. 20.

32. Ibid., p. 19.

33. Ibid., p. 177.

34. Ibid., p. 268.

35. Ibid., p. 269.

36. See Carol Barash, "Introduction," in *An Olive Schreiner Reader: Writings on Women and South Africa* (London: Pandora, 1987), and Berkman, *The Healing Imagination of Olive Schreiner*, ch. 4.

37. Nancy Stepan, *The Idea of Race in Science: Great Britain, 1800–1960* (London: Macmillan, 1982).

38. Schreiner, *Woman and Labour*, p. 248.

39. Swiney, *The Awakening of Women*, p. 197.

40. Ibid., pp. 120–121.

41. See Vron Ware, *Beyond the Pale: White Women, Racism, and History* (London: Verso, 1992), and Sander Gilman, *Difference and Pathology: Stereotypes of Sexuality, Race, and Madness* (Ithaca: Cornell University Press, 1985).

42. Swiney, *The Awakening of Women*, p. 67.

43. See, e.g., Antonia Raeburn, *The Militant Suffragettes* (London: Michael Joseph, 1973).

44. Emmeline Pethick Lawrence, "No Thoroughfare(?)," *Votes for Women*, 2, 66 (June 11, 1909): 785.

45. Emmeline Pankurst, "Why We Are Militant," in *Suffrage and the Pankhursts*, p. 153.

46. Vicinus, "Male Space and Women's Bodies," p. 250. My reference to the relationship between the feminist movement and the avant-garde draws on Janet Lyon's discussion in "Militant Discourse, Strange Bedfellows."

47. Emmeline Pethick Lawrence, "Is It Peace?" *Votes for Women*, 2, 39 (December 3, 1908): 168.

48. Pankhurst, "Why We Are Militant," p. 155.

49. Lyon, "Transforming Manifestoes," p. 102.

50. See Claude Abastado, "Introduction à l'analyse des manifestes," *Littérature*, 39 (1980): 6.

51. Tickner, *The Spectacle of Women*, pp. 205–212.

52. Quoted in Marcus, "Re-reading the Pankhursts," p. 8.

53. Pankhurst, "Why We Are Militant," p. 160.

54. This invocation of history as a suprapersonal validation for individual struggles was

also evident in the feminist fiction of the period. See Wim Neetens's discussion of Sarah Grand and Elizabeth Robins in *Writing and Democracy: Literature, Politics, and Culture in Transition* (New York: Harvester Wheatsheaf, 1991), in particular p. 123.

55. Emmeline Pethick Lawrence, "Is It Right? Is It Wrong?" *Votes for Women,* 2, 81 (September 24, 1909): 1205.

56. Pankhurst, "Why We Are Militant," p. 156. In a similar vein, Emmeline Pethick Lawrence wrote, "women, in direct opposition to their instinct, tradition and normal character, have thus been forced into a revolution in defence of their rights and liberties, and for this the Government is responsible and not the women. Women, even more than men, hate war. Women, even more than men, love peace. But there is one thing better even than peace. It is honour." See Lawrence, "Is It Right? Is It Wrong?" p. 1205.

57. Marcus, "Women, War, and Madness," p. 144; Tickner, *The Spectacle of Women,* note 73, pp. 306–307; Vicinus, "Male Space and Women's Bodies," p. 263.

58. For brief discussions of the *pétroleuse,* see Susanna Barrows, *Distorting Mirrors: Visions of the Crowd in Late Nineteenth-Century France* (New Haven: Yale University Press, 1981), p. 50, and Daniel Pick, *Face of Degeneration: A European Disorder, c. 1848–c. 1918* (New York: Cambridge University Press, 1989), p. 92. For contemporary interpretations of feminism as a form of hysteria, see Tickner, *The Spectacle of Women,* pp. 192–204, and Elaine Showalter, *The Female Malady: Women, Madness, and English Culture, 1830–1980* (London: Virago, 1987), ch. 6.

59. Vicinus, "Male Space and Women's Bodies," pp. 260–261.

60. Gianni Vattimo, *The End of Modernity: Nihilism and Hermeneutics in Postmodern Culture* (Baltimore: The Johns Hopkins University Press, 1988), p. 99.

61. See, e.g., Theodor W. Adorno, "Progress," in *Benjamin: Philosophy, Aesthetics, History,* ed. Gary Smith (Chicago: University of Chicago Press, 1989), and Jean Baudrillard, "Modernity," *The Canadian Journal of Political and Social Theory,* 11, 3 (1987): 63–72.

62. Lyon, "Militant Discourse, Strange Bedfellows," p. 109.

63. For a critique of this purported dissolution of history, see Lutz Niethammer, *Posthistoire: Has History Come to an End?* (London: Verso, 1992).

64. Vattimo, *The End of Modernity,* p. 7.

7. The Art of Perversion

Epigraph: Kaja Silverman, *Male Subjectivity at the Margins* (New York: Routledge, 1992), p. 187.

1. See, e.g., Carolyn J. Dean, *The Self and Its Pleasures: Bataille, Lacan, and the History of the Decentered Subject* (Ithaca: Cornell University Press, 1992), and Susan Rubin Suleiman, *Subversive Intent: Gender, Politics, and the Avant-Garde* (Cambridge: Harvard University Press, 1990).

2. Jean Pierrot, *The Decadent Imagination, 1880–1900* (Chicago: University of Chicago Press, 1981), p. 133.

3. Michel Foucault, *The History of Sexuality,* vol. 1 (Harmondsworth: Penguin, 1981), p. 47. See also Arnold I. Davidson, "Sex and the Emergence of Sexuality," *Critical Inquiry,* 14 (1987): 16–47.

4. Jonathan Dollimore, *Sexual Dissidence: Augustine to Wilde, Freud to Foucault* (Oxford: Clarendon Press, 1991).

5. Richard von Krafft-Ebing, *Psychopathia Sexualis* (New York: Pioneer Publications, 1953), p. 79.

6. Dollimore, *Sexual Dissidence*, p. 144.

7. Some of these recent works which I have found useful are Emily Apter, *Feminizing the Fetish: Psychoanalysis and Narrative Obsession in Turn-of-the-Century France* (Ithaca: Cornell University Press, 1991); Deborah L. Silverman, *Art Nouveau in Fin-de-Siècle France: Politics, Psychology, and Style* (Berkeley: University of California Press, 1989); and Jan Goldstein, "The Uses of Male Hysteria: Medical and Literary Discourse in Nineteenth-Century France," *Representations*, 34 (Spring 1991): 134–165.

8. Dean, *The Self and Its Pleasures*, p. 196. Foucault's own historical analysis of technologies of the sexed self did not, however, exclude an ongoing fascination with a disruptive aesthetics of transgression. In this context, see David Carroll, *Paraesthetics: Foucault, Lyotard, Derrida* (New York: Methuen, 1987).

9. Mario Praz, *The Romantic Agony* (Oxford: Oxford University Press, 1970).

10. Claude Dauphiné, *Rachilde* (Paris: Mercure de France, 1991), p. 325.

11. Krafft-Ebing, *Psychopathia Sexualis*, p. 131.

12. For negative responses to Rachilde, see, e.g., Jennifer Birkett's detailed and suggestive but overly dismissive chapter on Rachilde in *The Sins of the Father: Decadence in France, 1870–1914* (London: Quartet, 1986) and Bram Dijkstra's brief discussion in *Idols of Perversity: Fantasies of Feminine Evil in Fin-de-Siècle Culture* (Oxford: Oxford University Press, 1986), pp. 337–341. Recent reappraisals of Rachilde include Janet Beizer, "Venus in Drag, or Redressing the Discourse of Hysteria: Rachilde's *Monsieur Vénus*," in her *Ventriloquized Bodies: Narratives of Hysteria in Nineteenth-Century France* (Ithaca: Cornell University Press, 1994); Rae Beth Gordon, "Ornament and Hysteria: Huysmans and Rachilde," in her *Ornament, Fantasy, and Desire in Nineteenth-Century French Literature* (Princeton: Princeton University Press, 1992); Dorothy Kelly, *Fictional Genders: Role and Representation in Nineteenth-Century French Narrative* (Lincoln: University of Nebraska Press, 1989), pp. 143–155; Jennifer Waelti-Walters, *Feminist Novelists of the Belle Epoque: Love As a Lifestyle* (Bloomington: Indiana University Press, 1990), ch. 9; Melanie C. Hawthorne, "*Monsieur Vénus*: A Critique of Gender Roles," *Nineteenth-Century French Studies*, 16 (1987–88): 162–179, and "The Social Construction of Sexuality in Three Novels by Rachilde," *Michigan Romance Studies*, 9 (1989): 49–59; Micheline Besnard-Coursodon, "Monsieur Vénus, Madame Adonis: Sexe et Discours," *Littérature*, 54 (1984): 121–127; Renée A. Kingcaid, *Neurosis and Narrative: The Decadent Short Fiction of Proust, Lorrain, and Rachilde* (Carbondale: Southern Illinois University Press, 1992), ch. 5.

13. Apter, *Feminizing the Fetish*, p. 35.

14. Frank J. Sulloway, *Freud, Biologist of the Mind: Beyond the Psychoanalytical Legend* (London: Burnett, 1979), ch. 8.

15. Robert A. Nye, *Crime, Madness, and Politics in Modern France: The Medical Concept of National Decline* (Princeton: Princeton University Press, 1984).

16. Lawrence Birken, *Consuming Desire: Sexual Science and the Emergence of a Culture of Abundance, 1871–1914* (Ithaca: Cornell University Press, 1988).

17. Teresa de Lauretis, *The Practice of Love: Lesbian Sexuality and Perverse Desire* (Bloomington: Indiana University Press, 1994), p. xvii.

18. Jan Goldstein, *Console and Classify: The French Psychiatric Profession in the Nineteenth Century* (Cambridge: Cambridge University Press, 1987), p. 324.

19. Elaine Showalter, *The Female Malady: Women, Madness, and English Culture, 1830–1980* (London: Virago, 1987), p. 129. See also George Frederick Drinka, *The Birth of Neurosis: Myth, Malady, and the Victorians* (New York: Simon and Schuster, 1984), and Stephen Heath, *The Sexual Fix* (London: Macmillan, 1982).

20. Goldstein, *Console and Classify*, pp. 373–374. See also pp. 329–330 for a discussion of statistical variation in the diagnosis of hysteria.

21. See Goldstein, "The Uses of Male Hysteria."

22. Ibid., pp. 153–154.

23. Krafft-Ebing, *Psychopathia Sexualis*, p. 197.

24. Apter, *Feminizing the Fetish*, pp. 106–7. See also Jann Matlock, "Masquerading Women, Pathologized Men: Cross-Dressing, Fetishism, and the Theory of Perversion, 1882–1935," in *Fetishism as Cultural Discourse*, ed. Emily Apter and William Pietz (Ithaca: Cornell University Press, 1993).

25. Sigmund Freud, "'Civilized' Sexual Morality and Modern Nervous Illness," *The Standard Edition of the Complete Psychological Works of Sigmund Freud*, vol. 9 (London: The Hogarth Press, 1955), pp. 191–192.

26. Sulloway, *Freud*, p. 197.

27. See, e.g., Kingcaid, *Neurosis and Narrative*. For a more equivocal reading, see Gordon, "Ornament and Hysteria," and Beizer, "Venus in Drag."

28. See Goldstein, "The Uses of Male Hysteria."

29. See Birkett, *The Sins of the Fathers*, p. 166.

30. Rachilde, *La marquise de Sade* (Paris: Mercure de France, 1981), p. 295. I quote here from Jennifer Birkett's excellent translation in *The Sins of the Fathers*, p. 167.

31. Rachilde, *La marquise de Sade*, p. 297.

32. Angela Carter, *The Sadeian Woman: An Exercise in Cultural History* (London: Virago, 1979), p. 89.

33. Gilles Deleuze, *Coldness and Cruelty*, in his *Masochism* (New York: Zone Books, 1989), p. 20.

34. Jean Baudrillard, *Seduction* (London: Macmillan, 1990), p. 2.

35. Jeannette Foster, *Sex Variant Women In Literature* (Baltimore: Diana Press, 1975), p. 89. For a discussion of the relationship between the lesbian and the masculine woman, see Esther Newton, "The Mythic Mannish Lesbian: Radclyffe Hall and the New Woman," *Signs*, 9, 4 (1984): 557–575; George Chauncey, Jr., "From Sexual Inversion to Homosexuality: Medicine and the Changing Conceptualization of Female Deviance," *Salmagundi*, 58–59 (1982–83): 114–146; and Carroll Smith-Rosenberg, "Discourses of Sexuality and Subjectivity: The New Woman, 1870–1936," in *Hidden from History: Reclaiming the Gay and Lesbian Past*, ed. Martin Duberman, Martha Vicinus, and George Chauncey, Jr. (Harmondsworth: Penguin, 1991).

36. Rachilde, *La marquise de Sade*, p. 273, and *Monsieur Venus*, trans. Liz Heron (London: Dedalus, 1992), p. 50.

37. Mary Ann Doane, *Femmes Fatales: Feminism, Film Theory, Psychoanalysis* (New

York: Routledge, 1991), p. 2. See also Annemarie Taeger, *Die Kunst, Medusa zu töten* (Bielefeld: Aiesthesis, 1987).

38. See Dean, *The Self and Its Pleasures*, chs. 4 and 5, for a survey of the various interpretations which have either conflated de Sade's texts and his life or divorced them from each other.

39. I take my phrasing here from Abigail Solomon-Godeau's suggestive article "The Legs of the Countess," in *Fetishism As Cultural Discourse*, ed. Emily Apter and William Pietz (Ithaca: Cornell University Press, 1993), pp. 279–280.

40. John Berger, *Ways of Seeing* (Harmondsworth: Penguin, 1972), p. 47.

41. Rachilde, *Monsieur Venus*, p. 54.

42. Ibid., pp. 31–32. See also the discussion of this passage in Hawthorne, *"Monsieur Vénus."*

43. Beizer, "Venus in Drag," p. 250. See also Gordon, "Ornament and Hysteria," p. 233, and Kelly, *Fictional Genders*, p. 154, for discussions of Rachilde's aestheticization of the male body.

44. Rachilde, *Monsieur Venus*, p. 68.

45. Ibid., p. 144.

46. Naomi Schor, *George Sand and Idealism* (New York: Columbia University Press, 1993), p. 20.

47. Anne McClintock, "The Return of Female Fetishism and the Fiction of the Phallus," *New Formations*, 19 (1993): 21.

48. Elisabeth Bronfen, *Over Her Dead Body: Death, Femininity, and the Aesthetic* (Manchester: Manchester University Press, 1992), pp. 95–109.

49. Rachilde, *La jongleuse* (Paris: Des Femmes, 1982), pp. 50–51. I quote here again from Birkett's excellent translation in *The Sins of the Fathers*, pp. 182–183.

50. On this point, see Kelly, *Fictional Genders*, and Beizer, "Venus in Drag."

51. Rachilde, *Pourquoi je ne suis pas féministe* (Paris: Les Editions de France, 1928), p. 6.

52. Louise Kaplan, *Female Perversions: The Temptations of Emma Bovary* (New York: Doubleday, 1991), p. 40.

53. Mandy Merck, *Perversions* (London: Virago, 1993).

54. Parveen Adams, "Of Female Bondage," in *Between Feminism and Psychoanalysis*, ed. Teresa Brennan (London: Routledge, 1989), pp. 262–263.

55. Danae Clark, "Commodity Lesbianism," *Camera Obscura* 25/26 (1991): 181–201. On this issue, see also the excellent collection *The Lesbian Postmodern*, ed. Laura Doan (New York: Columbia University Press, 1994).

56. See the discussion of Barrès's preface in Beizer, "Venus in Drag."

Afterword

1. Friedrich Nietzsche, "On the Uses and Disadvantages of History for Life," in his *Untimely Meditations* (Cambridge: Cambridge University Press, 1983). See also Hayden White's discussion of this text in *Metahistory: The Historical Imagination in Nineteenth-Century Europe* (Baltimore: The Johns Hopkins University Press, 1973), ch. 9.

2. Carl E. Schorske, *Fin-de-Siècle Vienna: Politics and Culture* (Cambridge: Cambridge University Press, 1981), p. xxii.

3. Carol J. Clover, *Men, Women, and Chain-Saws: Gender in the Modern Horror Film* (Princeton: Princeton University Press, 1992), p. 99.

4. Peter Stalleybrass, "Modern," unpublished ms.

5. Steven Connor, *Theory and Cultural Value* (Oxford: Basil Blackwell, 1992).

6. Homi K. Bhabha, *The Location of Culture* (New York: Routledge, 1994); Trinh T. Minh-ha, *Woman, Native, Other: Writing Postcoloniality and Feminism* (Bloomington: Indiana University Press, 1989); and Gayatri Chakravorty Spivak, *In Other Worlds: Essays in Cultural Politics* (New York: Methuen, 1987).

7. Paul Gilroy, *The Black Atlantic: Modernity and Double Consciousness* (Cambridge: Harvard University Press, 1993), p. 198.

Index

Actresses, 4, 19–20, 75, 107, 110–111
Adams, Parveen, 204
Adorno, Theodor, 55, 189; *Dialectic of Enlightenment*, 5–7
Advertising, 64, 73, 75, 83, 88, 97, 140
Aestheticism, 22, 92–97, 99, 102–109, 112, 178, 193, 196, 199–201
American Revolution, 167
Andreas-Salomé, Lou, 50, 53, 57–58; "The Consequences of the Fact That It Was Not Women Who Killed the Father," 52; "The Human Being As a Woman," 52
Aristocracy, 74–75, 95–96, 98, 130, 144, 195, 200–201
Armstrong, Nancy, 18, 56
Athena, 166
Au Bon Marché, 66
Autoeroticism, 178, 199
Avant-gardism, 14, 22–23, 25, 27–29, 31, 91–92, 99, 119–120, 174–177, 179, 185, 202, 210
Aveling, Edward, *The Woman Question*, 154

Bachofen, J. J., *Myth, Religion, and Mother Right*, 50–51
Balzac, Honoré de, 82–83, 86
Barney, Nathalie, 192
Barrès, Maurice, 206
Bartlett, Neil, 104
Baudelaire, Charles, 2, 12, 20, 94, 96, 108, 110, 112, 140, 179
Baudrillard, Jean, 63, 190
Baym, Nina, 141–142
Bebel, August, 50, 159; *Woman in the Past, Present, and Future*, 154

Beizer, Janet, 197
Benjamin, Walter, 20, 99, 110
Berman, Marshall, *All That Is Solid Melts into Air*, 1–4, 16
Bernheimer, Charles, 109, 112–113
Bersani, Leo, 81–82
Bhabha, Homi, 211
Birken, Lawrence, 181–182
Bisexuality, 52–53, 182
Bloch, Iwan, 180
Bloomsbury group, 27
Boadicea, 166
Bourgeois subjects and values. *See* Middle class
Bowlby, Rachel, 18, 97, 106
Bradbury, Malcolm, 23
Braidotti, Rosa, 113
Brantlinger, Patrick, 137
Broch, Hermann, 118
Bronfen, Elisabeth, 198
Brooks, Peter, 75, 121–122, 124–125, 132
Brummel, Beau, 96
Buci-Glucksmann, Christine, 18–19, 110
Buddhism, 136
Bureaucracy, 9, 11, 28, 55–56
Burke, Edmund, 119
Butler, Judith, *Gender Trouble*, 205

Cahoone, Lawrence, 12
Calinescu, Matei, 13, 27
Campbell, Colin, *The Romantic Ethic and the Spirit of Modern Consumerism*, 61, 78
Capitalism, 157; and modern development, 2, 9, 13, 65, 69, 88; dehumanizing nature of, 5, 18, 75, 79; domination by, 11; logic of, 26,

Capitalism (*continued*)
31, 99; destruction of tradition by, 47; and
women, 64–67, 69, 77, 88–90, 106; and
patriarchy, 66, 72, 74; relationship to sex,
67, 71
Carpenter, Edward, 156
Carter, A. E., 107
Carter, Angela, 188
Charcot, Jean Martin, 183
Christianity, 109, 130, 132–134, 155, 159
City life, 37, 55; transitory nature of, 13; and
men, 17, 70; anonymity in, 19; and women,
19–21, 64, 75, 107; realities of, 38, 42, 50,
72, 79, 107, 181; exotic images of, 61, 177;
crowds, 73; elites, 103
Clark, Danae, 205
Clark, Suzanne, *Sentimental Modernism*, 115,
126
Class, 75; hierarchy of, 21, 143–144, 201;
blurred distinctions, 67, 72–73, 115, 132;
interests and privileges of, 105–106. *See also*
Aristocracy; Middle class; Working class
Clérambault, Gatian de Gaetonde de, 184
Clover, Carol, 209
Cohen, Ed, 97–98, 103
Colonialism. *See* Imperialism
Commodities: erotics and aesthetics of, 4–5,
19, 67, 97–101, 105, 118; and female desire,
63–66, 124; shopping for, 65–71
Connor, Steven, 211
Conrad, Joseph, 24
Consumerism. *See* Consumption
Consumption, 32, 123, 157; in modern society,
5, 13, 57, 61–62, 66–68, 87, 99–100, 171;
and postmodernism, 15; blurring of private/
public distinctions, 19, 74; erotics and aes-
thetics of, 61–90, 94; and women, 63–65,
70, 74–79, 88–90, 96–97, 124; and produc-
tion, 63, 157; of books, 81, 106; relationship
to sex, 181–182
Copernicus, Nicolaus, 12
Coprophilia, 180
Corbin, Alain, 26
Corelli, Marie (Mary Mackay), 33, 115–144,
180; *Ardath*, 133; *Barabbas*, 130; *A Romance
of Two Worlds*, 133, 135; *The Sorrows of
Satan*, 115, 122–123, 128; *The Soul of Lilith*,
133; *Temporal Power*, 127, 129–130; *Ziska*,
138–140
Cosmetics, 19, 63, 94
Crosby, Christine, 148
Cross-dressing. *See* Transvestism
Cubism, 28

Cultural studies, 21–22, 29, 32–33, 63, 141
Cvetkovich, Ann, 120, 130, 142
Cyborgs, 15, 20, 197–199

Dada, 28
Dandies, 16, 96–97, 103–110, 112, 114, 191
Darwin, Charles, 33, 39, 133, 155, 160, 181
Dauphiné, Claude, 178–179
Dean, Carolyn, 177
Decadence, 20, 146; of modern urban life, 30,
75, 92, 104, 123; capitalist, 79; and aes-
thetics, 91, 94–96, 100, 178–179; of high
society, 128; feminine, history as, 158; of
sadists, 186, 193
Decor, 96, 100
DeKoven, Marianne, 23–24
Deleuze, Gilles, 93, 100, 102, 111, 113, 188–
190, 200
Dellamora, Richard, 103
Department stores, 19, 28, 57, 61, 64, 66–74,
89–90
Derrida, Jacques, 113–114
Descombes, Vincent, 12
Desire, 32, 83, 91; modern forms of, 4, 20, 57,
174; female, 7, 17, 47, 63–66, 69–79, 86,
88–90, 180, 188–190, 192–193; nostalgic, 37,
59; and authority, 52; for commodities,
62–66, 69–79, 88–90; and romantic love, 87,
128, 138; homosexual, 93, 192; and aestheti-
cism, 94, 178, 203; women as objects of, 97,
195; constituted through symbols, 102;
repressed, 126; instinctual, 160, 200; perverse, 174–206; psychoanalysis of, 175, 177;
modernization of, 180–185
Dijkstra, Bram, 77
Doane, Mary Ann, 63–64, 193
Dollimore, Jonathan, 103–104, 176
Donzelot, Jacques, 56
Duffin, Lorna, 148
Dumas, Alexandre, 86

Eden, 18, 40, 158–159
Eliot, T. S., 23
Ellis, Havelock, 156, 159–160, 180; *Man and
Woman*, 154
Engels, Friedrich, 50; *The Origins of the Family*,
154
Enlightenment, 7, 12, 17, 38, 41, 45, 50, 57,
112, 136, 166, 189
Equality: democratic basis of, 14, 17, 166–167,
202; between sexes, 19, 143, 149, 157, 159,
162, 188; and consumerism, 68, 88
Erotic sublime, 138

Evolution, 31, 39–40, 51, 145, 147–149, 154–165, 170–172, 181

Exhibitionism, 178, 180, 194–195

Exoticism, 64, 70, 82, 98–100, 104, 136–141, 145

Exotic sublime, 131, 136–141

Eymery, Marguerite. *See* Rachilde

Factories, 19, 28, 55

Faderman, Lilian, 20

Family relations, 3, 16, 21, 39, 51, 55, 65, 90, 131

Fashion, 13, 19, 22, 49, 57, 62–64, 75, 87, 94, 96, 102, 110, 168

Faust, 1–4, 43

Fee, Elizabeth, 51

Femininity: of modernity, 1–6, 9, 18–22, 42, 61–63, 90; and subjugation, 2, 20; otherness of, 6–8, 17, 21, 31, 49; as outside history, 16; aesthetic of, 24–29, 33, 48, 94; nondifferentiated, 36, 40–49, 51–53; demodernizing role of, 38–39; archaic, 49–54; mass-produced images of, 64; masculine identification with, 72, 91–93; and feminized male, 94–97; and abominable woman, 105–111; in popular romances, 117, 120–121, 123, 126–131, 134–138, 141; and the sublime, 119–120; evolutionary and revolutionary, 146, 156, 158, 161, 164, 168–169, 171; and perversion, 175, 180–185, 187, 189–200

Feminism: critique of male subjects, 2; and hysteria, 3; and gender, 6, 42; theories of modernity, 8–10, 15–16, 211; on literary history, 24–33, 92–93, 113, 129, 131, 141–142, 144, 179–180, 207–209; and nostalgia, 45, 55–56, 58–59; theories of consumption, 63, 66, 85, 89; on evolution and revolution, 145–173; and psychoanalysis, 175; and desire, 180–185, 195; and perversion, 198, 202–206

Feminist theory. *See* Feminism

Femme fatale, 65, 75, 139, 179

Feré, Charles, 180

Fetishism, 4–5, 25, 64, 67, 100, 102, 109–110, 173, 178–179, 184, 196, 198, 204

Fin de siècle, 3–4, 9–10, 15, 22, 30–31, 36, 49–50, 54, 58, 65, 91–94, 96, 99–100, 102–104, 106, 133, 136, 139, 145, 148, 157, 163, 170, 172, 174, 178, 181–183, 186, 188, 192, 201–203, 208

Finney, Gail, 2–4

Flâneur, 2, 16, 37, 70, 98, 107

Flaubert, Gustave, 140, 185; *Madame Bovary*, 32, 65, 78–87, 144

Foster, Jeannette, *Sex Variant Women in Literature*, 192

Foucault, Michel, 12, 175, 177

Frankfurt School, 63, 141

Fraser, Nancy, 32

French Revolution, 14, 147–148, 150, 163, 166

Freud, Sigmund, 4, 6, 27, 41, 47, 50, 52–54, 177, 181–182, 184; *Civilization and Its Discontents*, 51–52; *Totem and Taboo*, 52

Frevert, Ute, 58

Frisby, David, 37

Fundamentalism, religious, 59

Future: commitment to, 13–14, 147, 149, 172; as female, 154–163

Futurism, 28

Gans, Eric, 82

Garber, Marjorie, *Vested Interests*, 205

Gasché, Rodolphe, 109

Geddes, Patrick, *The Evolution of Sex*, 154, 156, 159

Gemeinschaft, 55

Gender: historicity of, 1, 4, 7; of modernity, 1, 9–10; technologies of, 21; identities, 92–93, 101–103, 106, 112. *See also* Femininity; Masculinity

Gesellschaft, 55

Gide, André, 104

Gilbert, Sandra, 18

Gilroy, Paul, *The Black Atlantic*, 211–212

Gladstone, William, 115

Goethe, Johann Wolfgang von, *Faust*, 1–4

Goncourt, Edmond and Jules, 85

Guattari, Felix, 113

Gubar, Susan, 18

Habermas, Jürgen, 11–12

Haggard, H. Rider, 136; *She*, 139

Haraway, Donna, 20

Hegel, G. W. F., 12, 38, 45–46, 53, 207–208

Heidegger, Martin, 55

Hekman, Susan, 45

Hellenism, 51

Henke, Suzette, 24

Hinduism, 136

History: gendering of, 1, 4, 7; as domination, 6–7, 11, 14; as progress, 14–15, 18, 30, 101; and women, 21–22; feminist discourses on, 145–149; as evolution, 154–163; and feminine decadence, 158

Hobbes, Thomas, 12

Homer, 5
Homosexuality: and modernity, 20–21, 78;
    female, 130, 178, 180, 184, 192, 204–205;
    male, 93, 101–105, 178, 180, 200, 204
Hopkins, Gerard Manley, 103
Horkheimer, Max, *Dialectic of Enlightenment*,
    5–7, 189
Horney, Karen, 58
Hunt, Lynn, 150
Huysmans, J. K., *Against the Grain*, 92–93,
    95–96, 98–102, 105–109, 111
Huyssen, Andreas, 18, 20, 80, 106
Hysteria, 2–3, 69, 116, 125, 130, 183–185

Ibsen, Henrik: *A Doll's House*, 146; *Hedda
    Gabler*, 3
Idealism, 12, 79, 117–118, 126–131, 160
Imperialism, 14, 59, 137, 140, 171, 211
Individualism, 1, 3–5, 13–14, 98–99, 108, 177,
    188, 203
Industrialization, 13, 20–21, 38–39, 55, 99, 160
Islam, 136

Jameson, Fredric, 80
Joan of Arc, 166
Jordanova, Ludmilla, 30
Joyce, James, 24

Kant, Immanuel, 15, 84, 119, 178
Kaplan, Louise, *Female Perversions*, 203
Kellner, Douglas, 5
Kenney, Annie, 165
Kipling, Rudyard, 136
Kitsch, 118–121
Kittler, Friedrich, 56
Kleist, Heinrich von, *Penthesilea*, 179
Klimt, Gustav, 50
Krafft-Ebing, Richard von, 101–102; *Psycho-
    pathia Sexualis*, 176, 179–180, 184
Kristeva, Julia, 24

Lacan, Jacques, 38, 47, 53–54, 97
LaCapra, Dominick, 85
Landes, Joan, 14, 17
Lauretis, Teresa de, 182
Lawrence, Emmeline Pethick, 164–165
Leach, William R., 89
Leavis, Q. D., 117–118
Le Bon, Gustave, 73
Left Bank group, 27
Lepenies, Wolf, 35–36
Lesbianism. *See* Homosexuality, female
Lichtblau, Klaus, 48

Linton, Eliza Lynn, 129
Literary canons, 24–25, 142
Lloyd, Rosemary, 82
Lombroso, Cesare, 159
Lucia di Lammermoor, 84
Lulu, 3–4
Lunn, Eugene, 23
Lyon, Janet, 150, 166, 171
Lyotard, Jean-François, 119, 172
Lytton, Constance, 156

MacCannell, Juliet, 17
MacCarthy, Desmond, 125
Mackay, Mary (Minnie). *See* Corelli, Marie
Magazines, women's, 28, 63, 81, 83
Mallarmé, Stéphane, 185
Malthus, Thomas, 33
Man of the crowd, 16
Marcus, Jane, 150
Marriage, 129, 146
Marx, Eleanor, *The Woman Question*, 154, 156
Marx, Karl, 2, 4–5, 15, 55
Marxism, 6, 9, 25–26, 38, 42, 56, 58, 88–89,
    102, 157, 171
Masculinity: of modernity, 1–6, 16–17, 19,
    41–42; competitive nature of, 2, 27, 40; and
    domination, 2, 6–7, 20, 31, 44, 63, 71–72,
    74, 77–78, 139, 141; aesthetic of, 23–24, 43,
    94; of literary heritage, 24; identification
    with feminine, 72, 91–93; masking of,
    91–114; feminized male, 94–97; in popular
    romances, 120, 127–128, 134, 136–138; evo-
    lutionary and revolutionary, 148, 156, 168;
    and perversion, 175, 183, 189, 192
Masochism, 78, 93, 102, 111, 139, 174, 178,
    180, 188–189, 204
Masquerade, 104–105, 110, 129, 185, 190, 193,
    202, 205
Mass culture, 5, 28–29, 62, 80, 82–83, 89,
    98–99, 106, 118–121, 123, 126, 140, 142,
    144
Mass media, 17, 21, 83
Mass production, 19–20, 49, 64, 66, 80, 99,
    107, 118–119
Masters, Brian, 124
Matlock, Jann, 86
Matriarchy, rule by, 50–51, 160
McClintock, Anne, 53–54, 198
McFarlane, James, 23
Mechanical woman, 20, 107, 198
Medea, 7
Melodrama, 24, 29, 82, 101, 111, 117, 120–
    127, 132, 138, 142, 144

Merck, Mandy, *Perversions*, 203–204
Mercure de France, 179
Middle class, subjects and values of, 84, 123–124, 141, 144, 157, 194; individualism, 1; men, 2, 18, 26, 75, 91–93, 101, 208; and nature, 4–5; challenges to, 14, 27, 80, 106–107; women, 19, 62, 64–65, 88–90, 96, 117, 130, 133; and reason, 27, 95, 177–178; and shop employees, 72; and crowds, 73; industry and thrift, 78, 94–95; morality, 80, 143, 176; vulgarity of, 96, 107; reading habits, 133; and women's movement, 149, 168–169
Mill, John Stuart, 208
Mills, Patricia, 6–7
Mills, Sara, 137
Minh-ha, Trinh, 211
Modernism: defined, 13–14; and masculinity, 15, 24, 80; literary aspects of, 22–29, 79–80, 99–103, 112–113; and femininity, 80, 92–93; gender politics of, 112–113; sexualization of art, 178
Modernité, 12–13
Modernity: as contradictory, 1, 3, 9, 40; as feminine, 1–6, 9, 18–22, 42, 61–63, 90; gender of, 1, 9–10; as masculine, 1–6, 16–17, 19, 41–42; subjectivity of, 2–3, 5–6, 13, 90, 99, 174, 182; defined, 3, 8–9, 11–13, 15; multidimensional phenomena of, 12, 15; origins of, 12–13; and separation from the past, 13–14; and the new, 14, 30, 47, 146, 149, 158, 169–173; and sociology, 36; and differentiation, 42–43
Modernization, 3, 12–13, 16–18, 22, 29, 37, 39, 43, 69, 157, 160, 180
Modleski, Tania, *Feminism without Women*, 91, 114
Moers, Ellen, 96
Moll, Albert, 180
Morgan, Thais, 20–21
Morris, Meaghan, "Things to Do with Shopping Centres," 11
Morris, William, 50
Motherhood, 22, 39, 51–54, 56, 59–60, 129, 131, 191
Myths, 38, 165; Faustian, 4; as enlightenment, 5; gender roles, 7, 188; of modernity, 7, 10; edenic, 18; of femininity, 20, 50, 58; oriental, 140

Narcissism, 17, 52, 85–86, 97–101, 106–107, 126, 197
Narratives: historical, 1, 7, 40, 101; grand,

9–10, 61, 171–172; evolutionary, 51, 155, 164–165; popular romances as, 82; of sexual and colonial conquest, 137; of women's emancipation, 146, 155, 164–165
Naturalism, 29, 79–80, 108, 117, 121
Nature, 2, 4–5, 88, 99, 107, 112–114
Necrophilia, 178, 180, 199
Neoclassicism, 104
New Criticism, 23–24
New Historicism, 29
New Woman, 14, 92, 128, 146, 151, 158, 166
Nietzsche, Friedrich, 5, 50, 91, 207–208
Nisbet, Robert, 55–56
Nordau, Max, 95, 159
Nostalgia, 15, 18, 21, 35, 37–41, 45, 54–60, 63, 88, 107, 118, 140, 143–145, 195, 211

Oakes, Guy, 38
Odysseus, 5, 7
Oedipal complex, 2, 27, 39, 52, 126, 148, 168, 175, 184
Olalquiaga, Celeste, 120
Orientalism, 70, 131, 136–140
Osborne, Peter, 149
Otherness, feminine, 6–8, 17, 21, 31, 49

Pabst, G. W., *Pandora's Box*, 4
Pandora, 4
Pankhurst, Christabel, 164–165, 169
Pankhurst, Emmeline, 164–168
Paris Commune, 163, 169
Paris Exposition (1900), 64
Pastiche, 15
Past, the: repudiation of, 13–14, 161; desire for, 38–41
Pater, Walter, *Studies in the History of the Renaissance*, 101
Patriarchy: as the basis of modernity, 6; domination by, 7, 20, 52, 63, 71–72, 88, 90, 141; and religion, 17, 134; mystificatory discourses of, 26; and feminine Other, 31; on psychological superiority of men, 44; law, 51–52, 54, 111, 141; and psychoanalysis, 58; and capitalism, 66, 88; and families, 74, 191; male identification with feminine as subversive, 93; and history, 148
Pearson, Karl, 156
Perversity and perversion, 78, 102, 104; defined, 77, 174–180; and capitalism, 79; in modern urban life, 177; and modernization of desire, 180–185. *See also specific perversions*
Peterson, Carla, 83

Petro, Patrice, 18
Politics, symbolic, 150–154
Pollock, Griselda, 17
Poovey, Mary, 18
Popular culture. *See* Mass culture
Popular sublime, 119–120, 143–144
Pornography, 100, 179
Postcolonialism, 211
Postmodernism, 8–9, 15, 37, 58, 103, 171–173
Pound, Ezra, 23
Praz, Mario, *The Romantic Agony*, 177
Pre-Raphaelites, 50
Private sphere, 18–19, 22, 39, 41, 49, 61, 68, 74, 92, 94, 123, 155
Production, 95, 143; mass, 19–20, 49, 64, 66, 80, 99, 107, 119; women as laborers, 19–20; masculine nature of, 30, 43, 47, 61, 201; modern transformation of, 55; and consumption, 63, 157; of books, 80
Progress: history as, 14–15, 18, 101, 149; rhetoric of, 30; causes, 52; economic, 68–69, 72; as nineteenth-century ideal, 95; and women, 155–156, 158, 161–162; and men, 160; modern view of, 170–171
Prometheus, 3
Prostitutes, 4, 16, 19–20, 64, 72, 75, 107
Psychoanalysis, 3, 17, 26, 36, 39, 52, 54, 58, 77, 174–184, 202
Public sphere, 16–19, 22, 39, 41, 61, 68, 77, 90, 92, 94–95, 98
Pumphrey, Martin, 28

Queer theory, 204–205
Querelle des Anciens et des Modernes, 13

Race, 89; and modernity, 14, 56, 136–141, 161–163, 211–212; hierarchy of, 21, 143, 161–162; and access to commodities, 63; and cultural otherness, 137, 139–140, 161, 163; and miscegenation, 163; and slavery, 167, 211–212
Rachilde (Marguerite Eymery), 31, 174, 178–180, 184–203, 205–206, 207; *La jongleuse*, 193–195, 199–200, 202; *La marquise de Sade*, 179, 186–193; *Monsieur Vénus*, 179, 192, 195–198, 200–201, 206; *Pourquoi je ne suis pas féministe*, 180, 202–203
Radway, Janice, 81, 128
Rationality. *See* Reason
Realism, 24–26, 29, 36, 79–80, 100–101, 105, 115, 117, 121, 126, 132–133, 193
Reason: and irrationality of capitalism and

technology, 5, 17, 30, 43; and women, 6, 20; potential for, 11; and progress, 14–15; middle-class attitude toward, 27, 95, 177–178; and men, 30, 94; and aestheticism, 108, 112
Reekie, Gail, 66
Religious sublime, 134–135
Renaissance, 13
Reproduction, 16, 20, 55, 155, 157, 159–160, 178, 191, 197, 201
Revolution, 13–14, 31, 65, 145, 147–149, 151, 154, 163–173, 181, 206
Riggs, Larry, 81
Robbins, Bruce, 86
Romances, 22, 28, 31, 72, 79–83, 87, 120, 128, 131, 137–139, 144
Romanticism, 15–17, 37–39, 50, 57, 79, 81, 84, 86, 94, 98, 102, 107, 117–118, 120–121, 138, 140, 177–178, 212
Romantic love, 22, 68, 80, 82, 87, 111, 126–131
Roth, Michael, 40
Rousseau, Jean-Jacques, 38
Russett, Cynthia Eagle, 40
Ruthrof, Horst, 8

Sacher-Masoch, Leopold von, 188, 190; *Venus in Furs*, 92–93, 95, 97, 100, 102, 105, 108–111
Sade, Donatien-Alphonse-François de, 174, 188–191, 193, 200
Sadism, 71, 78, 81, 139, 174, 178–180, 185–193, 200, 204
Sainte-Beuve, Charles-Augustin, 144
Sand, George, 79, 83, 86
Schenk, Celeste, 25
Schor, Naomi, 79, 121, 198
Schorske, Carl, 208
Schreiner, Olive: *The Story of an African Farm*, 156, 158, 162; *Woman and Labour*, 152–154, 156–159, 161–162, 166
Science, 13, 15, 160
Scott, Walter, 82–83
Seduction, 62, 68–72, 75, 103, 190–191, 202
Sentimentality, 28, 43, 59, 80, 83–84, 117–118, 120–121, 126, 141–142, 188
Sexology, 77, 104, 174–184, 202
Sexuality: nineteenth-century preoccupation with, 3, 175; and economics, 19; loosening from traditional bonds, 19–20; hierarchy of, 21; female, 46–47, 65–78, 107, 157, 206; male, 46, 139, 182; and shopping, 66–74; perverse, 102–104, 174–182; and aestheti-

cism, 107–109; and spirituality, 123; and sexology, 174–184
Sheik, The, 139–140
Shoplifting, 68–69
Shopping, 19, 22, 55–57, 61–74, 77, 99. See also Commodities; Consumption
Showalter, Elaine, 18, 158, 182–183
Silverman, Kaja, Male Subjectivity at the Margins, 174
Simmel, Georg, 36–38, 41–49, 52–54, 56–58, 148; "The Metropolis and Mental Life," 42; "The Relative and the Absolute in the Problem of the Sexes," 44
Sociology, 12, 29–30, 35–37, 54–56, 155
Soulié, Frédéric, 86
Speeches, feminist, 31
Spencer, Herbert, 155
Spiritualism and spirituality, 82–84, 123–125, 131–136, 160
Spivak, Gayatri, 211
Stallybrass, Peter, 211
Stauth, Georg, 54–55
Steedman, Carolyn, 124
Stein, Gertrude, 24, 27–28
Stepan, Nancy, 161
Stern, Katherine, 147
Stewart, Susan, On Longing, 35
Stubbs, Patricia, 144
Subjectivity, modern, 2–3, 5–6, 13, 90, 99, 174, 182
Sublime, the, 82–83, 119–120, 125, 127, 131, 134–141, 143–144
Sue, Eugène, 83, 86
Suffrage and suffragettes, 3, 147, 149–154, 156, 159, 164–169, 171, 180
Sulloway, Frank, 181
Supernaturalism, 131–136
Swinburne, Algernon Charles, 103
Swiney, Frances, The Awakening of Women, 152, 154, 156, 159–164
Symbolic politics, 150–154
Symbolism, 22, 28, 94, 186, 194

Tarde, Gabriel, 73
Tarzan, 140
Technology, 9, 13–14, 17, 20, 98–99, 171
Tennyson, Alfred, 115
Tester, Keith, 59–60
Thomson, J. Arthur, The Evolution of Sex, 154, 156, 159

Tickner, Lisa, The Spectacle of Women, 145, 150–151, 153
Tompkins, Jane, 141–142
Tönnies, Ferdinand, 55
Tracts, feminist, 31
Tradition, 1–2, 13–14, 59, 78, 90, 145, 161
Transvestism, 15, 102, 113, 178–179, 184, 191, 203, 205
Turner, Bryan, 54–55

Urbanization. See City life

Vattimo, Gianni, 15, 169, 172–173
Verlaine, Paul, 179, 185
Vicinus, Martha, 150–151, 165, 169
Villiers de L'Isle Adam, Philippe Auguste, L'Eve future, 20, 198
Vivien, Renée, 192
Vizetelly, Henry Richard, 79
Votes for Women, 152, 164, 167–168
Voyeurism, 102, 178, 195
Vucht Tijssen, Lieteke van, 37
Vulgarity, 80–81, 85, 88, 96, 99, 105–108, 112, 116, 130, 141, 201–203
Vyver, Bertha, 130

Ward, Mary Augusta (Mrs. Humphry), 129
Ware, Vron, 163
Weber, Max, 5, 55–56
Wedekind, Franz, 4
Weininger, Otto, Sex and Character, 46–47
West, Rebecca, 166
Wilde, Oscar: The Picture of Dorian Gray, 92–93, 95–101, 103–105, 107–111; Salomé, 3
Williams, Rosalind, 62, 64, 99
Wilson, Elizabeth, 18, 68, 87–88
Wing, Nathaniel, 84
Wolff, Janet, 55
Women's Social and Political Union, 152, 164, 169
Woolf, Virginia, 24, 27
Working class, 2, 19, 75, 124, 133, 144, 195, 197, 201

Yaeger, Patricia, 120

Zola, Emile, 121, 157; Au bonheur des dames, 65–75; Nana, 32, 65, 74–79, 82

Lightning Source UK Ltd.
Milton Keynes UK
UKOW052019110112

185195UK00001B/89/P